The publisher and the University of California Press Foundation gratefully acknowledge the generous support of the Peter Booth Wiley Endowment Fund in History.

The Accidental History of the U.S. Immigration Courts

The Accidental History of the U.S. Immigration Courts

WAR, FEAR, AND THE ROOTS
OF DYSFUNCTION

Alison Peck

UNIVERSITY OF CALIFORNIA PRESS

University of California Press
Oakland, California

Library of Congress Cataloging-in-Publication Data

Names: Peck, Alison Elizabeth, author.
Title: The accidental history of the U.S. immigration courts : war, fear,
  and the roots of dysfunction / Alison Peck.
Other titles: Accidental history of the US immigration courts
Description: Oakland, California : University of California Press, [2021] |
  Includes bibliographical references and index.
Identifiers: LCCN 2020043064 (print) | LCCN 2020043065 (ebook) |
  ISBN 9780520381179 (cloth) | ISBN 9780520381186 (ebook)
Subjects: LCSH: Immigration courts—United States—History. |
  Emigration and immigration law—United States—History. |
  Emigration and immigration—Political aspects—United States.
Classification: LCC KF4821 .P43 2021 (print) | LCC KF4821 (ebook) |
  DDC 342.7308/20269—dc23
LC record available at https://lccn.loc.gov/2020043064
LC ebook record available at https://lccn.loc.gov/2020043065

Manufactured in the United States of America

25 24 23 22 21
10 9 8 7 6 5 4 3 2 1

For Dad

Contents

Acknowledgments

This book began with a question: After years of teaching courses in immigration law and administrative law and thinking out loud with my students about the structure and functions of the executive branch, I could not explain why the immigration courts would be located in the Department of Justice, a law enforcement agency. What began as a casual search for a satisfactory answer became a journey I had never anticipated taking. That journey took me not only to Hyde Park, Washington, Dallas, Amherst, and elsewhere, but also to another dimension, a place where past and present are contiguous, communicating, and fluid. It is a journey I hope never to complete.

Along the way, I have been assisted by many outstanding professionals, without whose work this book would not have happened. After a casual conversation about presidential history after class one morning, Jess Reed, WVU Law Class of 2021, jumped into the project mid-stream with only a year of legal training and proved to be one of the quickest, most thorough, and most astute research assistants I have ever had the pleasure of working with. Jeremy Cook, WVU Law Class of 2020, provided research support in the early stages, gamely joining me in combing through mountains of material at the National Archives. Mark Podvia, WVU Law's talented faculty services librarian, once again demonstrated his seemingly magic powers at locating every obscure source I asked for and pointing to others I had not considered. Nick Stump not only read and gave feedback on the manuscript but also ably spearheaded library acquisitions for a final proof in the middle of the extraordinarily destabilizing COVID-19 crisis.

Archivists and other staff at numerous presidential libraries and rare books collections guided my search and carefully policed my books, pencils, hands, and jackets in the diligent protection of our shared national treasures. I extend my thanks and admiration to the staff at the Franklin D. Roosevelt Presidential Library and Museum; U.S. National Archives and Records Administration in Washington, DC, and College Park, Maryland; George W. Bush Presidential Library and Museum; John F. Kennedy Presidential Library and Museum; Library of Congress; Amherst College Archives and Special Collections; Columbia University Rare Book & Manuscript Library; Albert Gore Research Center at Middle Tennessee State University; Princeton University Mudd Manuscript Library; and University of Michigan Bentley Historical Library.

Because of the haste with which the Homeland Security Act was developed and passed, the legislative record is scant, and most presidential records from that area are only now beginning to be opened to researchers. Because of the thin documentary record currently available, I am indebted to everyone who spoke to me about their experiences working on the Homeland Security Act, including those who spoke on background and cannot be thanked by name. Special thanks to David L. Neal and Esther Olavarria for sharing their recollections of that effort on the record.

Many people read and commented on early drafts of this work, and I am grateful to all of them. I am especially indebted to Valarie Blake, Amber Brugnoli, Amy Cyphert, Jena Martin, Caroline Osborne, Kirsha Trychta, and Elaine Waterhouse Wilson, who together convinced me to give this material book-length treatment. Family members with varied political leanings—Gary Dinzeo, Stephen Peck, Monica Peck, and Andrew Peck—served as my touch point and sounding board for many concepts in the book. If it resonated with them, I trusted it.

Thanks to Maura Roessner and everyone at University of California Press for valuing and promoting this work as both scholarship and story. Work on this book was supported by the West Virginia University College of Law and the Arthur B. Hodges Summer Research Grant.

Finally, I would like to thank the clients of the WVU Immigration Law Clinic. Your courage and fortitude are a daily inspiration.

Preface

"In essence, we are doing death penalty cases in a traffic court setting," immigration judge Dana Leigh Marks said.[1] *Why?* That is the central question that this book seeks to answer. To do so, this book asks two related questions: Why were the immigration courts assigned to their current location in the Department of Justice in the first place? And if those reasons are unconvincing in hindsight, are there good reasons for keeping them there today?

There has been widespread agreement among commentators and policy makers on both sides of the aisle that the immigration court system is broken. While most commentators have focused on troubling outcomes—long backlogs, summary procedures, inconsistent results—the primary focus of this book is on the *structure* of the immigration courts. Its premise is that the outcomes are strongly influenced by the structure, and that the structure is flawed from the perspective of good public administration.

The basic structure of the immigration courts has been in place for eighty years, and reexamination is overdue. Part 1 begins by focusing on the current state of the immigration courts. Those chapters take a look at the astonishingly broad scope of the attorney general's control over individual immigration cases under the current structure, the unprecedented ways in which attorneys general under the Trump administration have wielded that power, and the effects those policies have had on the lives of real people who have appeared before the courts as well as the working conditions of the immigration judges themselves.

How did America arrive at this anomalous court system within a law enforcement agency? To answer that question, part 2 looks closely at the two pivotal decisions that led to the current location of the immigration courts. First, in May 1940, President Franklin D. Roosevelt reluctantly decided to move the immigration services from the Department of Labor to the Department of Justice to catch a "fifth column" of German spies—a widespread fear that turned out to be a hoax perpetrated by the Nazi minister of propaganda, Joseph Goebbels. Second, despite reform efforts in the late 1990s, in the frenzy that followed 9/11 Congress transferred most immigration services to the new Department of Homeland Security. While the immigration courts were spared from being moved into this new security agency by one Republican holdout in the Senate, the opportunity for reform passed. As explored in part 2, this history suggests that the current structure of the immigration courts was motivated by fear and xenophobia in times of war, not sound public administration theory.

Even if the current structure arose by historical accident, there could be other reasons—political accountability, administrative efficiency, institutional expertise—for leaving the structure in place today. Part 3 analyzes potential arguments for the current structure and weighs their merits against the costs to individuals' lives and the reputation of the United States as a model of justice around the world. Finally, for the reader who emerges persuaded that the immigration court system is ripe for reform, part 3 describes and evaluates existing proposals for change and recommends the creation of an independent immigration court system akin to the U.S. Tax Court.

Moving the immigration courts out of a law enforcement agency and into an independent court system would not change the underlying immigration laws. Whether or how those laws need changing is a separate question not addressed by this book. What would change is how the immigration laws are administered, better insulating the immigration courts from the changing winds of politics and ensuring a fair hearing under the law for every person in every court of the United States.

PART I Crisis in the Immigration Courts

1 The Attorney General's Immigration Courts

Maybe you've seen those signs people would sometimes carry at rallies and protest marches aimed at President Trump's immigration policies, signs that say, "This is what 'Never Again' looks like." I first saw one in January 2018, in a photo in the *New York Times* that accompanied a story about the DACA program. In the photo, you can see about a dozen people standing close together, most of them holding up a photo—of themselves or possibly a loved one—printed over a Twitter hashtag like "#HereToStay" or "#DreamActNow." You can tell it's a chilly day because the people are dressed in light coats, scarves, and (for some reason) matching lime green gloves that punctuate the image throughout. Off to the right, one woman holds up a red sign with white lettering, bearing the slogan that Jews have long invoked to recall the Holocaust and stand against the persecution of any people.[1] Those signs, produced by a rabbinical human rights organization called T'ruah, cropped up with particular frequency after Representative Alexandria Ocasio-Cortez controversially referred to ICE detention facilities as "concentration camps," and now they seem to be pointing the finger primarily at U.S. government treatment of people in detention.[2]

When I first saw the sign in January 2018, though, the controversial family separation policy had not yet been announced, and the comparison

I felt challenged to was a different one: Do the conflicts now devastating Central America and Mexico amount to persecution and destruction of an entire people on a mass scale—a holocaust? Framing the question this way doesn't let U.S. immigration policy off the hook, either. Jewish leaders, historians, and others have criticized U.S. immigration policy of the 1930s and early 1940s for turning away large numbers of Jewish refugees from Europe.[3] If what's going on in Central America and Mexico today is mass persecution and the people fleeing it are like the Jews of yesterday, the sign suggested, then U.S. immigration policy deserves renewed scrutiny to avoid repeating the terrible mistakes of the past.

But what does "persecution" really mean? That question underlies some of the biggest debates in immigration law today, because that term is an essential element of any claim for asylum. When President Trump said that the asylum process is rife with abuse, he may have been conflating two separate issues.[4] The first is the need to shut down businesses that unabashedly seek to provide customers with entirely fictitious asylum petitions, which violate anyone's understanding of the asylum laws. Such operations have been prosecuted under Presidents Obama and Trump, though the Trump administration's proposal to deport potentially thousands of such operations' clients generated controversy.[5] The second, and more complex, issue that President Trump may have been raising is the fundamental question of what types of *truthful* claims should be considered "persecution," qualifying a person for asylum under U.S. statutes and treaty obligations.

A struggle for control over immigration law has broken out since the beginning of the Trump administration. The scope of the definition of "persecution" in asylum law is one of several hot-button issues over which the battle has been waged. While a few cases will end up before the U.S. Court of Appeals or, rarely, the Supreme Court, most litigants and their lawyers argue their cases before a different institution: the immigration courts. And it will be an immigration court that tells an individual whether her case fits within the constellation of fact situations that have been defined as persecution in the past. Unless the noncitizen has a lawyer—and most don't—the immigration court's word will usually be the last.[6] Even in those rare cases that are reviewed by the U.S. Court of Appeals, the appellate court will apply a high standard to overturn the decision below, generally accepting the immigration judge's view of the facts and deferring to reasonable interpretations of ambiguous legal terms. In other words, what happens in the immigration courts matters.

Actually, the immigration courts are not really "courts" at all, at least not in the sense we usually use the word. They're not part of the federal judiciary like the U.S. Supreme Court, the U.S. Courts of Appeals, or the U.S. District Courts, created under Article III of the Constitution. And they're not one of the court systems that Congress created to hear claims on certain specialized statutory issues, like the U.S. Tax Court or the U.S. Court of Appeals for the Armed Forces. Those are called Article I courts, since they are under the control of Congress, the branch of government defined by Article I of the Constitution.

Instead, the immigration courts are an arm of the attorney general, who heads the Department of Justice (DOJ). DOJ is part of the executive branch, defined by Article II of the Constitution, and the attorney general is a political appointee who answers directly to the president. Since 1940, the attorney general has had the responsibility of deciding whether a noncitizen was legally permitted to enter the country or is legally entitled to stay. Since that would be a lot of work for one person who has other important duties like prosecuting federal crimes, DOJ employees called "immigration judges" are tasked with hearing those removal cases. The immigration judges are now organized under an office of DOJ called the Executive Office for Immigration Review (EOIR). EOIR also includes the Board of Immigration Appeals (BIA), which hears appeals from decisions of the immigration judges. Collectively, the hearings and appeals directed by EOIR are often referred to in common parlance as "the immigration courts."

Since their function is to assist the attorney general in deciding removal cases, the immigration courts make decisions subject to his supervision and control. They're not Article III judges, so they don't have life tenure to make them independent of the political process. EOIR sets their performance standards and retention policies (though their salaries are set by Congress).[7] Because they are intended to function as an arm of the attorney general, he is free to disagree with them and overrule them at any time, in any case. In short, immigration judges and members of the BIA do not have—and are not intended to have—the independence that Article III or even Article I judges have. They are closely connected to political officers, and their decision-making authority is directly influenced by political goals.

This arrangement is an anomaly in the federal government. There are other federal agencies that adjudicate cases, but those adjudications arise under the statutes those agencies administer. For example, the Department of Labor (DOL) may sanction an employer for violating the Fair Labor Standards Act, and in adjudication before DOL's Wage and Hour Division an employer may contest the agency's reading of the statute or regulation upon which the agency action was based. As the agency that interprets and enforces the labor laws, it arguably makes sense for parties to be able to first challenge DOL's interpretation with DOL before seeking review of the agency's sanction by a court.

The immigration courts in DOJ are different. DOJ is a law enforcement agency that represents the United States. According to its mission statement, its job is

> [t]o enforce the law and defend the interests of the United States according to the law; to ensure public safety against threats foreign and domestic; to provide federal leadership in preventing and controlling crime; to seek just punishment for those guilty of unlawful behavior; and to ensure fair and impartial administration of justice for all Americans.[8]

According to Black's Law Dictionary (the classic source for legal terminology), "law enforcement" means "[t]he detection and punishment of violations of the law." All of DOJ's other functions—prosecuting federal crimes, enforcing federal civil laws, running the Bureau of Prisons—fit within this definition. Deciding immigration cases does not—especially where the cases being decided were brought by DOJ's "client," the United States, against an individual.

In addition, DOJ does not have special expertise in immigration law, apart from supervising the immigration courts themselves. DOJ, despite its law enforcement mission, doesn't enforce the immigration laws; that's done by the Department of Homeland Security (DHS). When you see on the news that Immigration and Customs Enforcement (ICE) is conducting raids or that Customs and Border Protection (CBP) is detaining people at airports, that's DHS, not DOJ or the immigration courts. Between 1940 and 2002, both the enforcement and the adjudication functions under the immigration laws were done by DOJ, but the Homeland Security Act of 2002 (HSA) recognized that this violated a basic tenet of due process: It is patently unfair to have the same party investigating, prosecuting, and deciding the case against you. The HSA formalized an important separation of functions by moving investigation and prosecution into the newly created DHS. Curiously, however, the HSA left the adjudication function within an agency whose purpose is law enforcement.

As long as the immigration courts remain under the authority of the attorney general, the administration of immigration justice will remain a game of political football—with people's lives on the line. While the aggressive actions of the attorneys general in the Trump administration exposed the political volatility of the system, the system itself invites political manipulation and a whiplash approach to the administration of immigration law that varies with the views of whoever happens to be in the White House.

THE ATTORNEY GENERAL'S SELF-REFERRAL POWER

The tension between law enforcement and removal adjudication has existed for over a century. So why is it only now becoming a concern?

It isn't. As early as 1931, a commission established by President Herbert Hoover studied exclusion and deportation procedures, then under the Department of Labor, and recommended that Congress replace them with an independent immigration court system like the U.S. Tax Court. The Wickersham Commission (better known for its separate report on Prohibition) cited many "objectionable features" of the process then, including the "despotic powers" of the immigration officers. "There seems to be no good reason," the Commission concluded, "why we should not proceed at least as far in the establishment of a satisfactory system with respect to the important personal rights involved in deportation as we have with respect to the property rights involved in taxation."[9]

The call for immigration court reform has been repeated over the decades, giving rise to some needed changes but never removing the immigration courts from the political control of law enforcement officers.[10] The issue has attracted renewed attention since 2017 because of the aggressive intervention by the attorneys general in the Trump administration into the day-to-day work of immigration judges. That intervention has affected both the substantive and the procedural operation of the law before the immigration courts in ways that have created chaos for immigrants and immigration judges.

The problem will not end with the Trump administration. The immigration courts' location within the Department of Justice will remain subject to abuse no matter who occupies the White House. Even if a new administration were to reverse some of the more controversial moves of recent attorneys general, the precedent set during the Trump administration could be followed by any administration at any time to achieve its political goals—restrictive or permissive—around immigration. While we expect shifts in policy from a new president, other tools—such as legislation, rulemaking, or executive orders on matters committed to presidential discretion—are available for that purpose. Those tools were designed to require participation by the public and deliberation by the executive branch over controversial issues. Adjudication, by contrast, is a blunt tool for changing policy—especially when people's lives are on the line. Individuals appearing before the immigration courts deserve some predictability about the standards that will be used to decide their cases. A system that allows politically appointed officers to suddenly change settled legal principles being used to decide pending cases—effectively moving the goalposts midway through a game with life-or-death consequences— impugns notions of fundamental fairness in adjudication.

The attorney general's power to rehear immigration court cases comes from a Department of Justice regulation, 8 C.F.R. § 1003.1, which prescribes rules for the organization, jurisdiction, and power of the BIA. That regulation provides

> (h) Referral of cases to the Attorney General.
> (1) The Board shall refer to the Attorney General for review of its decision all cases that:
> (i) The Attorney General directs the Board to refer to him.[11]

Section 1003.1(h)(1)(i) allows the attorney general to exercise plenary authority over the immigration courts, deciding on his own motion to "self-refer" cases from the BIA and redecide them himself. Through this

Administration	Time in Office	Self-Referrals	Possible Self-Referrals
Roosevelt	4 years, 8 months (from August 1940)	0	1
Truman	7 years, 9 months	0	3
Eisenhower	8 years	3	5
Kennedy	2 years, 10 months	2	0
Johnson	5 years, 2 months	0	0
Nixon	5 years, 8 months	0	0
Ford	2 years, 4 months	0	0
Carter	4 years	0	0
Reagan	8 years	0	0
G. H. W. Bush	4 years	0	0
Clinton	8 years	1	0
G. W. Bush	8 years	10	0
Obama	8 years	3	1
Trump	4 years	17	0

power, the attorney general can issue precedential decisions on common legal issues that immigration judges and BIA members must follow when deciding their cases.

The self-referral power has existed since the immigration courts were transferred to the Department of Justice in 1940, but the attorney general's use of that power has become more controversial since the beginning of the Trump administration due to both the frequency and the nature of its use by Trump's attorneys general. First, the frequency: During the twelve preceding presidential administrations, the self-referral power was used rarely, and never at a higher rate than about one a year. The table above indicates the frequency of attorney general self-referrals per administration. (The "Possible Self-Referrals" column includes decisions of the attorney general where the source of the referral was unspecified but the posture of the case suggests that the cases may have been self-referred.)

The spike in frequency, even taken by itself, raises questions regarding the propriety of locating the immigration courts within the Department of

Justice, acting as an arm of the attorney general. As a political appointee serving at the will of the president, the attorney general is subject to the changing winds of politics, and his primary duty is law enforcement, not adjudication. Because of the self-referral power, the attorney general maintains control over every ruling made by the immigration courts, and that control was exercised much more frequently under President Trump than in any prior administration—at a rate more than three times greater than even the relatively active George W. Bush administration. These frequent interventions reveal a tension between the constitutional ideal of an impartial decision-maker and the attorney general's control.

But the Trump administration's use of the self-referral power is remarkable for its nature as well as its frequency, turning the power into a tool to make sweeping policy changes to what were previously viewed as settled questions. This is a sea change from the past. In the first sixty years of its existence, the self-referral power, when used at all, was deployed only to make technical corrections, such as to amend the basis for relief in a particular case or to resolve conflicting decisions of the BIA.[12] Use of the power to make general immigration policy began with the George W. Bush administration. Early decisions by Attorneys General John Ashcroft and Alberto Gonzalez used the power primarily to narrow discretionary and humanitarian relief for people convicted of serious crimes.[13] In the final year of the George W. Bush presidency, Attorney General Michael Mukasey expanded the use of self-referral to establish DOJ's position on several controversial policy questions that were vexing the BIA and the immigration courts: whether the spouse of someone subjected to forced abortion or sterilization was per se eligible for refugee status; the proper test for determining whether a state court conviction should be considered a "crime involving moral turpitude" triggering removability under the Immigration and Nationality Act (INA); and whether a noncitizen had a right to effective assistance of counsel in removal proceedings.[14] Three other decisions from the Bush administration were technical adjustments in light of regulatory changes.[15]

Attorneys general in the Obama administration rejected the use of the self-referral power to make policy, preferring to use more traditional and participatory regulatory tools for that purpose. For example, a few months after taking office, Attorney General Eric Holder, Jr., "reconsider[ed]"

Attorney General Mukasey's decision that noncitizens did not have a right to effective assistance of counsel in removal proceedings. Attorney General Holder instead directed EOIR to initiate rulemaking proceedings under the Administrative Procedure Act (APA) to consider the issue. Rulemaking, which requires an agency to publish notice of its proposed policy change and to invite and consider comments from the public, would, Attorney General Holder stated, "afford[ ] all interested parties a full and fair opportunity to participate and ensure[ ] the relevant facts and analysis are collected and evaluated."[16] The other three self-referred decisions during the Obama administration involved changes prompted by federal court decisions.[17]

Self-referral decisions by the Trump administration are a horse of a different color. The second Bush administration had used the self-referral power to settle questions that the BIA and the federal courts were wrestling with—something like the certiorari power of the Supreme Court. The attorneys general in the Trump administration, in contrast, deployed the power to upset policies that had been viewed by everyone—including DHS—as settled. For example, immigration courts had for many years granted asylum to victims of domestic violence or gang violence, an issue that was suddenly thrown into confusion by Attorney General Sessions's decision in *Matter of A-B-*, as described in chapter 2.[18] Similarly, Attorney General Barr's decision in *Matter of L-E-A-* has raised legal uncertainty about the previously accepted rule that a family may be a "particular social group" under the asylum laws. Even DHS had not viewed that issue as raising any controversy, stipulating to the existence of a particular social group in the underlying case before the BIA. Members of the immigration bar were perplexed by the attorney general's instruction that the immigration courts engage in "rigorous" legal analysis of whether a family constituted a particular social group.[19] As one blogger quipped, "do we require rigorous mathematical analysis to the proposition that $2 + 2 = 4$?"[20]

In another set of cases, President Trump's attorneys general attempted to take away tools that immigration judges have used for years to manage their dockets to ensure that noncitizens had the opportunity to pursue other available forms of immigration relief and that both noncitizens and the government had a reasonable opportunity to prepare for hearings. These cases and other efforts by the attorneys general to control the decisions of immigration judges are described in chapter 3.

The decisions were remarkable in other ways as well. Many of the decisions reached back to overrule cases announced by the BIA years before. For example, Attorney General Sessions's decision regarding asylum based on domestic violence overruled a case decided four years prior; his decision regarding administrative closures overruled a case decided six years prior; and another decision regarding the granting of continuances reversed course on a body of law that had been relied upon since a BIA decision nine years earlier.[21] In another surprising procedural move, Attorney General Sessions referred the case of *Matter of A-B-* to himself while the case was still pending before the immigration court and the BIA, leading even DHS to delicately suggest that the case did "'not appear to be in the best posture for the Attorney General's review.'"[22] And in some cases, Attorneys General Sessions and Barr and Acting Attorney General Whitaker used the self-referral power to make new law on issues that were not even presented to the BIA in its underlying decision—especially to narrow access to asylum in unprecedented ways. While a new administration could find ways to reverse policies set by Trump's attorneys general and revert to previous understandings of the law, the decisions handed down by Trump's attorneys general will remain in effect in the meantime. More importantly, this quick back-and-forth depending on who occupies the White House leaves potential immigrants, as well as the immigration judges attempting to decide their cases, perpetually subject to the changing winds of politics.

To give a better picture of how the policies put in place by Trump's attorneys general are affecting the lives of real people, I'll go into several in more detail in the following chapters and give some specific illustrations. But giving examples in this context requires careful attention to privacy and confidentiality. Because these policies are only a few years old, many of the affected people still have cases pending—at least those who were fortunate enough to find a lawyer to help assert their rights. In addition, few decisions are publicly available—immigration judges' decisions are unpublished, and only a few decisions of the BIA are designated as "precedent decisions" and published by DOJ. Facts of individual cases can sometimes be drawn from these precedential decisions, from the few briefs and decisions on review before the U.S. Courts of Appeals, and from occasional statements to the media by noncitizens, speaking for themselves or through their lawyers.

For the most part, these are the types of sources I'll use to tell stories about people affected by the immigration court policies of the Trump administration. As background, I'm also drawing from my own experiences as a lawyer practicing in the immigration courts. As a law professor and codirector of the Immigration Law Clinic at West Virginia University College of Law, I work with a team of students and attorneys to represent clients in immigration matters. Because of attorney-client privilege, I won't describe our clients' individual cases, but the perspectives I'll offer draw on their experiences. Nearly all of the examples of attorney general intervention I'll describe have directly affected one or more of our clients. And that's in one small law practice. The immigration court policies of the Trump administration have had sweeping effects.

2 Whittling Away at Asylum Law

One of the first acts of Attorney General Sessions that roiled the immigration bar was his decision to refer *Matter of A-B-* to himself. Before the BIA, the parties had argued whether the respondent (a woman who, for her privacy, was referred to only by her initials) qualified for asylum based on the domestic abuse she had experienced for years at the hand of her husband—a series of crimes that the police in her country of origin, El Salvador, did nothing about. In referring the case to himself, however, Attorney General Sessions requested that the parties brief a much broader question: "Whether, and under what circumstances, being a victim of private criminal activity constitutes a cognizable 'particular social group' for purposes of an application for asylum or withholding of removal."[1] This question was never at issue before the BIA. It had long been accepted that a victim of private criminal activity might, upon a proper showing, be granted asylum as a member of a particular social group. The only question presented to the BIA in *Matter of A-B-* was whether Ms. A-B- had, in fact, made that showing.

In his decision on the case three months later, the attorney general seemed to announce a new standard. "Generally," the attorney general's opinion stated, "claims by aliens pertaining to domestic violence or gang violence perpetrated by non-governmental actors will not qualify for asylum."[2] To understand why this statement stirred so much controversy, we need to take a step back and consider the structure of asylum law.

What we call "the law of asylum" is not really a single law but a bundle of rules and standards drawn from several legal sources. The first is treaty law: In 1968, the United States acceded to the United Nations Protocol Relating to the Status of Refugees.[3] The Protocol, in turn, incorporates Article 33 of another treaty, the U.N. Convention Relating to the Status of Refugees, in which signatories commit not to return a "refugee" to a country "where his life or freedom would be threatened on account of his race, religion, nationality, membership of a particular social group, or political opinion."[4] The Convention and Protocol codified a fundamental principle of international law called *non-refoulement*, which arose out of recognition of the failure of many countries to accept Jewish refugees fleeing the Holocaust and the forcible (and often fatal) return of millions of refugees to the Soviet Union after World War II.[5]

The obligations undertaken by the United States in the U.N. Protocol were incorporated into U.S. law by the Refugee Act of 1980, which amended the Immigration and Nationality Act (INA).[6] As amended, the INA includes Section 101(a)(42)(A), which defines a "refugee" to include

any person who is outside any country of such person's nationality or, in the case of a person having no nationality, is outside any country in which such person last habitually resided, and who is unable or unwilling to return to, and is unable or unwilling to avail himself or herself of the protection of, that country because of persecution or a well-founded fear of persecution on account of race, religion, nationality, membership in a particular social group, or political opinion.[7]

The amendments to the INA also included a new Section 208, which provided procedures under which "any alien who is physically present in the United States or who arrives in the United States" may apply for asylum.[8] Those procedures include the right to apply "whether or not [arriving] at a designated port of arrival"; a burden of proof on the applicant to prove that he is a refugee as defined by Section 101(a)(42); and an obligation that the application be filed within one year of arrival, except in the case of changed circumstances that materially affect the applicant's eligibility for asylum or exceptional circumstances justifying delay in application.[9] The procedures permit the attorney general to deny asylum in certain specific cases, such as where the applicant has participated in the persecution of others or has been convicted of a "particularly serious crime."[10] The statutory procedures are outlined in further detail in regulations promulgated by the attorney general or the secretary of Homeland Security. For example, the attorney general, as the head of the department that contains the immigration courts, has promulgated regulations that specify how immigration hearings are to be conducted.[11] The DHS secretary has promulgated regulations relating to procedures for interviewing noncitizens apprehended at the border who claim a credible or reasonable fear of being returned to their country of origin.[12]

In addition to international obligations and statutory and regulatory rights and duties, the law of asylum includes the interpretations that the federal courts have given to those legal sources. As Chief Justice Marshall famously stated in *Marbury v. Madison,* "[i]t is emphatically the province and duty of the judicial department to say what the law is."[13] That statement in 1803 established the principle of judicial review: Although Congress makes the laws, the federal courts have the authority to decide what the laws mean for individual cases. Despite the doctrine of judicial review, however, the federal courts will not simply overturn just any decision made by an agency like DOJ or its immigration courts. In a case from 1984 called *Chevron v. Natural Resources Defense Council,* the Supreme Court held that federal courts should defer to an agency's interpretation of a statute it administers if the statute is ambiguous, as long as the agency's interpretation is reasonable.[14] *Chevron* deference has limits; for example, a court may decide the statute is unambiguous, and courts will not give the same deference to an agency interpretation announced in a document that does not have the force of law. Because of the *Chevron* doctrine, however, locating the immigration courts within a federal agency like DOJ means that the attorney general and the immigration judges and the BIA will have significant power to interpret the INA. Taken together, all of these sources of law—treaty, statute, regulation, decisions of the BIA or the attorney general, and federal court decisions—comprise "the law of asylum."

That brings us back to *Matter of A-B-.* In that case, Attorney General Sessions used his self-referral power to redecide a case that the BIA had decided a year and a half earlier granting asylum to the respondent, Ms. A-B-. The attorney general decided that the BIA had misapplied the law in finding that Ms. A-B- had stated a claim for asylum based on domestic violence that the police were unable or unwilling to control. In his decision from June 11, 2018, the attorney general made the controversial statement that victims of violence by nongovernmental actors would "generally" not be eligible for asylum. Attorney General Sessions's decision overruled an earlier case, *Matter of A-R-C-G-*, on which the BIA had relied in granting asylum to Ms. A-B-.[15]

I'd like to start my description of this case, as lawyers are trained to do, by telling you something about the life of the real person, Ms. A-B-, that underlies all the legalese. I can't, because the BIA decision is unpublished and the attorney general's reviewing decision tells us only this about her: "The respondent asserted that her ex-husband, with whom she shares three children, repeatedly abused her physically, emotionally, and sexually during and after their marriage."[16] Instead, I'll tell you something about Ms. A-R-C-G-, because we know a little more about her from the BIA decision in her case. I highlight the facts in *Matter of A-R-C-G-* not because they are unusual but precisely because they are typical of the stories that immigration lawyers often hear from clients, not only but especially women from the Northern Triangle of Central America.

Here is what the BIA tells us about the life of Ms. A-R-C-G- before coming to the United States, as she told the immigration court:

> The lead respondent is the mother of the three minor respondents. The respondents are natives and citizens of Guatemala. . . .
>
> The Immigration Judge found the respondent to be a credible witness, which is not contested on appeal. It is undisputed that the respondent, who married at age 17, suffered repugnant abuse by her husband. This abuse included weekly beatings after the respondent had their first child. On one occasion, the respondent's husband broke her nose. Another time, he threw paint thinner on her, which burned her breast. He raped her.
>
> The respondent contacted the police several times but was told that they would not interfere in a marital relationship. On one occasion the police came to her home after her husband hit her on the head, but he was not arrested. Subsequently, he threatened the respondent with death if she called the police again. The respondent repeatedly tried to leave the relationship by staying with her father, but her husband found her and threatened to kill her

if she did not return to him. Once she went to Guatemala City for about 3 months, but he followed her and convinced her to come home with promises that he would discontinue the abuse. The abuse continued when she returned. The respondent left Guatemala in December 2005, and she believes her husband will harm her if she returns.[17]

Undoubtedly, Ms. A-R-C-G- was in grave danger from her husband, and the attorney general in *Matter of A-B-* also acknowledged the "vile abuse" suffered by Ms. A-B- and the "harrowing experiences of many other victims of domestic violence around the world." Nevertheless, Attorney General Sessions emphasized, the "'asylum statute is not a general hardship statute.'" The language relied on by the immigration judges to grant asylum to both Ms. A-R-C-G- and Ms. A-B-, he said, was not intended to be "'some omnibus catch-all' for solving every 'heart-rending situation.'"[18]

That general statement about the asylum law is true, as far as it goes. Not everyone who has suffered hardship in their home country is entitled to asylum in the United States. As mentioned earlier, the INA provides that a person is only entitled to asylum if the person is unable or unwilling to return to their country of origin "because of persecution or a well-founded fear of persecution on account of race, religion, nationality, membership in a particular social group, or political opinion."[19]

But that doesn't mean that a victim of domestic violence can't qualify for asylum. Cases like *Matter of A-B-* and *Matter of A-R-C-G-* turn on the meaning of two terms in the asylum statute: "persecution" and "membership in a particular social group." As I described earlier, the parameters of the law are outlined by judges deciding, on a case-by-case basis, whether a particular litigant's factual circumstances fit within one of the defined terms. Because of the *Chevron* doctrine, the BIA has authority to interpret statutory terms that are ambiguous (though the U.S. Courts of Appeals and the Supreme Court have the final authority to decide whether the statute is clear). By looking at decisions of the BIA, the Court of Appeals, and, rarely, the Supreme Court, we can better understand what "persecution" means, and what it means to be persecuted "on account of . . . membership in a particular social group."

In his opinion, the attorney general defined "persecution" by stating, "[t]he prototypical refugee flees her home country because the government has persecuted her—either directly through its own actions or indirectly by being unwilling or unable to prevent the misconduct of nongovernment actors—based upon a statutorily protected ground."[20] The "unable or unwilling" standard is part of the definition of "refugee" at Section 101(a)(42) of the INA and was first recognized by the BIA in a case from 1985 called *Matter of Acosta.* In that case, the BIA held that the term "persecution" added to the INA in 1980 adopted a long-standing interpretation of the term, including that the "harm or suffering had to be inflicted either by the government of a country or by persons or an organization that the government was unable or unwilling to control."[21] That standard has since been adopted by the U.S. Courts of Appeals in a plethora of cases, finding asylum either where police failed to adequately control private violence that was reported or where the government was so notoriously unable or unwilling to control certain types of private violence that reporting the conduct would have been futile or might have merely subjected the respondent to increased violence.[22]

Without explanation, however, the attorney general two pages later seemed to all but write the "unable or unwilling" standard out of the asylum law. "While I do not decide that violence inflicted by non-governmental actors may never serve as the basis for an asylum or withholding application based on membership in a particular social group, in practice such claims are unlikely to satisfy the statutory grounds for proving group persecution that the government is unable or unwilling to address," the attorney general wrote. "The mere fact that a country may have problems effectively policing certain crimes—such as domestic violence or gang violence—or that certain populations are more likely to be victims of crime, cannot itself establish an asylum claim."[23]

If persecution includes being the victim of violence that the government is unable or unwilling to control, it doesn't follow that claims based on domestic violence or gang violence "in practice" will not satisfy the asylum standard. Under the law as defined by the BIA and the U.S. Courts of Appeals, the legal question is not whether "a country may have problems effectively policing certain crimes," as the attorney general wrote, but whether a government was "unable or unwilling to control" the harm inflicted by nongovernmental actors, such as a husband or a gang. To support his conclusion, the attorney general relied on *Velasquez v. Sessions,* a case decided by the U.S. Court of Appeals for the Fourth Circuit in 2017, which stated that "'[e]vidence consistent with acts of private violence or that merely shows that an individual has been the victim of criminal activity does not constitute evidence of persecution on a statutorily protected ground.'"[24] In *Velasquez*, however, the facts recited by the court do not include any claim that Ms. Velasquez attempted to report the violence and threats against her to the government or that she had any basis for believing that such reports would be futile.[25] In the case of *Matter of A-R-C-G-*, in contrast, Ms. A-R-C-G- did not merely say that the Guatemalan government had problems "effectively policing" her husband's violence against her. She said she reported the violence to the police; the police came to her home but failed to arrest her husband; and she was told the police "would not interfere in a marital relationship."[26] This evidence, which the immigration judge found credible, provides support for a ruling that the government of Guatemala was "unable or unwilling to control" the violence against her.

There is another phrase in the statute that is closely intertwined with the analysis in these cases, and that is "membership in a particular social group." The statute says that a person is a "refugee" if he or she experiences persecution "on account of" one of five specifically named factors: "race, religion, nationality, membership in a particular social group, or political opinion." In *Matter of A-R-C-G-*, the respondent was defined as a member of the particular social group of "married women in Guatemala who are unable to leave their relationship."[27] Similarly, in *Matter of A-B-*, the particular social group was defined as "El Salvadoran women who are unable to leave their domestic relationships where they have children in common" with their partners.[28] The protected ground does not have to be the only reason the persecutor inflicted harm on the person seeking asylum, but it must be "at least one central reason" why the person was targeted.[29]

The BIA has established a three-part test, adopted by the U.S. Courts of Appeals, to delineate what it means to be a member of a "particular social group." To satisfy that standard, a group must (1) have members who share an "immutable characteristic"; (2) be "defined with particularity"; and (3) be "socially distinct in the society in question."[30] For example, Ms. A-R-C-G- might have argued that she couldn't (or shouldn't be required to) change the fact that she was a woman and that she was unable to escape her husband's violence even by ending the relationship, that it could be clearly defined who fell into this group, and that people in Guatemala (such as the police) viewed her as a woman in a "marital relationship." Actually, even the attorney general's decision in *Matter of A-B-* acknowledged that every respondent—including a domestic violence victim—has the right to try to make this three-part showing. His narrow holding in the case was not that Ms. A-B- couldn't possibly establish membership in a particular social group, but only that the immigration judges in both *Matter of A-B-* and *Matter of A-R-C-G-*, on which it relied, had failed to make individual findings of fact on each of these three elements.

And yet, despite acknowledging that each respondent was entitled to demonstrate immutability, particularity, and social distinction, the attorney general made that blanket statement: "Generally, claims by aliens pertaining to domestic violence or gang violence perpetrated by non-governmental actors will not qualify for asylum."[31] This reinterpretation of the law, which appeared to contradict even his own decision, is what had immigration lawyers up in arms.

Even DHS officials were confused. The United States Citizenship and Immigration Service (USCIS) issued a guidance document to its asylum officers, who are in charge of reviewing asylum applications by foreign nationals who are not in removal proceedings before the immigration courts, including those arriving at the border. The USCIS guidance cited, in boldface type, the attorney general's conclusion that, "[i]n general, . . . claims based on membership in a putative particular social group defined by the members' vulnerability to harm of domestic violence or gang violence committed by non-government actors will not establish the basis for asylum, refugee status, or a credible fear or reasonable fear of persecution."[32] But a memorandum by ICE to attorneys who represent the government in immigration courts acknowledged that, "although the AG overruled *A-R-C-G-*, he did not conclude that particular social groups based on status as a victim of private violence could never be cognizable, or that applicants could never qualify for asylum or statutory withholding of removal based on domestic violence." ICE simply advised its attorneys to "ensure that [immigration judges] and the BIA rigorously analyze each claim such that protection is only granted where the alien has met his or her burden with respect to each and every element."[33] Immigration judges and BIA members were confused as well. One early decision of the BIA reportedly denied a claim where the particular social group was "'akin to the group defined in *Matter of A-R-C-G-*,'" saying that the attorney general's decision in *Matter of A-B-* "'has foreclosed the respondent's arguments.'"[34] Other immigration judges, however, have issued decisions since *Matter of A-B-* that granted asylum based on domestic violence after making the necessary individualized fact-findings consistent with the attorney general's actual holding.[35]

On December 17, 2018, asylum applicants filed a lawsuit against the attorney general and DHS, arguing that USCIS denials of asylum based on *Matter of A-B-* and the USCIS guidance violated the INA and the APA. The plaintiffs were twelve adults and children who had fled appalling violence in Central America and were detained while or shortly after trying to enter the United States. Each of the plaintiffs told immigration officials that they had a fear of being returned to their home country and requested asylum. Despite finding the plaintiffs' stories credible, the asylum officers in each case found that, based on *Matter of A-B-* and the USCIS guidance, their claims did not merit asylum. Those negative credible fear determinations were upheld by immigration judges, and the plaintiffs then brought this separate lawsuit challenging the underlying rule.[36]

The district court's decision described examples of the violence the plaintiffs had fled. Plaintiff Grace was raped, beaten, threatened, and disparaged for her indigenous heritage for more than twenty years by her partner, who also beat, sexually assaulted, and threatened to kill several of her children. When Grace complained to local authorities, they and her persecutor evicted her from her home. Plaintiff Mina left her country after gangs murdered her father-in-law for helping a family friend escape from the gang. When the police refused her husband's request for assistance, he went to a neighboring town to seek assistance from the police there. Knowing that her husband was away, gang members broke down Mina's door and beat her until she could no longer walk.[37]

In his argument to the district court in *Grace*, the attorney general stated that *Matter of A-B-* and the guidance document did not create a general rule against domestic violence–related or gang-related asylum claims, but that, if such a general rule did exist, it was a lawful exercise of the attorney general's discretion to establish it. The district court rejected the argument, holding that the USCIS guidance did create a general rule and stating that "there is no legal basis for an effective categorical ban on domestic violence and gang-related claims."[38] Based on that and other legal defects in the policies, the district court issued a nationwide injunction of the policies arising from *Matter of A-B-*, and ordered that Grace and the other plaintiffs should be returned to the United States and given new credible fear interviews.

The government appealed to the U.S. Court of Appeals for the DC Circuit. There, the government simply argued that *Matter of A-B-* does not contain a new rule against asylum claims based on domestic violence and gang violence at all but merely reminds judges to make findings as to the traditional elements of asylum law.[39] Thus narrowed, the court of appeals accepted the government's characterization of the rule. The court of appeals upheld the district court's injunction, however, on the grounds that *Matter of A-B-* and the USCIS guidance announced, without explanation, new and more stringent rules with respect to two aspects of asylum officers' decisions: First, both documents directed that asylum officers should find that the government was "unable or unwilling" to control the private conduct only where the government "condoned" it or showed "complete helplessness." Second, the USCIS guidance directed that asylum officers should apply the law of the circuit in which they were located, rather than the most favorable rule as previous policy had directed. The court noted, however, that the government was free to explain and reissue those new policies.[40]

It remains to be seen what the ultimate impact of *Matter of A-B-* will be on noncitizens in immigration court seeking asylum based on domestic violence or gang violence. As the court of appeals pointed out, DOJ and DHS relied on *Matter of A-B-* to propose a new regulation about asylum eligibility. Citing the attorney general's decision, DOJ and DHS proposed a new rule that those agencies, "in general, will not favorably adjudicate the claims of aliens who claim persecution based on . . . interpersonal animus in which the alleged persecutor has not targeted, or manifested an animus against, other members of an alleged particular social group in addition to the member who has raised the claim at issue." The commentary explained that this category applied to victims of domestic violence where the abuser had not harmed other group members.[41]

Even if the rule is not finalized and a new administration reverses course, Attorney General Sessions's decision in *Matter of A-B-* remains in effect for the immigration courts. The multiple interpretations of the scope and effect of that decision will likely leave immigration judges, and the noncitizens and lawyers who appear before them, in confusion for months or years to come. More broadly, with decisions like *Matter of A-B-* as examples, the attorney general's structural authority to dictate immigration court decisions may be wielded by any future administration, and crucial decisions about individual cases can still be decided based on politics rather than law at any time.

ASYLUM FOR MEMBERS OF TARGETED FAMILIES

While the effect of *Matter of A-B-* was being hashed out between DOJ and the courts, the attorney general continued to use the self-referral power to narrow asylum claims in other contexts. On July 29, 2019, Attorney General Barr decided a self-referred case regarding whether a family was a "particular social group" for purposes of asylum. In *Matter of L-E-A-*, the respondent claimed that he was persecuted by a drug cartel, La Familia Michoacana, after his father refused to sell the cartel's drugs out of his father's store in Mexico City. The respondent was shot at from a black SUV while walking near his home; about a week later, armed members of the drug cartel driving the same vehicle approached him and asked him to sell drugs from his father's store. When he refused, they threatened him; shortly thereafter, he was kidnapped by four masked men in the same vehicle. He managed to escape, fleeing to Tijuana and later the United States.[42]

In its initial decision in 2017, the BIA had found that the "immediate family" of Mr. L-E-A-'s father qualified as a particular social group—but his asylum claim nevertheless failed because the BIA held that his family membership was not at least one central reason for the harm he suffered from the drug cartel.[43] Even though the BIA had denied asylum, Acting Attorney General Whitaker referred the case to himself, inviting briefing on "[w]hether and under what circumstances, an alien may establish persecution on account of membership in a 'particular social group' under [the INA] based on the alien's membership in a family unit."[44]

This question surprised the immigration bar. Not only was it a different question than the one presented to the BIA, it was an issue that, in the words of one blogger, "had acquired a 'the sky is blue' certainty."[45] The first BIA decision that defined "particular social group" in 1985 recognized that the common, immutable characteristic shared by all particular social group members "might be an innate one such as sex, color, or kinship ties." Although the requirements of particularity and social distinction have since been added to the definition of "particular social group," that conclusion has not changed. Every U.S. Court of Appeals that has decided the question—eight out of the eleven circuits—has concluded that a family can be a particular social group.[46] In 2014, the First Circuit stated that "[t]he law in this circuit and others is clear that a family may be a particular social group simply by virtue of its kinship ties, without requiring anything more."[47]

As in *Matter of A-B-*, the attorney general's actual holding in *Matter of L-E-A-* was narrow, merely concluding that the BIA erred in relying on DHS concessions rather than performing a fact-based inquiry to determine that the respondent had demonstrated that his father's family was a particular social group.[48] Again following the lead of *Matter of A-B-*, however, the attorney general's decision in *Matter of L-E-A-* contained broad, general statements that purported to radically change the commonly accepted meaning of "particular social group." For instance, the attorney general stated that, "unless an immediate family carries greater societal import, it is unlikely that a proposed family-based group will be 'distinct' in the way required by the [INA] for purposes of asylum."[49] In other words, the attorney general proposed that the "kinship ties, without anything more" cited by the First Circuit would no longer be sufficient. "Under his proposed interpretation," one blogger wryly concluded, "an asylum seeker must be a Kardashian to satisfy the [particular social group] standard."[50]

To support his conclusion, the attorney general reasoned that interpreting "particular social group" to include any family "would render virtually every alien a member of a particular social group."[51] As legal commentators have pointed out, however, this interpretation would not make the term "particular social group" any more broad than the other four factors on which an asylum claim may be based. Virtually every noncitizen will also have a "race, religion, nationality, . . . [and] political opinion," yet the attorney general does not suggest that those terms are overbroad. To qualify for asylum, a noncitizen must still demonstrate that the persecution was on account of the protected characteristic, a showing the courts refer to as "nexus"—the very reason the BIA had originally denied asylum to Mr. L-E-A-.[52]

The tussle over the meaning of "particular social group" will continue in the months and years to come, as immigration judges and DHS asylum officers struggle to make sense of the attorney general's decision and unsuccessful respondents seek review by the federal courts. In light of the *Chevron* doctrine, courts will have to determine whether the phrase "particular social group" in the INA is ambiguous in a way that allows room for Attorney General Barr's interpretation in *Matter of L-E-A-*. Even if the courts ultimately decide that the statute does not permit the attorney general's reading, however, immigration judges must attempt to make sense of it in the meantime, and anyone deported while confusion reigns may have no second chance. And while a new attorney general could reverse the rule of *Matter of L-E-A-*, the nature of attorney general control means that a future attorney general could simply change it back again, and so on—resulting in a whiplash approach to justice that defies the ideals of fair and impartial adjudication.

The power of the attorney general to reinterpret the substance of asylum law has resulted in subjecting thousands of peoples' lives to uncertainty. But it may be the attorney general's authority to manipulate the *procedures* used by immigration courts that has created even more political volatility in the administration of immigration justice.

3 Policing the Immigration Courts

In late June 2014, a Guatemalan youth named Reynaldo Castro Tum entered the United States. He was seventeen years old. On June 26, Mr. Castro Tum was apprehended by CBP. Because Mr. Castro Tum was under eighteen, arrived without a parent or guardian, and did not appear to have a parent or guardian in the United States, CBP designated him as an "unaccompanied alien child" (UAC).[1] Under the law, a UAC is not detained by DHS but instead is placed in the custody of the Office of Refugee Resettlement, part of the Department of Health and Human Services (HHS-ORR). Children placed in HHS-ORR custody can be released to the care of a family member or, if none is found, placed in a youth facility operated by HHS-ORR.[2]

The UAC program dates back to the reorganization of the immigration services when DHS was created in 2002. At that time, Congress determined that minors arriving here alone required services such as education, health care, family reunification, and special protection from exploitation that could be better provided by a social service agency than by law enforcement. HSS-ORR policy is to place the child "in the least restrictive setting that is in the best interests of the child, taking into account danger to self, danger to the community, and risk of flight."[3]

Mr. Castro Tum told CBP that he planned to live with his brother-in-law and provided them with an address in rural Pennsylvania. Two days later, a DHS officer gave Mr. Castro Tum a notice to appear (NTA), which is the document that officially commences removal proceedings in immigration court. Following DHS practice at the time, the NTA told Mr. Castro Tum where to appear in court, but it didn't tell him when. It merely instructed him to be at the court address on "a date to be set at a time to be set." The NTA listed the address that Mr. Castro Tum had given for his brother-in-law and instructed him to inform DHS if he moved to another address. On August 20, HHS-ORR released Mr. Castro Tum to the custody of his brother-in-law.[4]

Not much is publicly known about Mr. Castro Tum or why he came to the United States. The website of HHS-ORR says that reasons that children arrive unaccompanied "may include rejoining family already in the U.S., escaping violent communities or abusive family relationships in their home country, or finding work to support their families in home countries."[5] In our law practice, we often see teenagers from El Salvador, Guatemala, and Honduras coming to the United States to avoid recruitment by gangs or to escape retribution after they or their family members have refused to cooperate with gangs. A report from 2019 on crime and safety in Guatemala says that extortion by the two primary gangs there, Barrio 18 and MS-13, is "incredibly common." In addition to targeting businesses, "[t]he gangs also target schoolchildren, street vendors, and private citizens. . . . Gang members usually punish non-compliant victims with violent assault or murder, and their family members are also victimized as punishment."[6] There is no doubt that the years preceding Mr. Castro Tum's entry into the United States saw an explosion of unaccompanied child migrants. The number of unaccompanied children detained by CBP increased from 4,059 in fiscal year 2011 to 10,443 in FY2012 and 21,537 in FY2013. In 2014, the year Mr. Castro Tum entered, the number was estimated to be more than 68,000.[7]

But there is a darker way of viewing this increase in unaccompanied child migrants. Attorney General Sessions, who would soon refer Mr. Castro Tum's case to himself for decision, said in several public statements that the UAC program was being used by gangs like MS-13 in the United States to import new recruits for gang activity here. For example, in

September 2017, he told federal law enforcement officers in Boston that MS-13 in Central Islip, New York, was "running rampant: killing victims, traumatizing communities, and replenishing its ranks by taking advantage of the Unaccompanied Alien Child program." Attorney General Sessions viewed the UAC program less as a means for youth to escape gangs in Central America than as a means for gangs to expand their reach in the United States: "This program continues to place juveniles from Central America into this gang controlled territory," he said. "It is clearly being abused."[8]

As for Mr. Castro Tum, neither DHS nor the immigration court had any information as to precisely why he left Guatemala. There was no evidence that he had a history of gang involvement or that he was more at risk of gang recruitment here than in Guatemala; nor do we know that he left specifically to flee gang violence. We simply don't know much about Mr. Castro Tum, because he didn't show up for his court hearings. And that's where the human crisis of gang violence and youth migration meets the formalities of legal procedure—with consequences for Mr. Castro Tum and thousands of other people, both children and adults, in immigration court proceedings.

Because the notice to appear that DHS personally gave Mr. Castro Tum didn't list a time or date of his hearing, when he left for his brother-in-law's home in Pennsylvania he didn't know when he was supposed to appear in court. DOJ's standard NTA form says, "YOU ARE ORDERED to appear before a judge of the United States Department of Justice at_____ on _____ at _____ to show why you should not be removed from the United States on the charge(s) set forth above." The last two blanks have the words "(Date)" and "(Time)" printed underneath. A DOJ regulation passed in 1997 said that a notice to appear only had to provide the place, date, and time of the hearing "where practicable."[9] As a result, DHS usually issued notices to appear without filling in the blanks indicating a time and date for the hearing, as they did in Mr. Castro Tum's case

Later, in June 2018, the Supreme Court in a case called *Pereira v. Sessions* would hold that "[a] putative notice to appear that fails to designate the specific time or place of the noncitizen's removal proceedings is not a 'notice to appear under [the governing statute].'"[10] The Court went on to conclude that such a defective NTA could not cut off the defense claimed by Mr. Pereira, called cancelation of removal, which involves a claim of hardship to a U.S. citizen spouse or parent. Later in 2018, the BIA would interpret *Pereira* as saying that an NTA that lacked a date was only defective in the specific circumstances considered by the Court in that case. Where the noncitizen later received notice of the hearing date, the BIA held, the NTA was adequate.[11] Since the Supreme Court's language did not expressly clarify the limits of its ruling, however, practitioners continue to challenge nonspecific NTAs in other contexts. Whether such NTAs will be deemed invalid across the board is a question that no doubt will end up before the federal courts again. Anticipating this challenge (at a minimum where a noncitizen asserts a defense of cancelation of removal), DHS now often lists a specific time and date for the initial court hearing in the NTA that it personally serves on the noncitizen.

At the time DHS served an NTA on Mr. Castro Tum, however, *Pereira* had not yet been decided and DHS followed its usual practice of not specifying the date or time of the hearing. This meant that, once the immigration court set the date and time, the court would have to mail a new and more specific notice to Mr. Castro Tum at the address provided by DHS. On November 26, 2014, the immigration court mailed a notice of hearing to the address that Mr. Castro Tum had provided to CBP. Mr. Castro Tum failed to appear on that hearing date on January 8, 2015, and immigration judge Steven A. Morley granted a continuance of the hearing until a later date.[12] A new hearing date was set for April and notice was mailed to Mr. Castro Tum at the same address, and again he failed to appear. On a third hearing date in October, counsel for DHS was unavailable and Mr. Castro Tum also did not appear. At a fourth hearing date on January 14, 2016, Judge Morley expressed concerns about the addresses provided by DHS in that and other cases involving unaccompanied minors. In many cases (although not in Mr. Castro Tum's) the hearing notices sent by the immigration court had been returned as undeliverable.[13] In fact, this was what would happen in the case of *Pereira v. Sessions,* which ultimately went to the Supreme Court (though Mr. Pereira was not a minor): DHS had sent the notice of hearing to Mr. Pereira's street address instead of the post office box address he had provided, and the notice of hearing was returned to sender.[14] At the hearing in January 2016 for Mr. Castro Tum, DHS requested additional time to confirm the addresses in all of the unaccompanied minor cases, and Judge Morley granted another continuance to allow them to do so.[15] Mr. Castro Tum again failed to appear at a hearing on April 18, 2016, and DHS could not confirm that it had mailed the notice of hearing to the correct address on file for him, leaving questions about whether the government had met its burden of proving notice.[16]

Unconvinced that DHS had provided fair notice to unaccompanied minors, Judge Morley temporarily closed Mr. Castro Tum's case and ten others in which unaccompanied minors had failed to appear.[17] In closing the cases, Judge Morley used a mechanism called administrative closure, which had been used by immigration courts since at least the 1980s. Administrative closure doesn't provide relief from removal or give the noncitizen any type of immigration status, but it allows the immigration judge to place the case on hold. Often, this happens because the respondent, while in removal proceedings before DOJ's immigration courts, is also waiting for USCIS to adjudicate his application for another type of immigration status—such as sponsorship by an employer or U.S. citizen relative. DHS would also request administrative closure from an immigration judge when it considered a case to be low priority, and occasionally an immigration judge would grant administrative closure to allow time to resolve administrative issues like the question of adequate notice that concerned Judge Morley. In a case from 2012 called *Matter of Avetisyan,* the BIA held that immigration judges could grant administrative closure even over the objection of either party if that party could not give a persuasive reason for its objection.[18]

DHS appealed Mr. Castro Tum's case and other similar cases to the BIA.[19] On review, the BIA held that the immigration court erred in "presum[ing] that addresses provided through the established HHS-ORR procedures are inherently unreliable," since that finding was not supported by evidence in the record in Mr. Castro Tum's case. The BIA also held that the immigration judge should have given a "presumption of regularity" to the statutory procedures used by DHS to obtain the address and mail the notice of hearing. The BIA vacated the administrative closure of Mr. Castro Tum's case and remanded the case to the immigration court to be put back on the docket.[20]

At this point, Attorney General Sessions referred the BIA decision to himself for review. Rather than reviewing the propriety of Judge Morley's administrative closure in that case, however, the attorney general asked for briefing on whether "Immigration Judges and the Board have the authority . . . to order administrative closure in a case."[21] The question whether immigration judges can *ever* administratively close a case was never presented to Judge Morley or the BIA.

The heart of the issue is how much independence the immigration judges and the BIA are meant to have. Where the law does not specifically provide a power—but does not specifically foreclose it either—does the immigration judge have leeway to do what he thinks is right, or does he merely follow the marching orders of the attorney general? Attorney General Sessions's answer was the latter. Beginning his analysis of the scope of immigration judges' power, Attorney General Sessions's decision cited numerous authorities that characterize the immigration courts as agents of the attorney general. Immigration judges "'shall be subject to such supervision and shall perform such duties as the Attorney General shall prescribe,'" he quoted from the statute, and may "'exercise the powers and duties delegated to them by the [INA] and by the Attorney General through regulation.'" Quoting Supreme Court precedent, Attorney General Sessions noted that the BIA, too, is "'a regulatory creature of the Attorney General, to which he has delegated much of his authority under the applicable statutes.'" Department of Justice regulations, he noted, provide that the BIA is limited to "'review of those administrative adjudications under the Act that the Attorney General may by regulation assign to it,'" and is "'governed by the provisions and limitations prescribed by applicable law, regulations, and procedures, and by decisions of the Attorney General.'"

Relying on these authorities, Attorney General Sessions rejected an alternative argument: that other broad delegations of power to immigration judges to manage their dockets and decide cases independently entailed the power to administratively close cases where, in the judge's view, circumstances warranted it. For instance, another DOJ regulation states that immigration judges and the BIA "shall exercise their independent judgment and discretion and may take any action consistent with their authorities under the [INA] and regulations that is appropriate and necessary for the disposition of such cases." Although noting that federal courts have interpreted these provisions as providing "'a reasonable degree of latitude in conducting . . . proceedings,'" the attorney general held that such latitude did not extend to administrative closure of proceedings. "Grants of general authority to take measures 'appropriate and necessary for the disposition of such cases' would not ordinarily include the authority to suspend such cases indefinitely. Administrative closure in fact is the antithesis of a final disposition." Another regulation defining the jurisdiction of immigration judges in removal proceedings gives them the authority to "take any other action consistent with applicable law and regulations as may be appropriate." Because this section appears in a statute that defines jurisdiction, the attorney general interpreted the rule as applying only to the scope of an immigration judge's authority to issue final orders, not to the scope of her authority to make procedural rulings within a proceeding.

The attorney general held that immigration judges and the BIA do not have authority to administratively close cases because no statute or regulation expressly provided for a general administrative closure power. He noted six instances in which regulations or court settlements *had* provided for a power of administrative closure, but concluded that such authority was limited to those specific circumstances.[22]

The immigration bar reacted with alarm. "Many immigrants who had claims for immigration relief relied on government assurances that they wouldn't be deported if they agreed to let their cases be closed," said Jeanne Atkinson, executive director of Catholic Legal Immigration Network (CLINIC). "Now, years later, the Trump administration is changing the rules on immigrants who did exactly what the government instructed them to do." Reopening administratively closed cases could add as many as three hundred thousand cases to an immigration court system already facing a backlog of seven hundred thousand cases, a CLINIC article noted.[23] A spokesperson for the National Immigrant Justice Center expressed outrage over what the organization viewed as an assault on both immigrants and immigration judges' independence. "The Attorney General has one agenda with this unnecessary ruling—to reduce immigration judges to deportation machines," said Chuck Roth, director of litigation for the organization.[24]

By pushing immigration judges to enter final orders of removal as quickly as possible, Attorney General Sessions's ruling in *Matter of Castro Tum* could force immigration courts to enter deportation orders even where the individual has a good claim to legal immigration status being heard by another federal agency. Although Attorney General Sessions concluded that administrative closure is "effectively permanent" because immigration courts had recalendared fewer than one third of cases, he did not indicate how often those cases were not recalendared because the respondent had been granted legal immigration status by USCIS in the meantime. Under *Matter of Castro Tum*, individuals may now be deported while waiting for a ruling on their family member's or employer's petitions to sponsor them legally. It has also been the practice of USCIS in the Trump administration to issue numerous requests for additional evidence, resulting in delays of months or longer, before granting even the most straightforward of visa applications.[25] Taken in combination, the delays from USCIS and the attorney general's decision in *Matter of Castro Tum* are likely to deprive many noncitizens of their legitimate rights to legal status under the immigration laws.

Shutting down administrative closure can't be justified on grounds of efficiency, either—quite the opposite. You can see why by looking at *Matter of Avetisyan*, one of the two cases the attorney general overruled in *Matter of Castro Tum*. In *Matter of Avetisyan,* Ms. Avetisyan had married and was expecting a child while in removal proceedings, and her husband was in the process of becoming a naturalized U.S. citizen. Ms. Avetisyan presented proof that her husband had filed a visa petition on her behalf and that USCIS had interviewed her and her husband in connection with the visa petition but had not yet ruled on the petition. The immigration judge granted several continuances to allow USCIS to rule on the petition, but each time Ms. Avetisyan advised that they were still waiting. At one of the hearings, counsel for the government admitted that she did not even have the case file, that it was probably at USCIS while they considered the visa petition. Finally—after five continuances—counsel for DHS explained that USCIS had not been able to rule on the visa petition because the file kept being transferred back and forth between USCIS and DHS Office of Chief Counsel every time the case came up again on the court's calendar. Ms. Avetisyan and her family were stuck in limbo. In order to avoid this absurdity, the immigration judge administratively closed the case so that USCIS could hold on to the file and finish its work. If the visa application were denied and Ms. Avetisyan did not have lawful immigration status,

DHS could then move to recalendar the case in immigration court, saving time and expense for all concerned. The BIA upheld the immigration judge's solution.[26] After *Matter of Castro Tum*, immigration judges facing this situation have only two choices: allow the case to keep bouncing back and forth between USCIS and immigration court hearings indefinitely, or order the individual removed even if she might be entitled to lawful immigration status that USCIS never got around to granting. This is this stuff of a Kafka novel.

DISCIPLINE OF IMMIGRATION JUDGES

Matter of Castro Tum was about to spiral even further, sparking not just displeasure but an outright war between the attorney general and the immigration judges—with Judge Morley as its poster child. In his decision on May 17, attorney general Sessions ordered Judge Morley to issue a new notice of hearing within fourteen days and indicated that an order of removal was required under the INA if Castro Tum again failed to appear. But confrontation mounted when the director of EOIR, James McHenry, ordered Judge Morley not just to give notice but to hold the hearing within fourteen days of the attorney general's decision. On May 19, 2018, a new notice of hearing was mailed to Mr. Castro Tum, directing him to appear at a hearing on May 31. Not surprisingly, he did not appear.

By this time, the immigration bar was tracking the case with interest. An immigration lawyer named Matthew Archambeault was in Judge Morley's courtroom in Philadelphia that day, appearing as a "friend of the court" on behalf of the Philadelphia chapter of the American Immigration Lawyers Association and other immigration lawyers. Archambeault requested a continuance, offering to help the court locate Mr. Castro Tum and to prepare a "friend of the court" brief about the legal adequacy of the HHS-ORR notices. Judge Morley granted the continuance for two reasons: First, the two-week period between service of notice and the hearing date was not enough time for the notice to be returned as undeliverable if the address was incorrect, and such return service would be an important piece of evidence for the court to consider in deciding whether to enter an order of removal without the individual present, called an *in absentia* removal order. The continuance would also allow time to receive a brief from Archambeault and the immigration bar about whether the HHS-ORR notice procedures were legally adequate as a basis for entering an *in absentia* removal order, an issue that the BIA and the attorney general had not addressed.[27]

"During the hearing, . . . the court administrator was seated behind Judge Morley's left shoulder, out of his view," Archambeault later recalled. "Toward the end of the hearing, Judge Morley joked, 'am I in trouble?' Though he said it in jest, it turned out he was in trouble."[28] On July 19, 2018, Judge Morley received an email from Assistant Chief Immigration Judge (ACIJ) Jack H. Weil informing him that the Castro Tum matter had been reassigned because of his failure to enter a final order at the hearing on May 31. Later that day, ACIJ Weil telephoned Judge Morley to discuss the email. According to a later statement by Judge Morley, ACIJ Weil told him that "the AG's decision stated that if [Mr. Castro Tum] did not appear, the Judge 'should' proceed by way of an *in absentia* order of removal."[29] Actually, the attorney general's decision did not go so far as to direct Judge Morley to enter an order of removal if Mr. Castro Tum failed to appear—indeed, the decision would probably have violated federal regulations about immigration judges' independence if it had—but the effect was the same. Judge Morley later learned that *Matter of Castro Tum* and dozens of other unaccompanied minor cases—approximately eighty-six in total—had been reassigned to other immigration judges (including two cases represented by our clinic).

This was a whole new world in the history of labor relations between the attorney general and the immigration judges. The National Association of Immigration Judges (NAIJ)—the immigration judges' labor union—took notice. On August 8, 2018, Judge Morley and the NAIJ filed a grievance against EOIR under their collective bargaining agreement. The grievance alleged that the reassignment of *Matter of Castro Tum* and the other unaccompanied minor cases violated Judge Morley's "decisional independence," including rights granted by some of the regulations mentioned earlier, such as an immigration judge's discretion to grant continuances for good cause, and his ability to take any action he deemed appropriate under law. In particular, the grievance cited a regulation that directs that the chief immigration judge of EOIR "shall have no authority to direct the result of an adjudication assigned to another immigration judge."[30]

That same regulation, however, also states that it does not limit the powers of the Chief Immigration Judge provided elsewhere in the regulation, such the right to "[i]ssue operational instructions and policy," to "[d]irect the conduct of all employees assigned to [the office] to ensure the efficient disposition of all pending cases," and to "[e]valuate the performance of the Immigration Courts . . . by making appropriate reports and inspections, and take corrective action where needed."[31] When the regulation was first being considered in 2000, members of the public expressed concern that the powers of the chief immigration judge might interfere with the due process rights of individuals in immigration court. EOIR responded that it "does not believe that the authority to establish time frames and guidelines 'directs' the result of the adjudication." The office pointed out that "[i]ndividual immigration judges set hearing calendars and prioritize cases," and assured the public that the judge "will take the time necessary for the case to be completed."[32]

At the next hearing for Mr. Castro Tum, Judge Morley had been replaced by the ACIJ. Reading from a prepared statement, the ACIJ ordered Mr. Castro Tum removed. "I was allowed to make a statement as Friend of the Court again, and the amicus brief was acknowledged," Archambeault recalled. Nevertheless, the final order was issued with Mr. Castro Tum not present.[33]

Maybe Mr. Castro Tum was confused by the NTA that failed to tell him when to appear in court. Maybe he received and ignored hearing notices, or maybe he moved and failed to update his address with DHS. Maybe the notices were sent to an incorrect address provided by DHS and did not reach him. It's unlikely he had an attorney to explain any of this to him. Although noncitizens have a right to counsel in removal proceedings, even minors are not entitled to a court-appointed lawyer—and usually can't afford to hire one and don't know how to look for one anyway. Had he appeared, maybe he would have had defenses to removal; maybe not. We know only one thing for certain: unless he has already been quietly arrested and removed, Mr. Castro Tum now lives somewhere in the shadows.

RESTRICTING IMMIGRATION JUDGES' DOCUMENT
MANAGEMENT TOOLS

The shutting down of administrative closure in *Matter of Castro Tum* was
foreshadowed by a curious decision of the attorney general two months
earlier, called *Matter of E-F-H-L-*. In that case, the government had
brought removal proceedings against Mr. E-F-H-L-, and he claimed asylum as a defense. The immigration court dismissed his asylum application
as legally insufficient just on the papers, without holding a hearing. Mr.
E-F-H-L- appealed. In 2014, the BIA overturned the decision of the
immigration court, holding that an asylum applicant had a right to a full
evidentiary hearing—to testify, present witnesses, and make legal arguments to the immigration judge. By the time the case was back before
the immigration court, Mr. E-F-H-L- had become eligible for a family-
sponsored visa petition, often a smoother path to legal immigration status
than asylum. Mr. E-F-H-L- withdrew his asylum claim with prejudice
(meaning he could not refile it later) and the court, following *Matter of
Avetisyan*, granted administrative closure to let USCIS adjudicate the
family-based visa petition.

Surprisingly, in March 2018, Attorney General Sessions suddenly
referred to himself the BIA's decision of 2014 and, without briefing or
argument, vacated the BIA's decision. The attorney general held the BIA's
decision was not valid because Mr. E-F-H-L-'s underlying asylum application was no longer pending, and ordered that his case be placed back on
the immigration court's docket.[34] This was astonishing for two reasons:
First, Mr. E-F-H-L- had done exactly what the immigration judge recommended he do in withdrawing his asylum application and moving forward
on the visa petition; now he was back in immigration court, apparently
with no right to refile his asylum application. Second, courts routinely
granted administrative closure so that USCIS could adjudicate a collateral
visa petition; if the attorney general had a problem with that, he would
have had to vacate thousands of cases. Members of the immigration bar
were left scratching their heads, wondering whether the attorney general
was now looking over the shoulders of immigration judges who granted
administrative closure.[35] As it turns out, he was. *Matter of Castro Tum*
was decided two months later.

The attorney general decided two other cases after *Matter of Castro Tum* that further limited the discretion of immigration judges to manage their cases based on concerns of efficiency or due process. In *Matter of L-A-B-R-*, Attorney General Sessions referred to himself three cases in which immigration judges had granted continuances at the request of the respondents, despite objections by DHS. In each case, the noncitizen was in removal proceedings and sought time to pursue other relief: In the case of Mr. L-A-B-R-, time for his U.S. citizen spouse to file a visa petition on his behalf before the immigration court resolved his claim for asylum; for Ms. Somphet, time to reassert an application for a waiver based on "extreme hardship" if she were removed; for Mr. McCalla, time to challenge past criminal convictions and pursue a pardon from the governor of Pennsylvania. Although the BIA had refused to hear the appeals because the immigration courts had not yet entered final orders in those cases, Attorney General Sessions nonetheless referred the case to himself to consider when an immigration judge could grant a continuance for a noncitizen to pursue other forms of relief.[36]

In his ruling, attorney general Sessions acknowledged that DOJ regulations expressly give immigration judges the authority to "grant a motion for continuance for good cause shown."[37] In deciding what is "good cause," however, the attorney general ruled that immigration judges should primarily look at two factors: the likelihood that the noncitizen will be successful in seeking other forms of relief, and whether that would change the immigration judge's decision in any event. The decision requires immigration judges to hold minihearings on a pending application before a different agency or authority to determine the likelihood of success, and emphasizes that efficiency concerns (like the number of previous continuances granted or how quickly the noncitizen acted to file her petition) may justify denial of a continuance. The decision also requires overburdened immigration judges to write detailed reasons for granting any continuance requested by a noncitizen to pursue a collateral proceeding, but not where a continuance is requested by DHS. Although the ruling did not overrule prior tests for granting continuances, the opinion "does appear to intend to make it harder for [immigration judges] to grant continuances to respondents who are seeking relief in other forums," according to a summary of the case by CLINIC.[38] Reacting to the decision, a group of retired immigration judges and BIA members called the decision "the Attorney General's latest blow to judicial independence." Because immigration judges may receive ten to fifteen requests for continuance each day, the retired judges stated, the requirement that judges give detailed reasons for granting continuances is "entirely unrealistic."[39] Failure to state reasons on the record or in a written decision would, according to *Matter of L-A-B-R-*, "leave the [BIA] no choice but to vacate the order granting the continuance if evidence supporting good cause is not clear from the record."[40] The practical effect is that immigration judges will be under workload pressure to deny continuances or see them reversed—even when they believe a continuance would be fair.

A month later, the attorney general further restricted immigration judges' authority to grant relief, holding in *Matter of S-O-G- & F-B-D-* that immigration judges had no authority to terminate or dismiss removal proceedings except in certain specific instances described in DOJ regulations. An immigration judge could dismiss a case, the attorney general concluded, only in two instances: when DHS made a motion that the notice to appear was "improvidently issued" or circumstances had since changed, or when the individual had an apparently valid application for naturalization pending *and* there were other "exceptionally appealing or humanitarian factors."[41] The attorney general distinguished the two cases before it from those situations: In *Matter of S-O-G-*, DHS had moved to dismiss the proceedings after it found that the individual was already subject to a previous order of removal issued *in absentia*. The individual—now present in court and likely represented by counsel—was not entitled to an opportunity to present defenses and the court was entitled to dismiss the proceedings, the attorney general held. In *Matter of F-B-D-*, the immigration court had dismissed the proceedings because Ms. F-B-D- already had an approved family-based visa petition, had proven that her removal would cause "exceptional and extremely unusual hardship" to her U.S. citizen family member, and was merely waiting to be called for a green card interview at the U.S. consulate in Brazil, her country of origin. Nevertheless, the attorney general held that Ms. F-B-D-'s case should not have been dismissed. Even though Ms. F-B-D- was entitled to a green card to avoid harm to her U.S. citizen family member, the attorney general's ruling required that Ms. F-B-D- voluntarily depart from the country or face removal, which at best requires that families be separated—sometimes for years—while waiting for a consular interview, and at worst could revoke immigration benefits already granted or trigger new bars to lawful immigration status.

Relying on the same logic used in *Matter of Castro Tum*, the attorney general held that the regulations permitting immigration judges to "take any other action consistent with applicable law and regulations as may be appropriate" did not include inherent authority to terminate or dismiss proceedings. Except upon DHS motion or certain pending applications for naturalization, the attorney general stated, the regulations provided that "'in *every other case*, the removal hearing shall be completed as promptly as possible.'"[42] In the attorney general's view, that regulation would appear to require immigration judges to rapidly process a case and enter a removal order even where the individual is entitled to lawful immigration status—status that could even include a right to naturalize but no "exceptionally appealing or humanitarian factors." Even being eligible for citizenship might not be enough to avoid being deported.

REWIRING PERFORMANCE METRICS

Even before that day in May 2018 when the EOIR administrator sat watching over Judge Morley's shoulder in Philadelphia, immigration judges were already feeling the administration breathing down their necks. On March 30, 2018, EOIR director McHenry had issued a memorandum to all immigration judges, announcing "new performance metrics for immigration judges."[43] Under these new metrics, EOIR would give all immigration judges a rating of "Satisfactory" or "Unsatisfactory." A Satisfactory rating required that an immigration judge complete seven hundred cases per year. In addition, an immigration judge had to meet six benchmarks that required them to dispose of matters in their cases within a certain period of time. For example, after a merits hearing where the individual was in detention and did not have any lawful immigration status, the judge had to issue a final order within three days; for a nondetained respondent, ten days. At least 85 percent of the time, Satisfactory judges must also decide motions within twenty days of receiving them. In

95 percent of cases, judges must complete individual merits hearings on the initial scheduled hearing date (that is, granting no continuances); the only exception was if DHS failed to produce a detained individual on the hearing date. Satisfactory performance required judges to complete reviews of asylum claims made at the border or before deportation on the initial hearing date 100 percent of the time, and again the only exception was if DHS didn't bring the individual from detention.[44] In the memorandum, Director McHenry stated that "[u]sing metrics to evaluate performance is neither novel nor unique to EOIR."

Immigration judges immediately protested the new performance metrics. The president of the immigration judges' union called the new standard "an egregious example of the conflict of interests of having the immigration court in a law enforcement agency" and said that no other administration had attempted to impose this type of metrics-based performance measure.[45] In a statement from June 2019, the NAIJ said, "Immigration Judges have been placed in the untenable position of having to choose between honoring their oath of office against ensuring their continued employment."[46]

Members of the immigration bar were quick to point out the tension between the new performance metrics and federal case law.[47] In *Hashmi v. Attorney General*, the respondent was in removal proceedings before DOJ while also awaiting adjudication of a visa petition filed on his behalf by his U.S. citizen spouse before USCIS. As in *Matter of Avetisyan*, the immigration case was delayed because his file kept being transferred back and forth between USCIS and DHS counsel for the immigration proceedings. Noting EOIR case completion metrics in effect at the time, the immigration judge refused to await the results of the USCIS adjudication and entered an order of removal. On appeal, the Third Circuit vacated the order of removal. "[T]o reach a decision about whether to grant or deny a motion for a continuance based solely on case-completion goals, with no regard for the circumstances of the case itself," the court of appeals held, "is impermissibly arbitrary."[48] Later, in his opinion in *Matter of L-A-B-R-* discouraging continuances, the attorney general would emphasize that *Hashmi* only precluded immigration judges from deciding cases based *solely* on case-completion metrics.[49] The scope of the Third Circuit's disapproval of case-completion metrics no doubt will be an issue fought out in the immigration courts and appealed to the federal courts unless those metrics are repealed by a new administration.

Until then, these metrics are the reality of immigration judges' daily lives. When an immigration judge logs on to her computer each morning, she sees a performance dashboard showing red, yellow, and green sections to indicate how she is doing in meeting the administration's speed goals.[50] While judges technically retain discretion to grant some continuances, the performance metrics create pressure for judges to deny that extra time— even when their judgment tells them that denying a request might be unfair.

THE FIGHT ESCALATES

If it seems strange to have a politically appointed administrator rating judges on how, or how fast, they decide their cases, it is. Judges on the federal courts have life tenure precisely so that they are not subject to this kind of political pressure, and even judges on Article I courts, though they serve for a term of years, cannot be removed based on how they decide their cases. But immigration judges are, in actuality, simply delegates of the attorney general. As such, the attorney general can rate, discipline, and terminate them for a number of reasons, including failure to decide their cases fast enough for his liking.

Immigration judges have a few protections against the control of the attorney general. One has been their union, the NAIJ, which filed a grievance on behalf of Judge Morley and has been outspoken in criticizing DOJ policies that limit immigration judges' discretion. But DOJ has attacked on that front as well. On August 9, 2019, DOJ filed a petition asking the Federal Labor Relations Authority to decertify the union. The petition argues that immigration judges are "management officials" and not entitled to organize and collectively bargain, according to news sources. Another motion to decertify the union had already been filed and rejected by the FLRA during the Clinton administration.[51]

The union struck back by filing two labor complaints the following month. The first complaint challenged the decertification motion; another involved a link sent by EOIR to its employees in August that, NAIJ claimed, included a link to a blog post from a white nationalist website with anti-Semitic descriptions of immigration judges.[52] News sources did not specify the specific labor violation that NAIJ alleged based on the incident. EOIR publicly acknowledged that it had found that its news aggregation service "contained non-news sources" and its contract would not be renewed. A spokesperson for EOIR said that the office "strongly condemns anti-Semitism and white nationalism."[53]

Also among the protections for immigration judges and the BIA are DOJ regulations that define their powers and duties—and decisions of the federal courts interpreting those regulations. On August 29, 2019, the U.S. Court of Appeals for the Fourth Circuit held that those regulations prohibit the attorney general from taking away the power of administrative closure, overruling *Matter of Castro Tum* within that circuit.[54] That case, *Romero v. Barr,* involved a common scenario—Mr. Romero, like many others, was in removal proceedings when his spouse, a U.S. citizen, filed a visa petition on his behalf with USCIS. The BIA initially held that Mr. Romero had a right to administrative closure while USCIS determined if he had a legal right to a visa; then, based on the attorney general's decision in *Matter of Castro Tum,* it reversed its decision and ordered Mr. Romero removed to Honduras. Mr. Romero took the case to the Fourth Circuit.

On review, the court held that *Matter of Castro Tum* violated regulations that require that immigration judges and BIA members exercise independent judgment and discretion and afford them the authority to take any action appropriate and necessary for the disposition of cases. The court of appeals didn't feel obliged to give deference to the attorney general's opinion that the regulations only allowed administrative closure in the handful of instances where it was specifically provided. Under *Auer* deference—a cousin of *Chevron* deference that applies when an agency is interpreting its own regulation rather than a statute—a court need only defer to the agency's interpretation where the regulation is ambiguous. "'If uncertainty does not exist, there is no plausible reason for deference,'" the court stated. "'The regulation then just means what it means.'"[55] Here, the court held, "any" means "any"—"Both regulations provide that [immigration judges] and the BIA 'may take *any action* . . . appropriate and necessary for the disposition' of the case."[56] That includes administrative closure, the court held.

While *Romero v. Barr* shifted some power from the attorney general back to the immigration judges, the decision has limits. Most importantly, it applies only in the Fourth Circuit, meaning only to cases heard by the immigration courts in Baltimore, Maryland; Charlotte, North Carolina; and Arlington and Falls Church, Virginia. While attorneys in other jurisdictions will no doubt point to the reasoning in that case, it remains to be seen whether other circuits will be persuaded to follow suit. Second, the case is based on regulations that were made—and could be changed—by DOJ. The attorney general still retains ultimate control over the scope of immigration judges' authority—and will as long as the immigration courts and the BIA remain in the Department of Justice.

What we call "the immigration courts" are, in fact, a group of employees within a law enforcement agency with no other regulatory authority over immigration, deciding cases brought by their own sovereign client against private individuals, and subject always to the control and review of the attorney general. How did this system come about? To find the answer, part 2 looks back to the moment when this architecture was put into place: May 1940, when deportations were conducted under the authority of the secretary of labor as the New Deal destabilized prevailing power structures and the fascist threat loomed.

PART II

From World War II to 9/11

THE GHOST OF THE FIFTH COLUMN

4 A New Type of Tough in the Department of Labor

Franklin D. Roosevelt was sworn in as president on March 4, 1933. In his urgency to tackle the Depression, he requested that his cabinet be sworn in the same evening. His new secretary of labor, Frances Perkins, canceled plans to return to New York and arrived at the Department of Labor building the next afternoon to begin work.[1]

Perkins, the daughter of a small businessman in Western Massachusetts with roots in the farmlands of Maine, graduated from Mount Holyoke in 1902. Soon afterward, she went to work in the settlement houses of Chicago and New York City. Settlement workers lived and interacted with residents of poor urban neighborhoods, many of them immigrants. Through this early form of social work, Perkins became intimately aware of the plight of the nation's industrial workers, who often worked nearly around the clock merely to survive with no safety net in the event of work reductions, disability, old age, or injury or death on the job. Her passion to improve working conditions led her from the settlement houses to lobbying the New York state legislature and eventually to appointed positions on the state Industrial Commission. Roosevelt appointed her Industrial Commissioner of the state when he became governor in 1928. When he became president, he considered her the natural choice for secretary of labor, the critical cabinet member who would help to give content to his then-aspirational idea of the New Deal.[2] "That phrase, 'new deal,' which gave courage to all sorts of people, was merely a statement of policy and emphasis," Perkins wrote in 1946. "When he got to Washington he had no fixed program."[3]

Perkins initially resisted the appointment. She was philosophically opposed to her own candidacy, telling Roosevelt that he should choose someone from organized labor "to establish firmly the principle that *labor is in the President's Councils.*" But privately, she also felt that the move to Washington and the demands of the job would be impossible for her. The same year Roosevelt was elected, Perkins's husband, Paul Wilson, entered a mental health institution after years of struggle with mood swings and drinking. Though a friend helped with his medical bills, Perkins was often his only visitor, and she remained solely responsible for maintaining a household in New York for herself and their daughter, Susanna. She obliquely mentioned to Roosevelt that her personal situation might "seriously impair" her effectiveness. Roosevelt, characteristically imperturbable, merely scratched out a note, "Have considered your advice and don't agree." In the end, Perkins was convinced by an Episcopal bishop that she had a duty to use her skills and experience to help the country. After confirming that Roosevelt was on board with some of her ideas for reform, she accepted.[4]

Through their advocacy in New York and Washington for workers as the Depression deepened, Perkins and Roosevelt would eventually become affectionate friends as well as political allies. Early indications would not have portended such a friendship, however, at least not to Perkins. Perkins recalled meeting Roosevelt at a few social functions in New York when she was still a graduate student at Columbia University, but said that "[t]here was nothing particularly interesting about the tall, thin young man with the high collar and pince-nez." She was no more impressed with the young Roosevelt when they began to cross paths a year or two later while she was a workers' rights advocate and he was a New York state senator. She recalled another prominent Democrat describing him as an "[a]wful arrogant fellow, that Roosevelt," and she herself recalled that "[n]o one who saw him in those years would have been likely to think of him as a potential President of the U.S.A." Always an astute observer of character, Perkins was highly critical of Roosevelt's in those early years: "[H]e really didn't like people very much" and "he had a youthful lack of humility, a streak of self-righteousness, and a deafness to the hopes, fears, and aspirations which are the common lot." Roosevelt himself would come to agree. Years later, Perkins recalled, he remarked to her, "'[y]ou know, I was an awfully mean cuss when I first went into politics.'"[5]

But life would be demanding of Roosevelt, and he would be the better person for it. "The marvel," recalled Perkins, "is that these handicaps [of character] were washed out of him by life, experience, punishment, and his capacity to grow." The vigorous, arrogant young man was brought down to Earth in 1921 by paralytic illness, then diagnosed as polio, though medical historians more recently have debated a diagnosis of Guillain-Barré Syndrome.[6] In 1928, Roosevelt remained doggedly focused on a full physical recovery and originally declined when New York governor Al Smith, the Democratic presidential candidate, implored the popular young politician with the influential last name to run for governor to help carry New York. Roosevelt, convinced only out of a sense of duty, surprised everyone with the energy he brought to and took from the campaign.[7] Congratulating him on his nomination for the office, Perkins—then more professional acquaintance than friend—added a comment on this inner victory, writing to Roosevelt, "may I dare to be quite personal and say that I believe it is your spiritual victory which has effected your physical improvement, and that this force in you will be augmented in this campaign and in this high office by the stimulus of leadership, and by the hopes and prayers of all the good people of this State who will help you to get well."[8]

Their bond, which Perkins described as "ties of affection, common purpose, and joint undertakings," would last to the end of Roosevelt's life, and beyond.[9] Three weeks after his death, Perkins responded to a letter of condolence from her friend, labor reformer Mary Dreier. "You are quite right that people throughout the world trusted him somehow to lead them to the actual accomplishment of freedom and righteousness," Perkins wrote. "This quality of his, as you know, came to him after his illness. That sympathy between him and the world and people was something he acquired out of suffering—not consciously, but just a result of it." Perkins's deep religious conviction, as well as her love for her departed friend, was evident in the stoic lesson she drew from those days: "A friend of mine wrote me," she told Dreier, "reminding me of the great episode described in the Old Testament when Moses had died and the Children of Israel were weeping on the Plains of Moab—'And the Lord spoke unto Joshua saying, Moses, my servant is dead; now therefore ye shall all rise, now therefore rise, go over this Jordan.' That, I guess, is the story. Thank you so much for writing me, dear Mary."[10]

In 1933, their work had just been promoted to the national stage when Roosevelt was sworn in as president. As the new secretary of labor, Perkins had been in her office no more than a couple of hours when she was informed of a cancer that had been growing in the immigration service— possibly with the encouragement or at least the acquiescence of the departing secretary, William Doak. Secretary Doak was still in the office when she arrived, expecting that business would carry on as usual for a time after the inauguration. As he introduced her to the employees—or, rather, as they introduced themselves, for it was clear to her that he didn't know or couldn't recall their names—seven different people told her, "I'm in charge of immigration." Although Perkins had lived and worked with immigrants, she had no direct experience with immigration law or policy.[11]

After firmly but politely disposing of Doak, Perkins had her first opportunity to speak privately with Doak's first assistant secretary, Robe Carl White. White approved of Perkins's actions in taking control of the office promptly. "I'm glad you have made the break, because it's going to be difficult," White told her. "There are some very serious situations here." Perkins instinctively trusted White and asked him to stay on for a while to help her understand the department. Soon, White told her about a terrible situation that had been festering: A group of special inspectors, answering only to Secretary Doak, were traveling around the country, raiding immigrants' lodgings and dance halls, and shaking people down for money by threatening deportation. The morale of the immigration service was extremely low, as the corrupt inspectors dominated operations and honest employees were overlooked. One longtime employee was reduced nearly to tears of gratitude when Perkins asked to meet with him personally about the problem. "I'm so glad to see the Secretary of Labor," he said. "I've been working in this Department all [these] years and haven't seen the Secretary."[12]

Perkins had been warned about the corrupt inspectors before she came to Washington. A New York City police detective had told her that the Department of Labor harbored "a little gang" of men who were extorting money from immigrants in New York and elsewhere. She had heard about the warrantless raids and arrests condemned by the Wickersham Commission but, the lieutenant said, "Wickersham didn't find out a quarter of it." Two brothers, Murray and Henry Garsson, were said to be the ringleaders of the operation.[13]

These jobs had been authorized by Section 24 of the Immigration Act of 1917, which created a special unit for investigation of contract labor violations. By 1933, contract labor was not a great concern, so instead Section 24 inspectors operated under a provision that allowed them to investigate other immigration law violations when no contract labor investigations were needed. It appears that Doak and several members of Congress had used the division as a dumping ground for unsavory characters that had gained government employment through means ranging from filial loyalty to possible blackmail.[14] An interdepartmental memo during the transition about the "contract labor investigators" stated that two had previously been fired as Prohibition inspectors—one for "beating up his dist[rict] director," another "for murdering 3 persons."[15]

Getting rid of them was not simple, however. In the last week of the Hoover administration, Doak had convinced Hoover to move the Section 24 inspectors into the civil service. This meant that they could only be fired by establishing cause individually—and there were more than eighty inspectors in the division. But White offered Perkins a solution, which she swiftly implemented with Roosevelt's approval: appropriations for the division would expire the following week, and she could eliminate it by simply not requesting renewal.[16]

Perkins's first major decision as secretary of labor would face resistance from inside and outside the department. One evening soon afterward, she came to the office after dinner to finish some work, an unusual practice at the time. Seeing activity in the building, she was informed that the Section 24 inspectors had returned, and she asked to be taken directly to their floor. When she stepped off the elevator, she encountered a room full of the former inspectors, sleeves rolled up, rifling through departmental files spread across the floor. The men insisted they were merely collecting their personal belongings. Perkins—the first female Cabinet member in U.S. history—told them to leave; they could return for any personal items during business hours. They left.[17]

THE IMMIGRATION SERVICES IN
THE DEPARTMENT OF LABOR

As secretary of labor, Perkins had inherited two jobs: one she wanted, and one nobody did. The immigration services had long been shuttled between various inhospitable government departments and by 1933 had arrived at their still unlikely and uncomfortable home in the Department of Labor. For most of the nation's first century, immigration was encouraged, not restricted, so there was no need for a department to oversee the administration of immigration laws. By the mid-nineteenth century, however, periodic waves of anti-immigration sentiment resulted in occasional legislation to discourage immigration by certain groups or for certain purposes. These early restrictions primarily targeted Chinese and Japanese nationals, especially for contract labor.[18]

By 1882, immigration laws began to include more generally applicable immigration restrictions, and the Immigration Act of 1891 created or continued numerous grounds of exclusion not based on race or national origin. Those to be excluded were persons "likely to become a public charge," those suffering from contagious diseases, those convicted of felonies or other crimes "involving moral turpitude," and polygamists. Such antiquated phrases will sound familiar to modern immigration lawyers, as they remain grounds for inadmissibility under the INA today. The statute created a presumption that persons whose passage was paid by someone else were excluded unless it was conclusively shown that they did not fall into any of the previously mentioned categories. If found inadmissible under these criteria, a person could be sent back on the vessel on which she came. Anyone who was found to have entered the United States unlawfully could also be removed within one year. Return was to be at the expense of the person, corporation, or vessel owner or the person or company bringing the person to the country, where possible. The Act made it unlawful to hire contract labor or for vessel owners to solicit immigration. Bringing a person into the United States unlawfully was a misdemeanor punishable by up to one thousand dollars and one year of imprisonment.[19]

Enforcement of these restrictions would require an administrative mechanism, and the Immigration Act of 1891 for the first time created one at the federal level. Administration of the early immigration laws had been conducted by state commissions at the ports, acting under contract with the secretary of the Treasury to collect the exacted fees and penalties. More than one secretary of the Treasury found this system unworkable. In 1890, Secretary William Windom canceled the contract with New York and appointed a superintendent of immigration at the port there. The Act of 1891 extended that system to all ports, creating one superintendent of immigration within the Treasury Department. The superintendent was supported by inspection officers—the first "immigration judges"—who administered oaths, took testimony, and made decisions on the record as to a person's admissibility. Decisions of such inspectors would be final unless appealed by the noncitizen to the superintendent of immigration, whose decision was subject to review by the secretary of the Treasury. No specific provision was made for the conduct of deportation proceedings of persons in the United States for less than a year, except that such return was allowed "as by law provided." The federal circuit and district courts were given concurrent jurisdiction over all civil and criminal cases arising under the Act.

Two years later, Congress passed a bill to improve administration of the 1891 law. The problem, explained the bill's sponsor in the House, was that inspection officers were making exceptions for people who would suffer extreme hardship if returned home. Rather than let these cases "appeal to his sympathy [and] warp his judgment," the Act of 1893 set up a system for "special inquiries" in cases where the inspection officer entertained doubt about the admissibility of the intended immigrant. Such cases were referred to a panel of four inspectors, who came to be known as "special inquiry officers," and admission was permitted only by agreement of the majority. The Act also remedied a perceived inequality in the Act of 1891, which permitted appeal only by the excluded person. Under the new law, a dissenting inspector could also appeal the admissibility decision to the superintendent of immigration, whose decision was subject to review by the secretary of the Treasury. The law also required informing emigrants of these laws upon purchase of passage and inspection for admissibility before departure, measures characterized as an effort to prevent extreme hardship to those who would be found inadmissible upon arrival and returned as well as to exclude those who did not meet the admissibility requirements.[20]

Thus, by 1893, the foundation of the modern immigration courts had been laid. In order to exclude persons that Congress found undesirable, the law set up a system of inspection by an administrative officer of an executive department, which included taking testimony and making a record. More difficult cases were referred to a board of such officers, and appeals of adverse decisions could be made to the agency head by either the noncitizen or the government. Persons discovered in the country who did not meet the admission criteria could also be removed, albeit only within one year.

It would be another twenty years before those functions—which had no natural home within any department—would be inherited by the Department of Labor. In 1903, Congress created the Department of Commerce and Labor and transferred the federal immigration functions to the new department. The Department of Commerce and Labor grew out of agitations in the late nineteenth century by the growing merchant and manufacturing sector that they deserved Cabinet-level attention comparable to the Department of Agriculture. The most important function of the new department was to provide information supporting expansion of American products into foreign commerce. The creation of the department was intended to help American businesses in part by lightening the load of the overburdened Treasury Department. The immigration service, by this time headed by a commissioner-general of immigration, was included in the reorganization on the theory that immigration was an important source of labor for American industry.[21]

The federal government's attention to labor in its own right officially began with the creation of the Bureau of Labor within the Department of the Interior in 1884.[22] Congress created an independent Department of Labor in 1888, but the commissioner of labor was not a member of the president's Cabinet. As the Industrial Revolution intensified into the twentieth century, labor conditions became the subject of increased attention and concern, and the existence of the Department of Commerce and Labor was an obviously inadequate solution to those concerned about ensuring a voice for labor against management. Investigation of labor problems and lobbying for legislation were led by organized labor and a growing class of professionals studying and assisting the movement. In 1906, the American Association for Labor Legislation was organized to lobby for legislation to improve working conditions. By 1913, these groups succeeded in lobbying for a Cabinet-level department of labor.[23]

In 1913, however, labor legislation was an uphill battle. The Supreme Court was still firmly entrenched in what legal scholars call "the *Lochner* era," named after a case in 1905 that rejected early labor legislation as a violation of due process—and left the Department of Labor with very little jurisdiction.[24] The do-nothing DOL became a bit of a joke among political scientists of the time. Introducing a chapter about the DOL in a book on public administration from 1936, Harvard political scientist E. Pendleton Herring began with a famous reference: "'Take some more tea,' the March Hare said to Alice, very earnestly. 'I've had nothing yet,' Alice replied in an offended tone: 'so I can't take more.' 'You mean you can't take *less*,' said the Hatter: 'it's very easy to take *more* than nothing.'"[25]

With so little to do, the Department of Labor was seen as a useful home for the federal Bureaus of Immigration and Naturalization. Indeed, the budget and personnel of the early Department of Labor were dominated by the immigration service: When established, the Bureau of Immigration and the Bureau of Naturalization combined to employ about eighteen hundred of the total two thousand staff members of the Department of Labor. Describing this period, Perkins would later tell a historian, "[t]hey transferred immigration to Labor on the wildest theory that all immigrants became laborers. . . . They were trying to think of something to give this department that would justify it being a department and paying grades of salaries and having Secretaries and Assistant Secretaries."[26]

In the dislocation in Europe that followed World War I, Congress introduced a system intended to drastically restrict immigration, especially from southern and eastern Europe. The Immigration Act of 1921 was the first act to regulate immigration based on a quota system, which limited the number of immigrants from any country to 3 percent of foreign-born persons of that nationality living in the United States in 1910. This system, originally intended to be temporary, was extended and modified by the Immigration Act of 1924. To preserve the Western European ethnic

majority of the U.S. population, the law of 1924 provided that immigration from each country would be reduced to 2 percent of persons in the
United States of that national origin—whether foreign- or native-born—
based on the 1920 census.[27]

Compared with the absolute racial or categorical exclusions of earlier
immigration acts, the new quota restrictions occasioned more illegal
immigration and required stepped-up enforcement activity, leading to the
creation of the U.S. Border Patrol in 1924. Greater enforcement gave rise
to a greater number of appeals and a new type of appeal from exclusion
decisions. To assist the commissioner-general of immigration with this
rising caseload, the secretary of labor created the Board of Review by regulation in 1921. The function of the Board of Review was to review
appeals from the Boards of Special Inquiry, which still heard exclusion
and deportation cases. Although the Board of Review held hearings upon
request, typically such appeals were considered only on paper, based on
the record made before the inspection officer. The Board of Review's recommendations were sent to an assistant to the secretary of labor for deter-
mination whether an order of deportation should issue, and the assistant
would usually accept the Board's recommendation.[28]

Special inquiry officers would later be called "immigration judges," and
the secretary of labor's Board of Review would evolve into the BIA. The
entities of the modern immigration courts were now in place, and the
country's first female Cabinet member would command them in an era of
unprecedented tension between industry and labor—many of whose leaders were also immigrants.

LABOR-IMMIGRATION TENSIONS IN THE NEW DEAL

Public reaction to Perkins's dismissal of the Section 24 inspectors portended criticism that would shadow Perkins throughout her tenure as
head of immigration enforcement. A press release prepared by a Seattle
labor union praised the Section 24 investigation unit, which "last year set
a record for deportations under Secretary of Labor Doak." The release
questioned Perkins's motivation in enforcing the immigration laws: "It is
said that Secretary Perkins never was in sympathy with the deportation of

aliens and the more readily seized the opportunity to bring about the destruction of the force."[29] The pressure would continue to mount throughout her tenure; the president, while typically unfazed, came to her defense when circumstances warranted. In April 1936, for example, Roosevelt forwarded her a letter sent to him by the Maryland state secretary of the Junior Order United American Mechanics—an organization that Perkins believed to be "a front for *something*" and seemed to support any statement by the chairman of the House Committee on Un-American Activities. The letter announced that the organization had enacted a resolution calling for the removal of Perkins "for failing to perform her duties according to the Laws and Constitution of the United States, regarding Immigration, and Deportation of Aliens." Roosevelt suggested she meet with the attorney general about a possible investigation into the organization and their specific charges against her—or lack thereof. "After all," Roosevelt wrote to her, "there comes a time when one can no longer take everything lying down or with a smile."[30]

Perkins faced resistance from within the administration as well, particularly in turf battles over immigration between Labor and State. Just weeks into her tenure, the persecution of Jews in Germany advanced from private acts of violence to officially sanctioned repression, as the Nazis boycotted all Jewish businesses on April 1, 1933, and soon dismissed all Jews from the civil service. As influential American Jews began to push the government to admit more refugees, Secretary Perkins learned that the quota for German immigrants—25,957 visas per year—was rarely met. One reason was a decision of the State Department to deny visas, even when available, to the majority of applicants on the theory that the absence of jobs during the Depression meant that most immigrants were "likely to become a public charge." State's restrictive interpretation was fueled in part by the opposition of the American Labor Federation to a liberal immigration policy. State convinced Roosevelt that no special action was needed for refugees because the quota was routinely unfilled. Perkins fought State on the policy, at one point arguing so forcefully that, according to another State Department official, "she quite blew our poor Under Secretary off his end of the telephone." In the end she prevailed, thanks to a memorandum by the young solicitor of labor, Charles Wyzanski, that persuaded Attorney General Homer Cummings. Wyzanski convincingly argued that the secretary of labor had the discretion to accept a bond by a friend or relative in the United States assuring that the immigrant would not become a public charge. The consuls were also told to interpret the public charge provision liberally with respect to refugees.[31]

Immigration policy was a prickly subject for both management and labor during the Depression. For groups like the American Federation of Labor, an influx of new immigrants spelled a threat to the few employment opportunities available to their current members. Management feared immigration for a different reason: recent immigrants in the work force were often important leaders in the labor movement, and management feared the spread of communist ideas by "un-American" new arrivals.

Perkins recognized an inherent tension in her dual responsibilities to support labor and to enforce the immigration laws. First was the sheer imbalance of resources: Shortly after her inauguration, Perkins told her soon-to-be commissioner-general of immigration, Daniel W. MacCormack, that "instead of finding a department concerned with the interests of labor she found one almost wholly preoccupied with matters concerning immigration." According to MacCormack, the immigration service in 1933 accounted for 3,659 of the departments' 5,113 employees.[32] Perkins had come of age as a warrior for workers' rights and had helped to push through reforms in New York such as maximum-hours laws and factory safety rules. As Roosevelt's secretary of labor, she would be instrumental in the development, passage, and implementation of transformative legislation to provide basic protections to workers on a national scale, especially the Social Security Act and the Fair Labor Standards Act. She felt the Immigration and Naturalization Service (INS) "ruined" the department because it distracted focus from labor problems.[33]

The second problem was the inherent conflict of interest between labor policy and immigration enforcement. MacCormack, speaking in 1934, described the process through which labor organizers or strikers were deported as Communists: Workers joined the National Miners' Union or the National Textile Workers' Union, which were affiliated with the Trade Union League, which was affiliated with the Red International of Labor Unions, which was affiliated with the Third International and with the Communist Party in Moscow. "Now, by that exceedingly tenuous thread they were connecting some poor miner, some poor textile worker, who had joined the union—perhaps the only union available to him—with the Communist Party at Moscow, and saying that he was subject to deportation as a Communist." Some commentators claimed the Department of Labor used deportation proceedings to quell labor unrest.[34] Perkins was aware of this conflict as she sought to respond to strikes in which foreign nationals played a leadership role for labor. "The conflict of interest within the Department was clear," she wrote. "On the one hand, we must enforce the immigration laws without fear or favor. On the other hand, in the effort to settle strikes and industrial disputes, we must deal with anyone who appeared to be effective and to represent the workers."[35]

The conflict was keenly felt when various parties began to agitate for the deportation of Harry Bridges, a mandolin-playing longshoreman who had become a leader of the nonunionized San Francisco dockworkers in 1934. Bridges, a native Australian, had become a sailor and entered the United States lawfully in 1920. When the transportation workers struck in sympathy with the longshoremen, both the public and the government became alarmed at the prospect of a "general strike" that might shut down the entire local economy. Public anger was stoked by Hugh S. Johnson, head of Roosevelt's National Recovery Administration, who happened to be speaking at the University of California at Berkeley as the strike got underway. Pounding the lectern, Johnson said, "If the Federal Government did not act, this people would act, and it would act to wipe out this subversive element as you clean off a chalk mark on a blackboard with a wet sponge."[36]

As the strike gained momentum, Attorney General Homer Cummings was acting president while Roosevelt was at sea. Cummings and Secretary of State Cordell Hull briefly considered calling in National Guard and Army troops to drive the San Francisco milk trucks or to order workers at gunpoint to drive them. Perkins foresaw a calamity of mass protests, shootings of citizens by federal troops, and irreparable damage to labor relations. She vociferously rebutted Hull and Cumming's opinion that the San Francisco unrest was a "general strike" that legally justified federal intervention. In the end, she convinced them that ordering such action while the president was at sea would cause political bedlam and prevailed upon them to send him a telegram. Her own telegram to Roosevelt explaining the situation reached him first. He agreed with her and suggested arbitration instead—

a step she knew would be unnecessary, as the sympathetic strikes were unorganized and were promptly conciliated.[37]

Though immediate crisis was averted, the reaction translated into a push to deport Bridges. Though the INS, FBI, and San Francisco police had found no evidence that Bridges was a subversive, in 1937 four witnesses submitted testimony to immigration officials that they had seen Bridges at Communist Party activities.[38] In the spring of 1938, the INS was preparing to hear the case when the U.S. Court of Appeals for the Fifth Circuit decided a case called *Strecker v. Kessler*.[39] The Fifth Circuit held that mere membership in the Communist Party of America was not sufficient to establish that a noncitizen advocated violent overthrow of the U.S. government and was thus subject to deportation. The statute under which Strecker had been deported provided for the exclusion of "[a]liens who believe in, advise, advocate, or teach, or who are members of or affiliated with any organization, association, society, or group that believes in, advises, advocates, or teaches ... the overthrow by force or violence of the Government of the United States or of all forms of law." Under Section 2 of the statute, noncitizens within the country who fell within any of the excluded classes in Section 1 were subject to deportation.[40]

Because the federal circuit courts were split on how to interpret the statute, the Department of Labor petitioned for and the Supreme Court granted a writ of certiorari—a conventional legal response for a government agency faced with having to comply with conflicting federal court precedents. Acting on legal advice and her own beliefs about the limits of executive power, Perkins concluded it would be wrong to force Bridges to defend a deportation proceeding brought under a legal theory that was currently being tested before the Supreme Court, and she postponed the case to await the Court's ruling.[41] The Supreme Court ultimately held that the statute permitted deportation of a noncitizen for present, but not former, membership or affiliation with an organization that advocates for overthrow of the government by force or violence, and remanded the case for further proceedings.[42] The Bridges case was eventually heard under this standard, and the presiding official, Harvard Law School dean James M. Landis, determined that Bridges was not deportable under the standard announced by the Supreme Court.[43]

But the delay in the Bridges case provoked public outrage. In February 1938, the *Detroit Free Press* published an editorial criticizing Perkins for failing to push forward with the Bridges hearing. "[T]he woman has so persistently appeared in the role of defender of Mr. Bridges," the editors wrote, "that a committee of the Senate finally has felt obliged to act." The editorial was laced with condescension. Perkins "does not seem able to comprehend the compelling nature of her responsibilities to the Country in dealing with such matters," the editors wrote. While conceding that she may be "sincere," "well meaning," and "honest," the editors decried what they saw as "her incurable emotionalism, her high susceptibility to prejudice, and her instinctive partisanship."[44] A constituent who forwarded the editorial to Perkins put the matter more bluntly: "I can't understand though why [the president] appointed a woman to hold the office of Secretary of Labor when it is so decidedly and distinctly a job—and a big one at that— for a red blooded HE MAN." The letter, signed by "A DETROITER," went on to criticize Perkins for using her maiden name. "When you took your marriage vows you became Mrs. So and So. Are you ashamed of your husband's name? What right have you to allow yourself to be addressed and spoke of as MISS."[45] Gender stereotypes often publicly attributed to Perkins appear to be without foundation; a Roosevelt administration consultant who interviewed all of Roosevelt's Cabinet members while studying executive reorganization described Perkins as "the most logical and objective" of all of them in her arguments, and "less emotional" than some of her male colleagues.[46]

Among those to seize on the hysteria over the Bridges case were Republicans in the House of Representatives. On January 24, 1939, Representative J. Parnell Thomas of New Jersey introduced a bill to impeach Perkins, as well as INS commissioner James L. Houghteling and Department of Labor solicitor Gerard D. Reilly. Perkins, Houghteling, and Reilly were accused of failing to enforce the immigration laws by not deporting Bridges and "conspir[ing] to defer and to defeat the deportation of the aforesaid alien." Remarkably, the bill even accused the three of high crimes and misdemeanors for seeking a writ of certiorari in the *Strecker* case—a decision that would have undermined the Department of Labor's position that Bridges should be deportable.[47] Moreover, in her statement to the committee, Perkins noted that the Department of Labor and the solicitor general had sought the writ of certiorari in part because of the extraordinary remedy ordered by the Fifth Circuit—remanding the case to the district court for findings of fact, a function reserved by statute to the Department of Labor.

Perkins testified before the House Judiciary Committee on February 8, 1939. She began by emphasizing that she believed the government should take steps against threats to its existence, and that she did not share the views of the Communist Party. Perkins, a deeply religious person, particularly found in the Communists' insistence on party authority, class struggle, working-class dictatorship, and contempt for religion "the negation of that individual liberty and that development of the human personality for which this country and every democracy must stand." She noted that the secretary of labor was charged with an extraordinary function among executive branch officers. "The Secretary of Labor has the power, in certain specific situations, not even involving a crime, to issue a warrant for the arrest of any alien in the United States; he has the power virtually to imprison that person; and he has the power to order that person to be sent back to the country of his nationality even though he recognizes that in some circumstances this is tantamount to sending an alien to his death." The secretary, she pointed out, "is investigator, prosecutor, jury and judge."[48]

On March 24 of that year, the Judiciary Committee reported to the House that it had found insufficient evidence to support the resolution, which was then permanently tabled.[49] The report of the committee, however, included a statement by the Republican committee members that Perkins, Houghteling, and Reilly had been "lenient and indulgent to Harry Bridges" and that their actions called for "the official and public disapproval of this Committee."[50]

Despite the unanimous vote of the committee clearing Perkins and her colleagues of wrongdoing, the political attacks continued. On March 29, Representative Thomas, the congressman who initiated the impeachment inquiry, gave a radio address stating that "Frances Perkins, our present Secretary of Labor, has abused [her] powers to such an extent as to create not only an economic burden upon our people, but also a dangerous menace to our national existence."[51] Thomas proceeded to distort the case against Perkins, the *Strecker* opinion, and the House Committee's findings. This prompted a Democratic senator from New York, James M. Mead, to

deliver a radio address two days later in defense of Perkins. Mead emphasized the unanimous vote of the committee, the testimony of immigration
investigators in support of Perkins, and Perkins's own statements rejecting
the Communist Party and expressing faith in the American people to do
the same. "These you will agree are the sincere views of a patriotic and
God-loving American public official holding high and responsible office.
And that is what Frances Perkins is first, last and all the time," Mead
concluded.[52]

But Congress was not done pillorying Perkins. On July 24, 1939, the
Senate Immigration Committee proposed an investigation of INS;
Roosevelt himself called a supportive senator to help block the $50,000
appropriation.[53] A White House memorandum to the president said,
"[t]here have already been 17 investigations of the Immigration Service.
Miss Perkins thinks that is enough."[54] Public opprobrium of Perkins continued, much of it laden with sexism, xenophobia, and anti-Semitism. As
late as 1941, magazines continued to perpetuate the misconception that
Perkins was a communist sympathizer of Russian-Jewish heritage. There
were even rumors that her daughter was married to Bridges.[55]

Perkins was deeply troubled by these events, but Roosevelt was not. He
made light of the matter to Perkins, saying, "'Who is this fellow J. Parnell
Thomas? . . . Who bothers about him? Don't pay any attention to him.'"
According to Perkins, Roosevelt exhibited "his complete confidence that if
you do the thing that seems right to you, you'll come out all right."[56]

5 Refusal

In light of Roosevelt's characteristic equanimity about politics and his respect and affection for Perkins, it is unlikely that the Bridges case or the bill of impeachment changed his opinion of her or her competence to administer the immigration laws. But perceptions matter, and the public perception of Perkins had soured by 1939. With Perkins's credibility wounded, the INS, still under her charge, became especially vulnerable to political attack as war in Europe accelerated and fear of sabotage grew. Perkins's biographer concluded that, even after the end of the Bridges affair and bill of impeachment, "[u]nquestionably the continuing suspicion and slander decreased her effectiveness. Possibly by 1940 no legislation with which she was closely associated, such as unemployment insurance or the minimum wage law, could have passed Congress."[1] Roosevelt was no doubt aware of Perkins's reputation and the fragile legacy of their New Deal legislation, still subject to reversal by the Supreme Court or repeal by Congress.

He was also aware—long before many in the country—of the exigency of the fascist threat. Roosevelt had been pushing the public and Congress to abandon the myth that the United States was protected from attack by geography, that it could take cover behind isolationism or "neutrality." In a speech on October 5, 1937, at the dedication of Chicago's Outerlink Bridge (since replaced by Lake Shore Drive Bridge), Roosevelt publicly took his stand. He warned listeners that the spread of "terror and international lawlessness" would not leave the Americas untouched. Roosevelt quoted from James Hilton's epic novel *Lost Horizon*, published in 1933, in which a British diplomat finds inner peace in the fictional Tibetan utopia Shangri-La with the help of the enlightened High Lama. Hilton's and Roosevelt's words are a reminder of just how closely annihilation would, in fact, brush by. Standing at the mouth of the Chicago River, Roosevelt spoke:

> To paraphrase a recent author, "perhaps we foresee a time when men, exultant in the technique of homicide, will rage so hotly over the world that every precious thing will be in danger, every book, every picture, every harmony, every treasure garnered through two milleniums, the small, the delicate, the defenseless—all will be lost or wrecked or utterly destroyed."
>
> If those things come to pass in other parts of the world, let no one imagine that America will escape, that America may expect mercy, that this Western Hemisphere will not be attacked and that it will continue tranquilly and peacefully to carry on the ethics and the arts of civilization.
>
> No, if those days come "there will be no safety by arms, no help from authority, no answer in science. The storm will rage till every flower of culture is trampled and all human beings are leveled in a vast chaos."[2]

These two concerns—the political vulnerability of his New Deal reforms and congressional isolationism in the face of the growing crisis in Europe and Asia—weighed heavily on Roosevelt in 1938 and 1939. He needed congressional support, and badly. But his standing with Congress was precarious after it had rejected both his "court-packing plan" in 1937 and his first attempt to reorganize the executive branch in 1938, amid cries of executive aggrandizement.[3] When Germany annexed Austria in March 1938, many Americans grew even more anxious about affording greater power to Roosevelt, lending strength to the president's political opponents.[4]

But the unsinkable Roosevelt managed to convince Congress to pass a revised reorganization bill in March 1939 that gave Roosevelt the power to make long-desired changes in the structure of the executive branch.[5] The version from 1939 included a policy innovation that undermined claims of president-as-dictator: the first-ever legislative veto. Rather than making changes by executive order, as the bill from 1938 had proposed, the president would be required to submit a "reorganization plan" to Congress, which Congress could nullify by passing a concurrent resolution within sixty calendar days. Soon after passage of the Reorganization Act of 1939, members of Congress began to urge Roosevelt to use his authority to move INS out of the beleaguered Department of Labor and into the Department of Justice for national security reasons. For over a year, Roosevelt resisted.

It wasn't because he didn't take the threat seriously. March 1939 brought an ominous reminder of the possibility for sabotage on U.S. soil: For nearly a decade, the U.S.-Germany Mixed Claims Commission had been considering a claim that the government of Germany was responsible for the bombings of two munitions plants in New Jersey in 1916 and 1917. Just after 2 AM on July 30, 1916, a thousand tons of munitions bound for the Allies in Europe had exploded on Black Tom Island in New Jersey, causing an impact equivalent to an earthquake measuring 5.5 on the Richter scale. People in Manhattan and New Jersey had been thrown from their beds, as shattered glass from the impact and a mist of ash from the explosion had rained down. Although fewer than ten people died, the blast had caused $20 million in damage, equivalent to about half a billion dollars today.[6] On January 11, 1917, carloads of dynamite and artillery shells had exploded at a munitions factory in Kingsland, New Jersey.[7]

After the war, the Mixed Claims Commission was created to determine the amount of reparations to be paid by Germany to the United States.[8] At hearings in 1930, an attorney for the U.S. government ascribed the Black Tom and Kingsland explosions to German sabotage, complete with sulfuric-acid "pencils" that exploded when the tip was cut. Introducing last-minute evidence, however, Germany managed to discredit the testimony of the German-American spies who described the sabotage.[9] The resulting opinion of the Mixed Claims Commission referred to the secret agents, Fred Herrmann and Paul Hilken, as "liars, not presumptive but proven," and the claims were denied.[10]

Watching the hearings at The Hague, an American lawyer named John J. McCloy from the law firm of Cravath, Henderson, and de Gersdorff became intrigued. Over the next several years, McCloy became Cravath's answer to James Bond, traveling to Germany and Britain to meet with spies, double agents, and code breakers. He learned the ways of espionage and intelligence, still largely unknown in the United States. McCloy became convinced that dealing with deception required deception, including the interception of the enemy's wire communications and letters.[11]

By 1933, McCloy succeeded in persuading the Mixed Claims Commission to reopen the case by presenting evidence of substantial fraud by the German parties. In 1936, McCloy and his wife Ellen traveled to Munich and Berlin to negotiate a settlement in a "terrifying" atmosphere of Nazi oppression that still haunted Ellen's nightmares years later. The settlement, however, was scuttled by interference from previously successful American claimants before the Mixed Claims Commission such as Chase Bank, which objected to the possibility of having to take a smaller share of the pie. Despite McCloy's urgings, the Department of Justice declined to charge Chase with interference with foreign relations because such a suit would depend on the absurd notion of top Nazi officials testifying in U.S. courts.[12]

But McCloy was not defeated. In 1938, he and his colleagues discovered an incriminating postscript in a letter to Hilken. When read using well-established code words, the postscript clearly congratulated Hilken on his successful sabotage at Kingsland. McCloy convinced the Mixed Claims Commission to reopen the case, and the new hearing ended in January 1939.[13] On March 1, the German commissioner abruptly "retired" rather than render a decision. The umpire, U.S. Supreme Court Justice Owen Roberts, entered a decision for the American claimants in the German commissioner's absence.[14] The U.S. Supreme Court would eventually uphold the award and authorize payment of the claims.[15] These decisions, and the vivid reminder of German sabotage they invoked, crossed Roosevelt's desk in 1939 and 1940 as he weighed what to do about the immigration services.[16]

CONGRESSIONAL PRESSURE

Once the Reorganization Act of 1939 looked likely to succeed, Roosevelt wasted no time in preparing reorganization plans for Congress. Even before final passage of the bill on April 3, Roosevelt called together members of the former President's Committee on Administrative Management (better known, happily, as the Brownlow Committee after its chairman, public administration expert Louis Brownlow). The committee had been studying the structure of the executive branch for the president since 1936, but so far had been foiled by Congress in most of its efforts. Holed up in Brownlow's suite at the Hay-Adams Hotel at 16th and H Streets—"where nothing is overlooked but the White House," as the hotel's website now reads—Brownlow and other public administration experts quickly crafted a reorganization strategy to seize the opportunity provided by the new legislation. Reorganization Plan No. I would create the Executive Office of the President and several new "agencies" under existing departments in light of a prohibition on creating new departments. Reorganization Plan No. II would make some fairly uncontroversial interdepartmental transfers.[17] Those first two plans were submitted to Congress on April 25 and May 9, 1939.[18] During the same work session, the president and the Brownlow Committee members were already discussing Plan III, which would ultimately be sent to Congress in April 1940, to consolidate or abolish a handful of overlapping or duplicative agencies within existing departments.[19]

At no point in its study process from 1936 onward did the Brownlow Committee consider the transfer of any immigration services from Labor to Justice. For the most part, the Brownlow Committee focused on presidential management and left the question of interdepartmental reorganizations to a joint congressional committee established around the same time.[20] One internal draft, however, presented two alternative plans for departmental reorganization. The "ideal" plan would have transferred INS to the Department of State; the alternative plan would have left it in a revamped Department of Labor and Security (which would also have included the Social Security Administration). Neither plan contemplated moving any part of INS to the Department of Justice.[21]

The first documented suggestion to the president to transfer INS from Labor to Justice came on April 25, 1939, from a freshman congressman from Tennessee named Albert Gore. After referring in the cover letter to the president's powers under the pending reorganization bill, the young representative Gore wrote:

It is respectfully submitted for your consideration, Mr. President, that the Immigration and Naturalization Service no longer has anything more than a remote and indirect bearing upon or relationship to labor; that the principal duties of the Immigration and Naturalization Service are now law enforcement, apprehension, investigation, criminology, registration (finger printing proposed), naturalization, and deportation; and that upon analysis one cannot escape the conclusion that the overwhelming proportion of the duties devolving upon the Immigration and Naturalization Service are more nearly within the purview of activity of, and more directly related to the functions of the Department of Justice than to the Department of Labor.[22]

Supporting this conclusion, the brief cited the "working relations" between the Department of Justice and the courts; the "record of performance" of the FBI for investigation, registration, apprehension, and "criminology"; and the declining role of immigration as a source of cheap labor. "Now," Gore wrote, "even more than protection of American workers, our immigration and deportation laws are a protection of our standards of living, of our form of government, of the caliber of American citizenship, and of our way of life." Intimating a link between these values and the fear of sabotage, Gore added that "[t]his need of protection is accentuated by the international disturbance in Europe."

The memo seems to have received scant attention from Roosevelt at the time it was sent; a year later, it had generated no response and could not be located in the president's files.[23] That, perhaps, is less surprising than the fact that Gore sent the letter at all. Gore was not a member of the House Select Committee on Government Organization or the Committee on Immigration; the first committee assignment of his career that year was the Committee on Banking and Currency. As a former Tennessee commissioner of labor, Gore may have recognized the poor fit between the duties of Labor and INS.[24] But freshmen congressman were not encouraged to wield influence. Gore noted that in Congress, "[a]s in my father's household, the youngsters were to be seen and not heard."[25]

Gore's regular radio addresses and newspaper columns summarizing the events in Washington for his constituents at home in Tennessee during his first term show a congressman aware of the immigration and refugee issues of 1939, but not unusually focused on them. Like most Americans of his time, his attitude was generally isolationist. Three days before sending the letter to Roosevelt, Gore commented on a "terrific drive" in Congress to admit twenty thousand German refugees. While stating that the relief effort was commendable, Gore concluded that "it does appear that those who profess to be so charitably inclined could look about them and find thousands and thousands of good, healthy, intelligent American children who cry out for encouragement and opportunity."[26]

Perhaps more important than *what* the young congressman knew was *whom* he knew. Gore may have been prompted to the task by another member of the Tennessee delegation, Senator Tom Stewart. On July 19, 1939, Stewart introduced a bill in the Senate to require the registration and fingerprinting of noncitizens already within the country.[27] A week after Stewart introduced the Senate bill, Gore introduced a House bill to provide for the registration of aliens.[28] Aside from Stewart, another Tennessean may have had a hand in Gore's decision to write to Roosevelt. Gore's biographer stated that, "[i]n the early stages of his career, Gore's most significant influence was Cordell Hull."[29] Secretary of State Hull had been a family friend of the Gores back in Carthage, Tennessee, and Gore kept a picture of Hull prominently displayed in his office throughout his career.[30] In light of the turf wars between State and Labor over immigration, Gore may have been influenced by his mentor in 1939.[31]

The Gore brief may not have attracted much attention from the president, but Congress was not done pressing the issue. The second request came from Representative Lindsey Warren, Roosevelt's House ally on the reorganization bill of 1939. On May 6, 1939, the president met with Representative Warren and Senator James Byrnes, chairs of the House and Senate reorganization committees, and his own reorganization team. Reorganization Plan No. I had caused some ripples in Congress, and the president in this meeting sought to do a little path-paving for Reorganization Plan No. II. The president's team was now headed by the new director of the Bureau of the Budget, Harold D. Smith, and included Brownlow and Department of Justice attorney Newman A. Townsend. After the president's team had presented their plan, Representative Warren made two related suggestions: moving the Bituminous Coal Commission from the Department of the Interior to the Department of Labor, and moving the Immigration and Naturalization Service out of Labor and into Justice.[32]

After some discussion of the proposal, Roosevelt asked Smith to consult with Perkins and Secretary of the Interior Harold Ickes. "I suspected that the President was not very enthusiastic about the proposals," Smith noted, "and therefore wanted me to serve notice to the respective

Secretaries in anticipation that their reaction would give him a clue to the answer." When Smith reached Perkins later that day, she told him that the immigration service "might be most anywhere but that she saw no point in moving it from Labor to Justice." A more sensible home, Perkins thought, might be the new Federal Security Agency, which had been created to manage health and social welfare programs.[33]

Perkins's opposition to the move seemed motivated not by any jealousy over control of immigration but by a concern about criminalizing immigration matters. That July, Perkins developed a statement titled "The Relation of the Immigration and Naturalization Service to the Department of Labor." In the statement, she outlined three reasons why INS should remain in the Department of Labor rather than being transferred to the Department of Justice. First, she said, the issue of immigration is "basically an economic one" closely related to labor (a view she later disavowed). Second, the immigration and naturalization functions are closely related and should not be separated between different departments. Finally, she wrote, "immigration is a civil process and should not be confused with criminal procedure." She distinguished between the administrative process of determining an individual's immigration status and the urgency and danger associated with apprehending and isolating criminals. "Indeed, more often than not, the individual investigated [for immigration violations] is a person of good moral character and in no sense undesirable from the moral point of view," the statement said. "He has merely entered without inspection or first securing a visa."[34]

Roosevelt declined to heed Gore's and Warren's suggestion, at least for the moment. On May 9, 1939, Roosevelt sent Reorganization Plan No. II to Congress, recommending various executive branch reorganizations for efficiency and cost savings.[35] The president's message to Congress in transmitting the plan noted that he had "considered the desirability of transferring the jurisdiction over deportable aliens from the Immigration and Naturalization Service in the Department of Labor to the Department of Justice," but he concluded that "this matter will require further study, or perhaps legislation, and therefore is not included in this plan."[36]

Uninterested in moving INS from Labor to Justice, Roosevelt would take a different approach to increase government control over noncitizens. In late June 1939, Attorney General Frank Murphy presented to Roosevelt a proposal for handling countersabotage and counterespionage operations within the executive branch.[37] To that point, these operations had been handled by an informal committee comprising representatives of State, Treasury, War, Justice, the Post Office, and the Navy. This cumbersome arrangement proved inefficient, and critical information was often delayed before reaching the FBI in the Department of Justice. Murphy and his Department of Justice wanted all such operations to be handled only by the FBI, the Army's Military Intelligence Division, and the Office of Naval Intelligence.[38]

Murphy's presentation must have impressed Roosevelt, because he sent to all involved agencies a memo that Murphy delivered to him for that purpose.[39] Decades later, a Senate select committee on governmental intelligence would refer to Roosevelt's memorandum of June 26, 1939, as "the closest thing to a formal charter for FBI and military domestic intelligence."[40] The coordinated operation was not made public until after Britain declared war on Germany on September 3, 1939.[41] In a press conference on September 8, 1939, Roosevelt expressly described the FBI's new authority as an attempt to protect the country against sabotage of the type that occurred prior to World War I.[42]

But Warren and Gore were not through pressing the issue. On November 16, Representative Warren sent a letter to the president's secretary with thoughts on further reorganization. After discussing the abolition of several boards, Warren added, "I hope you will also tell the President that nothing he could do would please Congress more than to move the Bureau of Immigration and Naturalization from the Department of Labor to the Department of Justice where we think it properly belongs."[43] The president forwarded the letter to Brownlow a month later and, in early January, requested a meeting with Representative Warren.[44]

Warren's letter may have stoked the president's interest in transferring INS to DOJ, because around the same time Roosevelt asked Attorney General Murphy to have his staff study the question. An unsigned memorandum reporting back to the attorney general was dated November 28, 1939. After a lengthy overview of the various functions of INS, the author reached an unequivocal conclusion: "It does not appear appropriate to transfer to the Department of Justice the administration of the immigration laws." DOJ, the author stated, was divided between the legal division, which prosecuted and defended criminal and civil matters and gave legal advice, and the FBI and Bureau of Prisons, which principally dealt with enforcement of criminal laws. The report continued:

> To transfer the immigration service might well create in the public mind a confusion between immigration matters and criminal matters. Such a result would be unfortunate. It is hardly desirable, therefore, that the department which administers the criminal law should, at the same time, administer immigration laws. Moreover, the enforcement of laws, such as the immigration laws, which are not connected with the administration of justice is a subject that is foreign to the primary purposes of the Department of Justice and would transform it from the legal department of the Government to a department charged with the administration of various miscellaneous laws. The desirability of such a consummation is highly doubtful.[45]

The president did not receive this report promptly, possibly because of his decision to nominate Murphy to the Supreme Court on January 4, 1940, and to promote Robert H. Jackson to attorney general. In the transition, the president apparently said nothing to Jackson about the possible expansion of the duties of his new office. Two weeks after taking office, on February 1, Jackson sent a memo to DOJ attorney Townsend, part of the president's reorganization team. "I have heard rumors of a proposed transfer of the immigration service from the Department of Labor to this Department," Jackson wrote to Townsend. "If you hear anything tangible about it, I should like to be advised."[46]

Indeed, talk was afoot about such a transfer, and another push would soon come from Congress. On February 6, Representative Gore again sent a letter to the president, urging him to transfer INS from Labor to Justice and referring him to his memorandum of the previous April. "This letter is to further and respectfully call to your attention that the overwhelming proportion of the current duties devolving upon the Immigration and Naturalization Service are more nearly within the purview of, and more directly related to the functions of the Department of Justice than to the Department of Labor," Gore wrote.[47]

But the president's top legal advisors disagreed. Just three days after the Gore letter, Jackson forwarded to Roosevelt the memorandum from November 28 that DOJ lawyers had prepared on the subject. In his cover memo, Jackson noted that the legal memorandum "deals at some length with the subject and reaches the conclusion that the general administration of these statutes should not be transferred to the Department of Justice."[48]

Roosevelt apparently listened to Jackson. The DOJ memorandum was labeled "Plan 3" in the White House files, and Reorganization Plan Nos. III and IV were submitted to Congress on April 2 and April 11 with no mention of a transfer of INS.[49] To the contrary, Plan No. III further consolidated the Immigration and Naturalization Service within the Department of Labor by abolishing separate immigration offices in the ports and immigration and naturalization offices in various districts, placing their functions under the supervision of the secretary of labor. As these were the last reorganization plans that Roosevelt intended to send, the subject appeared to be closed: the immigration services would remain in the Department of Labor.

6 Invasion

At 5:30 AM on May 10, 1940, Hitler's Wehrmacht invaded Luxembourg and began *Blitzkrieg* on Belgium, Holland, and northern France. By May 13, a German Panzer division broke through the French front at Sedan, opening a path to the English Channel. Learning the news at the North-East Front headquarters of the French High Command, General Alphonse Georges broke down and wept. On May 14, a Blitzkrieg on Rotterdam killed nine hundred and left nearly eighty thousand homeless despite ongoing surrender negotiations, and the Netherlands surrendered to Germany the next day. By May 20, General Heinz Guderian's Second Panzer Division reached Abbeville, twelve miles from the English Channel. From May 26 to June 4, the Allies evacuated 366,131 soldiers and other personnel at Dunkirk. More than sixty-eight thousand were lost in the evacuation, many to spend five years as Nazi prisoners of war.[1]

Since the spring of 1939, members of Congress had been pressing Roosevelt to transfer the Immigration and Naturalization Service from the Department of Labor to the Department of Justice. He had repeatedly rejected the idea, despite attempts by Congress to impeach his secretary of labor. The following winter and spring, he again resisted pressure from

Congress to make the transfer, heeding a warning from two attorneys general that it would cause the public to equate immigration with crime.

The simple explanation offered by the administration for the transfer of INS to DOJ in the reorganization plan sent to Congress on May 22, 1940—that it was a necessary response to the war situation—does not quite tell the story.[2] War in Europe was already underway and expected to accelerate by April 11, 1940, when Roosevelt sent his fourth, and supposedly final, reorganization plan to Congress with no transfer of INS.[3] The "fifth column" strategy, in which undercover German agents who appeared to be locals would attack from within while German armed forces invaded from without, had already been rumored to be responsible for Norway's defeat. The fifth column threat was familiar to the White House and the State Department and was being monitored daily on the home front by the FBI. So how did the events of May 1940—which were not entirely unforeseen—change Roosevelt's mind about transferring INS from Labor to Justice?

By May 7, State Department officials knew the storm was coming. Adolf A. Berle, Jr., assistant secretary of state for Latin American Affairs, called it an "extraordinarily difficult" day. "The cables outside are indicating that there is going to be trouble somewhere, though it is not clear exactly where," he wrote in his diary. Berle worried about German concentrations on the Hungarian border, as well as "renewed activity towards the West."[4]

Berle's experience and expertise were considerable, if largely academic. After graduating from Harvard Law School at the prodigious age of twenty-one, he had a short career as an intelligence officer for the Army in the Dominican Republic and a lawyer in private practice before becoming a law professor at Columbia, noted for his expertise on corporate law. He was part of Roosevelt's "Brain Trust" of academic advisors on the early New Deal and joined the State Department in 1938. Roosevelt relied on him for speechwriting as well as advice on international and economic issues.[5]

In the first few days of May 1940, Berle had been working urgently to transfer funds held by the Norwegian government and banks into the account of the Norwegian ambassador, Wilhelm von Munthe af Morgenstierne, before Germany seized control of Norway. The Dutch chargé d'affaires, Alexander Loudon, was another matter still. By May 3, Berle feared Loudon was on the verge of a nervous breakdown; there was little Berle could do but try to console him. Late in the day of May 7, Loudon phoned Berle, again beset with worry. "He thinks there is something brewing—and perhaps it is," Berle wrote.[6]

By the end of the following day, word came that Germany would soon invade Belgium and Holland. Berle learned that Roosevelt had received a telegram from Queen Wilhelmina of the Netherlands. She had mentioned an invitation Roosevelt had once made to her that she could find asylum in the United States if the need were to arise. In her cable, she said that she had decided to stay, but asked whether the offer might be extended to her daughter, the Princess Juliana, then twenty-one years old and mother of two young daughters. Berle phoned the White House for details, and Roosevelt told him that he had asked Under Secretary of State Sumner Welles to answer the telegram.[7]

"Since I thought this indicated that German troops might be on the march," Berle wrote, "I came down to the Department to find Welles, who had gone to bed with a couple of sleeping powders, been routed out, taken some black coffee and showed up very tired, and quite unhappy." Berle suggested they send a cruiser to Iceland to meet the princess and her daughters there since they could no longer send a cruiser into the war zone. Welles had a more practicable suggestion: The Princess might fly to Lisbon and meet a U.S. cruiser that regularly stopped there. Berle and Welles sent the message and, as May 9 dawned in Holland, waited for word of Nazi activity. There was none.[8]

The two men, exhausted and on edge, left the State, War, and Navy Building next to the White House at Seventeenth Street and Pennsylvania Avenue, now the Eisenhower Executive Office Building. Walking a block north to H Street, they stopped at the exclusive Metropolitan Club and quickly downed four scotches. They swapped stories about old times in the Dominican Republic, considered their career prospects, and wondered where they would all be in a year. "In any event, it doesn't matter," Berle, then forty-five years old, concluded in his journal entry for the day. "[I]f we can help to pull the country through, ambitions of any individual amount to very little."[9]

On the night of May 9, Roosevelt had just finished dining with his secretary Grace G. Tully and the heir and philanthropist Vincent Astor and was resting in his study when the call came that would end the months of waiting. The U.S. ambassador to Belgium, James Cudahy, reported that Germany had invaded Holland, Belgium, Luxembourg, and France.[10] For the next four hours, Roosevelt monitored the situation—or attempted to, as phone calls to Europe were not going through.[11] Shortly after midnight, he phoned Treasury Secretary Henry Morgenthau, Jr., and asked him to issue exchange controls on property of Holland, Belgium, and Luxembourg first thing in the morning. The president's alarm, while abundantly justified, was at that hour of confusion slightly misdirected. Morgenthau noted that the president "[t]hinks there is a big raid on in England," and is "[a]fraid they will attack Sweden." Ten minutes later, Morgenthau talked to Secretary of State Cordell Hull, saying he thought he should freeze the exchanges on a voluntary basis first thing in the morning and wait for more information before issuing mandatory orders. Hull agreed, but apparently Roosevelt did not. At 2 AM, Roosevelt called back and said Morgenthau should "[d]efinitely" issue mandatory orders by 8:30 the following morning and be at the White House at 10:30.[12]

In those first hours of May 10, Secretary Hull and his top officers were at the State Department, watching the wires and feeling powerless. Many of the State officials had come, still in formal attire, directly from a dinner party hosted by shipping magnate Basil Harris. Hull had phoned the Harris estate to speak to Jay Pierrepont Moffatt, chief of the division of Western European Affairs, and word slowly spread among the guests that the U.S. ambassador at The Hague had called to report the German attack. The Belgian ambassador, despite having a son and son-in-law at the front, calmly continued to flirt with the women. For Berle, the moment evoked a canonical scene in *Vanity Fair:* fashionable and conniving Becky Sharp dominates a Brussels ball on June 16, 1815, before word arrives that the British and Belgian officers in attendance have been ordered to Waterloo to face an advancing Napoleon.[13] According to Thackeray's narrator, "[t]here never was, since the days of Darius, such a brilliant train of camp-followers as hung round the Duke of Wellington's army in the Low Countries, in 1815; and led it dancing and feasting, as it were, up to the very brink of battle."[14]

Moffatt and Berle quietly left the party and headed for the office, along with Assistant Secretary of State Breckinridge Long and James Clement Dunn, an advisor and de facto press spokesman for Hull.[15] Hull was there when they arrived, and around 1 AM Welles joined them, again having been jarred by a phone call from a chemically induced sleep. The news was spotty. The wire from The Hague wasn't working much, but one telephone call went through. They failed to connect with anyone in Paris. The news they could get was bad; in Belgium and Holland, they were told, fifth column German agents had attacked airfields, followed by troops parachuting in to seize the fields and air raids to secure them. Radio reports and the occasional cable confirmed to the State group that the Blitzkrieg "lived up to the convictions of horror" long anticipated. By 2:30 AM, Berle decided "there was no point in spending all one's strength on sight-seeing" and went home. Dunn stayed all night and arrived at a meeting the next morning still in a tuxedo.[16]

Within days of the Nazi invasion, telegrams arriving from the royal families of Belgium and Luxembourg sounded poignant notes of the defeat that was soon to come. On May 13, a cable from King Leopold III of Belgium thanked the president for an earlier offer of refuge but concluded that "the Belgian people have resolved to accept the most extreme sacrifices for the maintenance of their liberty. . . . Express to the American people their gratitude. . . . Your loyal friendship is particularly precious to me in these hours of trial."[17] Roosevelt and Welles, to whom the cable was forwarded, may have recalled this message ruefully after the Belgian king's unconditional (and controversial) surrender to the Nazis on May 28.[18]

On May 14, as the Nazis were breaking through the French front at Sedan, the Duchess and the Prince of Luxembourg sent a telegram to Washington from their exile in Paris. The monarchs asked the Luxembourgish ambassador in Washington, Hugues Legallais, to "express to the President their profound gratitude for the offer of hospitality to their children." The offer, however, was declined: "Parents and children wish to remain together not far from their country during this cruel test. Please thank the president for the sentiments of sympathy shown by him and the United States Government with regard to the people of Luxembourg."[19]

"WE HAVE SEEN THE TREACHEROUS USE
OF THE 'FIFTH COLUMN'"

At 1 PM on Thursday, May 16, the president rose before Congress—a physical ordeal for Roosevelt under any circumstances—and delivered an address that would be met with cheers by most members in attendance (and stony silence by a few). "These are ominous days," the president began. The "swift and shocking developments" of those days, he said, required neutral nations to consider their defenses anew. "Let us examine, without self-deception, the dangers which confront us," he continued. "Let us measure our strength and our defense without self-delusion." The dangers enumerated by the president began with the realities of modern warfare, as demonstrated in the previous week: Motorized armies traveling two hundred miles a day through enemy territory. Parachute troops dropping behind enemy lines. "We have seen the treacherous use of the 'fifth column,'" he continued, "by which persons supposed to be peaceful visitors were actually a part of an enemy unit of occupation." The new warfare was capable of destroying defense production facilities far behind enemy lines, he said, his warning echoing the Black Tom and Kingsland sabotage cases he'd reviewed nine days earlier.[20]

On that Thursday in May, Roosevelt was performing a delicate task with each hand: on the one, galvanizing an isolationist Congress around the national defense and the possibility of war; on the other, maintaining Congress's insistent neutrality by resisting England's plea for assurances of American weaponry and support. On Wednesday, Roosevelt had received a telegram from Winston Churchill, then a mere five days into his tenure as prime minister. Churchill appealed to Roosevelt with all the force and eloquence for which he would soon be legendary, and the pressure was not subtle:

> We expect to be attacked here ourselves, both from the air and by parachute and air borne troops in the near future, and are getting ready for them. If necessary, we shall continue the war alone and we are not afraid of that. But I trust you realize, Mr. President, that the voice and force of the United States may count for nothing if they are withheld too long. You may have a completely subjugated, Nazified Europe established with astonishing swiftness, and the weight may be more than we can bear.[21]

Churchill made six specific requests: forty or fifty destroyers until those already under construction could be completed; several hundred of the latest aircraft, which might be paid for out of the order then under construction in the United States; antiaircraft equipment and ammunition; a guaranteed supply of American steel even if England could no longer pay for it in dollars; an American squadron in Ireland to defend against an anticipated parachute attack there; and American use of Singapore to forestall attack by Japan. With regard to the antiaircraft equipment and ammunition, Churchill chillingly assured Roosevelt that this was a stop-gap measure, as "there will be plenty [in England] next year, if we are alive to see it."

As Roosevelt was beginning his speech to Congress on Thursday, the U.S. Embassy was wiring his response to Churchill. Sympathetic to the cause but unable to promise anything in light of Congress's unbudging policy of neutrality and the increasing fear of attack on U.S. soil, Roosevelt denied nothing and promised nothing. While "giving every possible consideration" to Churchill's "suggestions," each was deflected based on concerns ranging from lack of congressional authorization to American defense needs to lengthy turnaround time. With preposterous coolness, the message closed, "The best of luck to you. Franklin D. Roosevelt."[22]

The question of what it meant to be an American hovered in the background of everything. The same day he warned Congress of modern warfare's "fifth column" threat, Roosevelt sent Secretary Perkins "A Greeting to New Citizens on 'I Am an American Day.'"[23] Just two weeks earlier on May 3, Congress had authorized the president to proclaim the new holiday (now celebrated on September 17 as Citizenship Day), recognizing those attaining citizenship.[24] "It will be their responsibility and their duty always to think first of America and at the same time to think in terms of humanity," the president's message read. "This nation was created to insure the things that unite and to eliminate the things that divide."[25]

Roosevelt's mind that week was cluttered and tired; sleep was hard to come by. Late in the afternoon after delivering his address to Congress, Roosevelt called Berle at the State Department. He had been thinking about how to evacuate Americans in England when the time came, and he suggested that Bantry Bay, on the southern Atlantic coast of Ireland in County Cork, might be a suitable evacuation point.[26]

In the summer of 1918, Roosevelt had toured County Cork as part of his duties as assistant secretary of the Navy. During a trip to England and France, Roosevelt was invited by Sir Eric Geddes, first lord of the Admiralty of the British Royal Navy, to accompany him on a brief trip to Ireland to inspect operations there. On July 24, Geddes and Roosevelt, accompanied by two junior officers, traveled to Cobh—called "Queenstown" by the British in the occupied Ireland of 1918—"inspecting everything in the neighborhood," Roosevelt wrote.[27] That tour would likely have included a drive to nearby Bantry Bay and its flying stations at Berehaven and Whiddy Island, for which Roosevelt would submit reports to the department upon his return.[28]

Much had changed in Roosevelt's life since World War I. In August 1914, weeks after the assassination of Archduke Ferdinand in Sarajevo, a thirty-two-year-old Roosevelt had faced war with naïve bravado. Arriving at the Department of the Navy after a speaking engagement in Pennsylvania, Roosevelt had written to Eleanor that "[t]o my astonishment . . . nobody seemed the least bit excited about the European crisis—[Secretary of the Navy] Mr. Daniels feeling chiefly very sad that his faith in human nature and civilization and similar idealistic nonsense was receiving such a rude shock."[29]

In May 1940, Roosevelt was fifty-eight, paralyzed from the waist down, and much more sober. He had been sitting awake at night, Berle recalled, "facing the crashing truth that the British Empire might be passing out of existence and that we would have nothing between us and some pretty hostile Germans except the deep Atlantic." Roosevelt remembered, from that trip to Ireland twenty-two years earlier, driving along Bantry Bay and seeing beautiful Irish girls walking on the road. When the girls opened their mouths to curse the British officers in the vehicle, Roosevelt saw that their teeth were black and decayed.

"Wouldn't you think," Roosevelt mused to Berle in 1940, "that one's mind would make different kinds of pictures when things are going fast?" Berle wished him Godspeed, hung up the phone, and went to work on the evacuation plan.[30]

JOSEF GOEBBELS AND THE FIFTH COLUMN

Fifth column fear was spreading rapidly in all nations under Nazi threat. The origin of the term "fifth column" is disputed but is generally associated with the siege of Madrid during the Spanish Civil War. At least according to some Communist journalists of that era, Nationalist general Emilio Mola told reporters that his four columns of troops approaching Madrid would be supported by a "fifth column" of supporters within the city to undermine the government from within.[31] Whatever its provenance, the term was exploited by the Nazi minister of propaganda, Josef Goebbels, who spread the rumor that Germany had large colonies of spies in France and the Low Countries to confuse and distract from within.[32] This strategy was remarkably effective at undermining Allied morale. As British historian James Holland wrote, Goebbels had only to plant the seed and "the Allies themselves did the rest. The genius of the scam was that it made everyone suspicious."[33] Fifth column terror led the Poles to massacre at least fifty-five hundred ethnic Germans in September 1939.[34] The Dutch foreign minister claimed that German parachutists had arrived dressed not only as Dutch, Belgian, French, or British soldiers, but even as priests, nuns, and nurses.[35] In May 1940, the British Joint Intelligence Committee concluded that the German occupation of Norway and Denmark was the result of fifth column activity and warned of its possible use in any Nazi invasion of England.[36] The British Ministry of War recruited a quarter of a million volunteers in six days to defend against the possibility of parachutists and undercover agents who appeared to be locals.[37]

In the United States, J. Edgar Hoover and his agents at the FBI had been investigating rumors of undercover activity for months. In the first few months of 1940, reports sent by Hoover to the White House dealt with a variety of threats. The majority involved Communist activity or other sources of concern, although the files also contain several reports of Nazi activity: In mid-February, the FBI reported a German plan to destroy two electric power stations and two terminal transformer stations in Southern California as well as the aqueduct that supplied water to Los Angeles.[38] Later that month, a "reliable" informant told an FBI agent that German agents purporting to be German Jewish refugees were reporting to the German government, though only with regard to prevailing public opinion and not in connection with any planned sabotage.[39] The likelihood that spies would travel to Germany for training and might be detected by INS upon reentry into the United States was illustrated by a report about a former German professor at Smith College. Evidence suggested that the professor made a trip to Germany and upon his return was employed by the German Library of Information under the control of the German Consulate in New York City, an employment the professor variously claimed and denied.[40] And Roosevelt's friend and fellow Navy veteran Vincent Astor, with whom the president dined on May 9 before learning of the Nazi invasion of France and the Low Countries, had provided a report on an incident involving a private German-owned vessel that participated in the rescue effort for the SS *Athenia*, the first British vessel sunk by Germany in the war in September 1939.[41]

By late April 1940, the focus of FBI reports to the White House had changed. While occasional reports of Communist activity in the Americas were passed along, the overwhelming majority of reports from this point involved German spies or sabotage attempts on American war-manufacturing facilities. The turning point may have been a letter from April 23, 1940, from Hoover transmitting a memorandum received from a British secret agent regarding Canadian plans to protect Greenland and its desire for the United States to lead the effort.[42]

In North America, all eyes were on Greenland. On April 9, Denmark, Germany's northern neighbor, had been left surrounded when Oslo fell to the Nazis and King Haakon VII and his government retreated northward. The same morning, the German minister in Denmark, Cecil von Renthe-Fink, presented King Christian X a list of thirteen ultimata. The Danish king surrendered, albeit under the fiction that Denmark would merely be placed under the protection of the Reich.[43]

Danish surrender was a game-changer for North Americans, since it meant the Nazis now controlled Greenland, a Danish territory.[44] In the memo that Hoover forwarded to the White House later that month, the Canadian author reported evidence that Denmark had been "honeycombed" by fifth column forces and the same might well be the case in Greenland. The author cited frequent statements by Hitler and his geopolitical advisors "that North America should not be regarded as a preserve, closed off to Germany." Germany might establish a temporary air base in Greenland from which Canadian transportation, communication, and power systems could swiftly be destroyed. The Canadian memo proposed that the United States, joined by Canada, declare Greenland to be part of North America, which the United States would then be bound to defend under the Monroe Doctrine condemning European colonization of the Americas.[45]

The occupation of Denmark and the Greenland situation were forecasted in March in a memorandum prepared by the Council on Foreign Relations for the State Department. The memorandum was part of a larger project of the Council, "Studies of American Interests in the War and the Peace," funded by the Rockefeller Foundation and pitched as free expert foreign policy analysis to State in the fall of 1939.[46] The group's memorandum from March 17, 1940, "The Strategic Importance of Greenland," outlined the United States' waiver of any rights to Greenland in 1916 and Denmark's perfection of title in 1933; the "nuisance value" of Greenland for disrupting air navigation between North America and the British Isles; and the prospects and implications of Greenland's acquisition by Germany, Britain, or the United States. The memo concluded that the acquisition of Greenland by any European power would violate the Monroe Doctrine, and purchase by the United States might be advantageous if the status of neighboring Iceland were secure.[47] The president would have this memorandum with him at a Cabinet meeting that summer and would rely heavily on its details and opinions in forming his own judgment on the subject.[48] By late April, State had already chosen a U.S. consul to be sent to Greenland (who went under protest over the hardship).[49]

According to State Department analysis and American news reports that month, the rapid fall of Oslo was precipitated by the assistance of a robust fifth column of Nazi forces throughout the city. According to State Department memoranda, on April 15, the *Washington Star* reported that a Norwegian at the Horten naval base outside Oslo said, "[t]here was nothing we could do. The officers of our ships ran up white flags. We didn't know why and I still don't know why. We thought they had orders from the government."[50] The State analysis, relying on reports by a *Chicago Daily News* correspondent, claimed that German agents in Oslo had used "a gigantic conspiracy" of bribes and promises of position in the new government to obtain the cooperation of a small number of Norwegian officials in key defense positions. "[T]he capture of Oslo, with a harbor uniquely protected by impregnable fjords and narrows, stands as a significant and timely example of treachery to other peaceful nations," the State analysis concluded.[51] No longer could Americans assume that an ocean would be sufficient protection against Nazi invasion.

7 The Welles Mission

Reports of fifth column involvement in Norway had greatly disturbed the under secretary of state, Sumner Welles. By May 8, Welles had Berle at work on a plan to control noncitizens present in the United States. "Welles . . . wants to be sure that precautions are taken here; and he is right," wrote Berle after their meeting. At the heart of their plan was a deep suspicion of the culture of the Department of Labor. "[T]he blunt fact is that the Labor Department is so honeycombed with Left Wing and Communist intrigue that you can never quite trust what they are doing," Berle wrote in his diary that day. He regretted the displacement of "[t]he older men, who knew their business," with a new generation that he found prone not so much to disloyalty as to "inefficiency and sheer soft-headed foolishness."[1] As part of this plan to defend against a fifth column invasion, State officials debated the possible relocation of INS. On May 9, Ruth Bielaski Shipley, the head of the Passport Division, suggested to Berle that INS should be moved to the State Department. It was the last matter Berle would work on before learning of the Nazi invasion of the Low Countries late that night.[2]

Under Secretary Welles was nominally subordinate to Secretary of State Cordell Hull, but it was well known in Washington that the president relied much more heavily on Welles, whom Roosevelt would later call the "only man in the State Department who really knew what was going on."[3] Though Roosevelt needed Hull for his influence with Congress, it was Welles with whom the president discussed and developed his foreign policy views, often meeting daily for informal chats at the White House. In addition, Welles effectively acted as secretary during Hull's frequent absences due to illness, to the increasing consternation of Hull.[4]

Roosevelt did little to soften the appearance that Welles was his true advisor on foreign affairs. It was Welles whom Roosevelt sent as his "special envoy" to Europe in February and March 1940 for meetings with Hitler, Mussolini, Chamberlain, and others. Welles reported directly to Roosevelt from that mission, giving only selective briefings to Hull. As war drew nearer and Congress maintained its isolationist stance, Roosevelt would authorize Welles to give a speech announcing war and peace aims that Roosevelt was not yet free to articulate: the creation of a global international organization; international coordination of military, political, and economic planning; lowering of tariffs and other trade barriers; equal access to the world's resources, a slap against imperialism; and the restoration of independence, sovereignty, and self-determination to colonized peoples. And it was Welles, not Hull, who would advise Roosevelt at the pivotal Atlantic Conference in August 1941. At that meeting off the coast of Newfoundland aboard the HMS *Prince of Wales* and the USS *Augusta*, Churchill and Roosevelt would negotiate and announce many of these principles in the Atlantic Charter. The Charter was Welles's brainchild and the predecessor to the United Nations and the General Agreement on Tariffs and Trade, among other pillars of modern international governance.[5]

Welles's relationship with Roosevelt was long-standing. As a close family friend of Eleanor's, a twelve-year-old Welles had served as an attendant in the couple's wedding in March 1905.[6] An aloof outsider at Groton and Harvard, Welles had spent nine months of privileged idleness in Paris and on safari in Africa until the First World War erupted. Returning to Boston, he sat for the Foreign Service exam and immediately demonstrated his abilities, earning the highest score of all takers. In early diplomatic posts, including Japan, Argentina, and the Dominican Republic, Welles excelled. By the age of twenty-eight, he was a very able acting assistant secretary for Latin American affairs, known for his ability to work copiously and quickly. "He is brilliant, tireless," Secretary of State Bainbridge Colby said of him. "When there is work to be done—the clock does not exist."[7]

One colleague opined that Welles, respected but often disliked, wanted in State "only men whom he can absolutely dominate." He could be formal, even imperious: a lawyer visiting Welles on business once remarked that it was "the first time that [Welles] has not been so much overwhelmed with his own dignity that my suggestion of difference with him was not regarded as presumption."[8] Even Roosevelt was not spared these airs. On one occasion, after Welles had repeatedly complained that State needed more office space, Roosevelt asked Budget Director Harold D. Smith to accompany him on a late-afternoon visit to the State, War, and Navy Building.[9] Roosevelt asked Hull and Welles to take him from office to office, opening cabinets and leafing through files to demonstrate that State could create ample space by moving old files off site. Smith "observed with some amusement that Sumner Welles was making strenuous efforts to maintain not only his own dignity but the dignity of the State Department. When the President would ask to see in a room, although Sumner Welles would be a few feet from the door, he would not open it but would ask that it be opened by the Budget Officer of the Department or some other staff person."[10]

Eventually, Roosevelt's reliance on Welles would so threaten Hull that the secretary would support a malicious whispering campaign by the U.S. ambassador to France, William Bullitt, to force Welles out of the government over a sex scandal. Bullitt and Hull learned that a highly intoxicated Welles had propositioned Pullman porters while traveling with the president by train in September 1940. Ironically, Bullitt and Hull would seize on the national hysteria over espionage and sabotage to undermine Welles, arguing that Welles's sexual behavior made him uniquely vulnerable to manipulation by spies and blackmailers. While Roosevelt doggedly resisted attempts to drive out his most trusted foreign policy advisor, ultimately the political opposition over Welles was insurmountable. Roosevelt would announce Welles's resignation on September 25, 1943. The incident would end Welles's diplomatic career.[11]

Until that time, Roosevelt seemed to rely on his under secretary of state irrespective of the political liabilities it engendered—a trust that may have been owing to Welles's visionary foreign policy, the two men's longstanding acquaintance and similar cultural backgrounds, Hull's weaknesses, or some combination. In a sense, Roosevelt may have viewed Welles as his able-bodied alter ego. Welles's grueling travel itinerary—Italy, Germany, England, France, and Italy again in the space of four weeks—would have been impossible for the president. That Welles was in some sense traveling in the president's stead was suggested by Roosevelt's letter of introduction for Welles to Mussolini, which Roosevelt closed by saying, "I still hope to meet you one day, soon!"[12] It would never happen.[13]

The purpose of the Welles mission has been hotly debated since the moment it was announced. Publicly, the administration said Welles's journey was "solely for the purpose of advising the President and the secretary of state as to present conditions in Europe."[14] Welles later wrote that his charge from the president was to "find out only what the views of the four governments might be as to the present possibilities of concluding any just and permanent peace," while offering "no proposals and no suggestions."[15] The British and French feared that the United States sought to negotiate a truce that would capitulate to fascist demands.[16] Hull objected that the mission would only hold out false hopes of peace and give rise to innumerable rumors about its purpose.[17] In hindsight, motives likely included an effort to forestall Italy's entry into the war (a move that backfired) and, perhaps most importantly, to introduce the notion of U.S. leadership into the eventual peace and postwar order.[18] Regardless of motive, the assignment could not have been more delicate: Welles would meet with Mussolini and his foreign minister and son-in-law, Count Galeazzo Ciano; Hitler and his ministers Joachim von Ribbentrop and Hermann Göring; British prime minister Neville Chamberlain and First Lord of the Admiralty Churchill; and Pope Pius XII, among others.[19] Although Welles found that the time for talking had clearly passed, even the unsympathetic Hull wrote in his memoirs that "[n]o one could have gleaned more information from them than he."[20]

Welles's meetings with the Nazi officials were chilling. On being ushered into the Foreign Office, Welles passed two security guards in stained uniforms whose faces "were subnormal in their startling brutality." Von Ribbentrop proceeded to lecture him for more than two hours with his arms glued to the arms of his chair and his eyes continuously closed. His statement was "such an amazing conglomeration of misinformation and deliberate lies" that Welles managed to hold his tongue only for fear of jeopardizing his upcoming meeting with Hitler. The next day, Hitler repeated the identical misrepresentations of British aggression and Nazi innocence, as in subsequent meetings did Hitler's field marshal Göring and Nazi party deputy Rudolf Hess (the latter actually reading from type-written flash cards).[21]

Driving back to Berlin from Göring's palace filled with stolen artwork, Welles reflected that "never before in the history of Europe had the Western powers fought a more wholly defensive war than that in which they were now engaged." The allegations of Hitler and his ministers were "farcical," and whatever influence Mussolini may have had was gone. "There was only one power on earth which could give Hitler and his associates pause," Welles concluded. "That would be their conviction that, in a war of devastation forced upon Europe by Germany, the United States, in its own interest, would come to the support of the Western democracies." Welles also knew that such support was far from assured in the isolationist atmosphere that still prevailed at home.[22]

From the first days after the Nazi invasion of Western Europe, Welles was constantly back and forth between the State Department and the White House.[23] Recalling those tense days, Welles would later remark on "our realization for the first time of the extent of the assistance rendered the German Armies by its hidden accomplices within countries destined for invasion." His apprehensions about the fifth column threat may have been strengthened by his disturbing interviews with the Nazi officials just weeks earlier, as well as his observation, while passing through Switzerland during that trip, of the "all too apparent efforts of various categories of German agents to form some contact with myself or with the members of my staff."[24]

When Welles decided that the fifth column threat was real and must be stamped out, Roosevelt promptly heeded him, reversing course on a decision he had maintained for a year. At noon on Saturday, May 18, Welles delivered his report to the president. State had identified several ways in which noncitizens entered or remained in the country without detection, Welles reported. Under existing legislative authority, Roosevelt could remedy many of them: remove the visa exception extended to North American and Caribbean nationals; require all incoming noncitizens to be registered and fingerprinted; require arriving seamen to be registered and fingerprinted and to carry identifying documents that would be returned upon their departure; and verify the departure of all noncitizens. Additional legislation, Welles concluded, would be required to register and fingerprint all resident noncitizens, exclude some immigrants on public safety grounds, restrict the definition and requirements for foreign officials, and require all noncitizens to obtain departure permits.

The State memorandum and its summary cover letter were not marked confidential, but the papers Welles delivered to the president that day were fronted with a second cover letter, also signed by Welles—this one marked confidential. In that cover-to-the-cover letter, Welles recommended that "the present statutory and administrative activities in connection with the admission of aliens now vested in the Bureau of Immigration and Naturalization in the Department of Labor be transferred to the Department of Justice." He also recommended that the Department of State be given authority to coordinate the activities of all the agencies that would have to play a role in administering the immigration laws: State, Labor, Justice, Treasury, and the Post Office.

In the confidential cover letter, Welles enumerated four reasons to support his recommendation to transfer immigration from Labor to Justice. Welles wrote:

1. Immigration problems can most effectively be dealt with in a department which does not have also labor matters as its major function. As long as the Bureau of Immigration and Naturalization is in the Department of Labor, executive and administrative offices of that Department will have to deal with important policy matters in which they are faced by a duality of interest.

2. All aspects of naturalization would seem to fall more naturally within the province of the Department of Justice than of any other department of the Government.

3. There are various aspects of naturalization and of immigration problems, such as deportation, in which the collaboration and cooperation of the courts are essential. It would seem probable that administrative practice would be simplified by bringing immigration and naturalization under the jurisdiction of the Department of Justice.

4. In connection with individual immigration and naturalization cases, it is frequently necessary to undertake investigations which can be most

effectively carried out by the Federal Bureau of Investigation. In cases where this is necessary, better coordination and more effective results would presumably be obtained by having the Attorney General undertake jurisdiction of both activities.[25]

Welles was not a lawyer, and his rationales for transferring the immigration services from Labor to Justice fail to give weight to separation of powers or due process concerns. His first point, fairly enough, points to a conflict of interest in the Department of Labor that Perkins had frequently complained of. The second point was unexplained and is not self-evident; the naturalization of a foreign national might just as easily be considered the natural province of the Department of State, as Shipley had argued. But it is the third and fourth points that raise critical constitutional concerns. In a system in which the executive and judicial branches are intended to act independently as checks on each other, it is troubling to suggest that deportation efforts by the executive should be conducted with the "collaboration and cooperation of the courts." And since a central tenet of due process is the separation of investigative and adjudicative functions, it is of dubious constitutionality to "hav[e] the Attorney General undertake jurisdiction of both activities." The latter infirmity was recognized and remedied, first by creating EOIR as a separate office within DOJ in 1983, and, more completely, by transferring investigative functions to DHS in 2002. But the erroneous argument fails to support Welles's position that immigration functions should be controlled by the attorney general, then or now.

Roosevelt had been expecting this report, and he already knew from their exchange in February that his attorney general did not favor transferring immigration to the Department of Justice. At Roosevelt's request, Welles had shown Jackson the entire report about control of noncitizens—including the confidential cover letter recommending the transfer of INS. Jackson had responded with reluctance, but he appeared to concede defeat. Jackson's letter of response was delivered to the president by Welles with his report.

"I would not be entirely happy in accepting the responsibility for the Bureau of Immigration and Naturalization without some preliminary studies and understandings, as I indicated to you yesterday," Jackson had written to Welles on May 15. "Its problems are of a kind that I have no desire to assume except as it might be required as a matter of duty." But Jackson did not attempt to advance any opposing arguments, and he accepted the suggestion that State coordinate the activities of multiple departments. Jackson may have sought to buy time for a more cohesive alien enemy control policy, however. He concluded that they should take the steps that were authorized under existing legislative authority, as Welles had outlined. As for new legislation, Jackson noted the many ad hoc legislative approaches then heading toward the president's desk and suggested, "perhaps it would be wise for [the president] to suggest that a general legislative program is being formulated that would be more just and more uniform" than the various special acts then pending.[26]

Shortly after meeting with Welles on Saturday, Roosevelt received another entreaty from Churchill. "I do not need to tell you about the gravity of what has happened," Churchill wrote. "We are determined to persevere to the very end whatever the result of the great battle raging in France may be." Churchill anticipated an attack against England "on the Dutch model," meaning heavy bombing followed by parachute troops and gliderborne forces to distract attention from an invasion by sea, "and we hope to give a good account of ourselves. But if American assistance is to play any part it must be available [soon]."[27]

A PLEA, A SPY, AND A WARNING

Roosevelt did not take action on Welles's fifth column recommendation on Sunday or Monday. Two things happened on Monday, however, that may have increased his anxiety. Roosevelt and Churchill had been in communication through the British ambassador, Lord Lothian, who communicated Roosevelt's predicament with regard to the Prime Minister's previous requests. On Monday morning, Churchill sent another telegram, emphasizing the urgent need for fighter planes to counterattack the German forces. But Churchill's message this time was more emotional plea—or even tacit threat—than detailed request. He noted that he and his administration would under no circumstances consent to surrender, but he could not promise what would happen if the battle went poorly and he were removed (or worse). "If members of the present administration were finished and others came in to parley amid the ruins, you must not be blind to the fact that the sole remaining bargaining counter with Germany would be the fleet," Churchill wrote, "and if this country was left by the United States to its fate no one would have the right to blame those then responsible if they made the best terms they could for the surviving inhabitants." Churchill, who had hesitated before sending such a bald entreaty, made a personal appeal: "Excuse me, Mr. President, putting this nightmare bluntly. Evidently I could not answer for my successors who in utter despair and helplessness might well have to accommodate themselves to the German will. However there is happily no need at present to dwell upon such ideas." Thanking the president for his goodwill, he closed.[28]

Around 2 PM that afternoon in Washington, Joseph P. Kennedy, then U.S. Ambassador to Britain, informed the State Department that Scotland Yard that morning had arrested Tyler G. Kent, an American code clerk at the U.S Embassy in London. Kennedy reported that a search of Kent's apartment discovered "substantial amounts of confidential Embassy material," including some transcriptions of messages sent using confidential State Department codes. Around 6 PM, Sumner Welles and Breckinridge Long replied to Kennedy, asking only whether State's most secure codes had been compromised. An hour later, State waived Kent's diplomatic immunity by dismissing him as of five hours earlier. The documents in his possession included the correspondence between Churchill and Roosevelt, the mere existence of which would have been politically damaging in 1940 despite the fact that the messages do not demonstrate any violation of American neutrality. Moreover, Kent was an admitted friend and suspected co-conspirator of fascist sympathizer and spy Anna Wolkoff.[29]

If Welles's presentation on Saturday was not enough to convince Roosevelt that further precaution must be taken against a fifth column of alien enemies, Churchill's pleading messages and their interception by a suspected spy may have sealed the deal. With no further discussion with anyone in his administration, Roosevelt decided to transfer the immigration service from Labor to Justice.

But the logistics of the matter remained to be ironed out. The previous week, Roosevelt had received a message that the reorganization committee chair, Louis Brownlow, would be in town from Monday through Wednesday,

May 20 to 22. Roosevelt was accommodating, sending a message through his secretary that Brownlow should see him "when convenient."[30]

Brownlow arrived at the White House for a noon meeting with Roosevelt on Tuesday, May 21. The subject of the meeting was national defense coordination and organization; the plan included the implementation of an advisory commission and the appointment of a director of the Office of Emergency Management within the new Executive Office of the President.[31] The sequence of events of that afternoon suggests that the transfer of INS from Labor to Justice may also have been part of the conversation. Sometime that morning or early afternoon, the Department of Justice received a phone call from the White House requesting that Attorney General Jackson come to lunch with the president at 1 PM. Though this was hardly the type of message that would be ignored in any event, the caller was urgent; the phone message from Jackson's secretary said that "[t]hey would like an immediate response."[32]

May is a beautiful month in Washington. As Jackson went to the White House, it was seventy-six degrees, with only moderate humidity for the capital. There was a light breeze from the northeast. The six-block trip up Pennsylvania Avenue from the building that had been home to the Justice Department since 1935 would have been a pleasant one that day.

Jackson arrived at the White House and the two men sat down to eat. As soon as lunch had been served, the president got to the point. He handed Jackson a document that proposed the immediate transfer of INS from the Department of Labor to the Department of Justice. Then "[h]e turned to his soup and left the move to me," Jackson said.

After taking time to read the document, Jackson once again tried to dissuade Roosevelt from making the transfer. First, he found himself in an unenviable position, "one which no man could long perform acceptably in a period of public excitement." Or no woman, perhaps—Jackson could not have envied Perkins's ordeal of impeachment threats and public calumny over the Bridges case. Jackson made the sobering observation to Roosevelt that "there was somewhat the same tendency in America to make goats of all aliens that in Germany had made goats of all Jews."

Jackson suggested an alternative: Instead of transferring INS to Justice, the president should create a special wartime agency to deal with alien control, sabotage, espionage, and subversive activities. Those were more properly defense activities than the ordinary administration of justice, Jackson told Roosevelt, and their methods should be preventive, not remedial. "He was not, however, persuaded," Jackson recalled later that day. Roosevelt said that immigration needed to be in Justice, "as it was the only place that was prepared adequately to handle it."

That was the end of the matter. Roosevelt had rejected the advice of the government's top lawyer. Jackson accepted his president's decision and began making arrangements for Solicitor General Francis Biddle to handle the transition.[33]

After the lunch, Brownlow phoned for news, saying the president would have a message for him at 2 PM.[34] At 3:30, the president called the budget director, Harold D. Smith, whose office had developed and drafted all four previous reorganization plans. This time, Smith and his staff were not consulted as to substance. Roosevelt told Smith he thought it wise to transfer INS from Labor to Justice and asked if Smith and his staff could have a plan drafted for submission to Congress by noon the next day. Smith said they could. "In the conversation the President mentioned fifth column activities," Smith noted in his diary. The president promised to send Smith a sketch for the message to Congress and Smith and his staff quickly got to work.[35] After consulting with staff at Justice and Labor, Smith's team completed the draft the next morning and Smith presented it to Roosevelt at 11 AM. Apart from a jocular debate about split infinitives, Roosevelt approved the draft in full.[36]

REORGANIZATION PLAN NO. V

Roosevelt would waste no time announcing his decision publicly. At 4 PM Tuesday afternoon, just after calling Smith, Roosevelt held a press conference at the White House, and the questions went straight to the defense of the capital, the country, and the hemisphere. Roosevelt rebuffed questions about possible "coalition control in the cabinet," but confirmed that additional management would be added to deal with demands posed by the war and that some of the new hires would be Republicans.

In the discussion of wartime restructuring, one reporter asked whether Roosevelt planned to implement any further reorganization plans.

"No, there is only one thing coming up," Roosevelt began, then stopped. "Oh, I suppose it is all right to mention it now, though you should all wait until the thing actually goes to Congress." The following day, he announced, he would submit Reorganization Plan No. V for congressional approval.

"I held off last winter because there were very definitely two sides to the case," Roosevelt said. The new plan, only one page, would transfer INS from Labor to Justice. "Today the situation has changed, and it is necessary for us, for obvious national defense reasons, to make that change at this time." He said he hoped Congress would approve it before it recessed for the summer.

"Mr. President, does that fit in with the general measure to prevent espionage and sabotage?" one reporter asked.

"Yes."

"Are you contemplating any other measures of a similar nature?"

"No comments on that at the present time."[37]

It was late when the phone rang in the small study next to Secretary Perkins's bedroom. It was Roosevelt; he had a direct line so that he could reach her at all hours.

"Frances, I've got something to tell you," he said. "Maybe you won't like it." He told her he had decided to take the immigration service out of the Department of Labor. Far from being displeased, Perkins was relieved. She reminded the president that she had been recommending for years that he make a change.

"Where are you going to put it?" she asked.

"Well, on account of the war situation and the problems with saboteurs and spies, I'm going to put it in the Department of Justice," Roosevelt told her.

"Well, under ordinary circumstances, I think that's a bad place for it," she said. Immigration should be one of the humanitarian functions of the government, she told Roosevelt, assisting with the assimilation and adjustment of new immigrants and conducting deportations, where necessary, with justice and mercy. Still, she conceded, DOJ made sense under the circumstances. She had heard reports of people slipping into the country outside the usual ports of entry, avoiding detection by immigration officials.

Roosevelt told her that Biddle had discovered such cases and they knew some of the locations of those illegal entries. "So that's what I've got to do," he told her.

"That's all right with me," Perkins said. "You do it with my blessing."[38]

Perkins, describing the phone call from Roosevelt years later, did not seem to be aware of the Welles memo or the State Department's push on Roosevelt to make the move. She believed it had been Biddle who convinced Roosevelt. Yet the records do not support the notion that Biddle was a major player in the decision. No documents in the president's or Biddle's files link Biddle to the transfer, and Biddle himself, in his memoirs, disclaimed any role. "I cannot now remember the immediate cause of the transfer," he wrote. "[T]here was something about the Secretary's failing to furnish the President with information that he wanted urgently, the number of deportable aliens in the country—something of the sort. But that was probably no more than the spark to action."[39] Biddle's involvement seems to have been primarily after the fact: three weeks after approving the transfer of INS, Congress passed the Alien Registration Act of 1940, which required all noncitizens to register with the government at post offices across the country.[40] Because the transfer of INS and the registration of aliens were to happen during the summer when the Supreme Court was in recess and the Solicitor General would be less occupied, Biddle was placed in charge of implementing the move. His usual job, briefing and arguing cases before the Supreme Court, did not give much occasion to interact with law enforcement or intelligence officers who might have provided the kind of information that Roosevelt purported to have received from him. Even if Biddle had discovered information that influenced Roosevelt, however, it is clear that Welles, not Biddle, was the primary author of the transfer—a fact Roosevelt did not mention to Perkins.

Roosevelt was no doubt careful to put distance between the House's attempt to impeach Perkins the year before and his decision to transfer INS. Although her political weakness was inescapably relevant to Roosevelt's dilemma, his affection for Perkins and his desire to keep her in the Department of Labor to preserve the still-fragile innovations of the New Deal would likely have motivated him to present the decision as simply a matter of security, no more and no less.

Around noon on Wednesday, May 22, Smith sent Reorganization Plan No. V to Congress. The "Message of the President" that accompanied the plan varied significantly from the draft, dated May 20, which was located in the president's files with the Welles memorandum. The draft says that the transfer, which had been omitted from previous reorganization plans "because of the closeness of the argument," was now necessary because "the nation is confronted with matters relating to aliens in our midst." Because of the emergency, the draft stated, national safety required "measures and controls over aliens, which are not demanded in normal days." After a brief assurance that the measure was not intended to "tak[e] away any civil liberties or . . . affect[] the normal, human and legal rights of aliens," the draft stated, "I feel, however, that at this time it is best to make this transfer." Most significantly, the draft emphasized that the move was intended to be temporary: "After these days of emergency have passed, the Congress can and should, of course, consider whether the Bureau of Immigration and Naturalization should remain in the Department of Justice or be returned to the jurisdiction of the Department of Labor."[41]

The message Roosevelt actually sent was crafted by a more politically skillful hand. The substance of the president's intent is conveyed in two brief, decisive paragraphs. It begins:

When Reorganization Plan No. IV was submitted to Congress, I did not contemplate the transmittal of any additional plans during the current session. However, the startling sequence of international events which has occurred since then has necessitated a review of the measures required for the Nation's safety. This has revealed a pressing need for the transfer of the immigration and naturalization functions from the Department of Labor to the Department of Justice. I had considered such an interdepartmental transfer for some time but did not include it in the previous reorganization plans since much can be said for the retention of these functions in the Department of Labor during normal times. I am convinced, however, that under existing conditions the immigration and naturalization activities can best contribute to the national well-being only if they are closely integrated with the activities of the Department of Justice.[42]

After making the declarations required by the Reorganization Act of 1939, the president's message assured that, while the transfer "is designed to afford more effective control over aliens, this proposal does not reflect any intention to deprive them of their civil liberties or otherwise to impair their legal status. This reorganization will enable the Government to deal quickly with those aliens who conduct themselves in a manner that conflicts with the public interest." No monetary savings were anticipated. Because of the upcoming recess, Congress was asked to act quickly rather than waiting for the plan to take effect after sixty days without a resolution of disapproval, as provided by the Reorganization Act. No suggestion was made that Congress revisit the move after the war.

In his Fireside Chat four days later, Roosevelt extended the warning to all listeners. "Today's threat to our national security is not a matter of military weapons alone," Roosevelt said. "We know of other methods, new methods of attack. The Trojan Horse. The Fifth Column that betrays a nation unprepared for treachery. Spies, saboteurs and traitors are actors in this new strategy. With all of these we must and will deal vigorously."[43] Welles's mission to sound the alarm about the "fifth column" had been accomplished.

8 Alien Enemies

Transfer of the immigration courts to the Department of Justice was one element in a complex of policies adopted during the war to control "alien enemies." Those policies would eventually include the development of an intelligence apparatus that would become the CIA; the detention and internment of certain German and Italian nationals suspected of having sympathies with Germany or Italy; and, most infamously, the internment of all Japanese nationals and Japanese-Americans in the western states for much of the war. The term "alien enemies" comes from the notorious Alien and Sedition Acts passed by John Adams's Federalist government on the verge of war with France in 1798. The Alien Enemies Act provided that, if war were declared, any male of age fourteen or older who is a native, citizen, denizen, or subject of a hostile nation or government "shall be liable to be apprehended, restrained, secured and removed, as alien enemies." The Act gives broad powers to the president to issue proclamations regarding the treatment of alien enemies by the United States.[1] A version of the statute remains in effect today.[2]

Like most falls from grace, the slide into the infamous internment policy was a gradual one. Although Roosevelt resisted congressional calls to transfer the immigration services to DOJ in 1939 and early 1940, the

reality was that he led a government with no intelligence apparatus sufficient to defend against invasion, leaving him grasping for ways to protect
against sabotage. Roosevelt's order in June 1939 creating an interdepartmental coalition to handle domestic intelligence still left overseas counterintelligence operations up in the air. At first, foreign intelligence
was divided between the FBI (for the Western Hemisphere); the Navy (for
the Pacific region); and the Army (for Europe, Africa, and the Panama
Canal Zone). By late July 1941, however, Roosevelt was frustrated with
the lack of cooperation between the agencies. As an end run around the
disputes, Roosevelt created the Office of the Coordinator of Information
in the White House, appointing William J. Donovan to the post. The website of the CIA in 2020 attributed the creation of the new office to
Roosevelt's "fears of fascist and Communist 'Fifth Columns' in America."[3]
A year later, Roosevelt created the Office of Strategic Services, which, after
the end of the war, became the Strategic Services Unit in the War
Department.[4] To free the intelligence operations from resistance from the
Department of State and the armed services, SSU and its Central
Intelligence Group would be granted independent agency status and
named the Central Intelligence Agency in the National Security Act of
1947.[5]

Lacking this intelligence architecture as war accelerated in Europe in
1940, however, Secretary of War Henry L. Stimson had grown impatient.
By September 16, 1940, he directed the Army to hire John J. McCloy, the
lawyer-turned-intelligence-analyst from the Black Tom case, whom
Stimson had met while both men's families vacationed at the Ausable
Club in the Adirondacks.[6] "I have been trying to get the State Department
and the Department of Justice to connect with McCloy ever since I have
been here but they have made no progress on it, so I finally decided to take
him on in the War Department until they begin to realize how much he
knows," Stimson wrote in his diary.[7] McCloy originally came on as an
unpaid consultant while still a partner at Cravath, but after recognizing a
potential conflict of interest due to his representation of clients against the
federal government, he resigned the consultancy just over a month later.[8]
Rather than lose his valued new intelligence expert, Stimson managed to
have McCloy hired as special assistant to the secretary of war in December
1940 and McCloy resigned from his law firm.[9]

From the beginning, McCloy emphasized to Stimson that the priority should be to coordinate the intelligence gathering and analysis then being done by the FBI, the Army, and the Navy. "Unfortunately, they are in three different cabinet departments—always a fertile field for lack of cooperation," McCloy wrote.[10] Soon, McCloy became something of a Swiss Army knife to Stimson, working on matters ranging from lobbying for lend-lease legislation to outlining a new intelligence department.[11] A Department of War profile on McCloy in 1944 said (with McCloy's own edits), "[p]erhaps the logical title for McCloy would be 'trouble-shooter,' for frequently when there is a troublesome problem at the War Department he will be asked by the Secretary to take it on."[12]

From his experience on the Black Tom case, McCloy had developed a philosophy on counterintelligence and sabotage, one that treated the Constitution and civil liberties as largely dispensable in the face of executive powers during wartime. Although widely liked and respected, he became associated with a growing—and, to some, troubling—trend toward this approach in the administration. In October 1942, Assistant Attorney General James Rowe wrote to Attorney General Francis Biddle that the attitudes in the Department of War "indicate a disregard of the military mind for intellectual protest. I am perfectly aware that Jack McCloy is an intelligent, reasonable human being. I am even more aware of the terrific pressures exerted against him by the brass hats . . . but I do believe in adapting our techniques to defend ourselves." In the summer of 1942, Secretary of the Interior Harold Ickes put the matter much more bluntly. "I like McCloy a lot and I have seen him more than any of the other men in the Army but I have been told that he is more or less inclined to be a Fascist and this would not surprise me," Ickes wrote in his diary, adding, "I know of my own knowledge that he is strong and able."[13]

Paradoxically, fifth column fears have been shown to have contributed to the U.S. fleet's vulnerability to the Japanese air attack at Pearl Harbor. On February 7, 1941, Army Chief of Staff General George Marshall warned the new Commander of the Army Hawaiian Department, Lieutenant General Walter Short, that "the risk of sabotage and the risk involved in a surprise raid by Air and by submarine constitute the real perils of the situation." General Short, however, focused primarily on the first of these two perils, the risk of sabotage. Further orders to counter sabotage compounded

General Short's anxiety, and he ultimately developed a plan, called Alert No. 1, in which aircraft would be bunched together without fuel or ammunition to protect against sabotage. The plan adopted by Short also included Condition Easy 5, which required four hours' notice to prepare planes for combat. On November 27, 1941, the War Department sent a vaguely worded warning of Japanese air attack to General Short—which General Short misinterpreted as a warning against sabotage. Adopting Alert No. 1 and Condition Easy 5, General Short set up the fleet as a consolidated target for the Japanese attack and drastically delayed the Army's ability to mobilize in pursuit of the attacking Japanese planes.[14]

The day after the attack on Pearl Harbor, President Roosevelt issued Presidential Proclamation No. 2525 under the Alien Enemies Act, which declared all "natives, citizens, denizens, or subjects" of Japan over age fourteen to be alien enemies of the United States. The Proclamation gave the attorney general and the secretary of war the authority of "summary apprehension" of alien enemies "deemed dangers to the public peace or safety of the United States." The Proclamation also gave the attorney general and the secretary of war the authority to exclude alien enemies from a designated area whenever one of those authorities "deems it to be necessary, for the public safety and protection."[15] The following day, the president extended the order to Germans and Italians through Presidential Proclamation No. 2526 and 2527. On January 14, 1942, Presidential Proclamation No. 2537 required all alien enemies to register with the Department of Justice.[16] In a deep twist of irony, Presidential Proclamation 2524 on November 21, 1941, had established "Bill of Rights Day."[17]

Through the presidential proclamations, the legal stage was set for internment. Proclamation No. 2525 gave authority over "alien enemy" control primarily to the attorney general, but some key staffers in the Department of Justice fought against the idea of internment. Francis Biddle, recently promoted to attorney general upon Jackson's appointment to the Supreme Court, was reluctant but resigned to agree to internment if the Army was convinced that it was a military necessity. This left the Department of War in the driver's seat. Secretary Stimson assigned his troubleshooter, McCloy, to evaluate the intelligence and recommend a position. After a period of consultation with Army personnel, McCloy decided to recommend a wholesale internment of Japanese and Japanese-

Americans to President Roosevelt, over the dissent of the Army general headquarters and the FBI.[18]

McCloy did not make the decision lightly. On February 17, he made a note in his journal—usually just a bare record of meeting times, subjects, and attendees—notating a phone call with Army personnel in charge of the military evaluation. McCloy mentioned the Under Secretary of War's "vehemence that aliens should be *really* moved out with no half-way measures used on them," a position that Under Secretary Robert J. Patterson, Jr. had pressed upon McCloy the day before. But McCloy hesitated. "Danger, too, of the unwisdom of yielding to local pressures which demand drastic and unintelligent action," McCloy acknowledged in his notes. "No easy problem, and, I'm afraid, no easy solution,—or one which will not be criticized whatever way we move. It is clear, however, that we must act with full responsibility and dispatch." Uncharacteristically, McCloy added his initials to this notation.[19]

On February 19, 1942, the president issued Executive Order 9066, permitting certain military commanders to declare military zones from which any persons could be excluded.[20] On March 21, 1942, Congress enacted a law making it a misdemeanor for any person to remain in a military zone contrary to the orders of the military commander.[21] In subsequent weeks, the military commander of the West Coast region declared all of California, Washington, Oregon, Idaho, Montana, Nevada, Utah, and parts of Arizona to be military zones, excluded all persons of Japanese ancestry from those zones, and required them to report to "assembly centers" where they were detained for the remainder of the war.

When the Supreme Court upheld the detention of California native Fred Toyosaburo Korematsu in December 1944, it did so over three blistering dissents—two of them authored by justices who, as attorneys general, had participated in warning Roosevelt not to transfer the immigration services to DOJ. Justice Frank Murphy, the attorney general in November 1939 who ordered his staff to analyze the transfer, pierced through the rationalizations of military necessity and baldly called the Court's decision a "legalization of racism." Citing openly racist testimony of the commanding general ("'It makes no difference whether he is an American citizen, he is still a Japanese'") and the lack of any arrests of Japanese or Japanese-Americans for espionage or sabotage before their mass detention, Justice Murphy found no "reasonable relation between the group characteristics of Japanese Americans and the dangers of invasion, sabotage and espionage." Instead, he found the policy to be based on "misinformation, half-truths and insinuations that for years have been directed against Japanese Americans by people with racial and economic prejudices."[22]

Justice Jackson, who had warned Roosevelt less than five years earlier of the dangerous tendency in the United States to "make goats of all aliens," focused on the different roles of the courts and the military in a democracy. While he did not feel qualified or obliged to judge the military necessity of the exclusion order, he objected to the use of the courts "to execute a military expedient that has no place in law under the Constitution." Justice Jackson's reasoning includes one of the famous passages of constitutional history:

> Much is said of the danger to liberty from the Army program for deporting and detaining these citizens of Japanese extraction. But a judicial construction of the due process clause that will sustain this order is a far more subtle blow to liberty than the promulgation of the order itself. A military order, however unconstitutional, is not apt to last longer than the military necessity. Even during that period a succeeding commander may revoke it all. But once a judicial opinion rationalizes such an order to show that it conforms to the Constitution, or rather rationalizes the Constitution to show that the Constitution sanctions such an order, the Court for all time has validated the principle of racial discrimination in criminal procedure and of transplanting American citizens. The principle then lies about like a loaded weapon ready for the hand of any authority that can bring forward a plausible claim of an urgent need. Every repetition imbeds that principle more deeply in our law and thinking and expands it to new purposes.[23]

Korematsu v. United States was not overruled or repudiated by the Supreme Court until the 2018 case of *Trump v. Hawaii*, which upheld President Trump's travel ban. Justice Sotomayor, in a dissent joined by Justice Ginsberg, quoted from Justice Jackson's dissent in *Korematsu*, arguing that the executive order excluding nationals of certain countries was an example of the expansion of the principle of legalized racism for national security expedience permitted in *Korematsu*.[24] Rejecting Justice Sotomayor's analogy, the majority nevertheless took "the opportunity to make express what is already obvious: *Korematsu* was gravely wrong the day it was decided, has been overruled in the court of history, and—to be clear—'has no place in law under the Constitution.'"[25]

President Roosevelt's internment of Japanese Americans during World War II was the subject of a report issued by a congressional commission in the winter of 1982 and spring of 1983.[26] The commission censured the conduct of the U.S. government during the war and recommended reparations to survivors. In 1988 and 1992, Congress passed statutes awarding $20,000 to each surviving detainee, for a total of $1.2 billion.[27]

As the commission's report was making headlines, McCloy stewed in his office at One Chase Manhattan Plaza. In 1983, McCloy was eighty-seven years old and mostly retired from public life. As the commission's findings and recommendations rolled out, McCloy struck up a sympathetic correspondence with Frank A. Schuler, Jr., a diplomat to Japan for the State Department prior to and after World War II. Schuler had been marginalized at State during the war for stating three months before the bombing of Pearl Harbor that Japan planned to attack the United States—a view that conflicted with the opinion of U.S. ambassador Joseph C. Grew.[28] McCloy and Schuler bonded over their shared anger, their shared indignation—and perhaps their shared mortification. On April 4, McCloy sent Schuler a memorandum that he had dictated, not for any particular purpose but just "to get something off my chest." McCloy's memo was entitled "REGRETS." Its subtitle was "Japanese/American Relocation." McCloy began,

> In the clear light of perfect hindsight and with the passage of some 40 years, it can now be said that it is regrettable that those who had the responsibility for the security of the country in a critical period of its history, including the President of the U.S., Franklin Roosevelt, should have decided after careful consideration and as a direct result of the Japanese surprise attack on Pearl Harbor that it was imperative for them to take the steps they did to guard against the ominous consequences of that attack.

In the next paragraph, McCloy again calls the U.S. actions "regrettable," but also, in the same breath, "imperative" and the "direct consequence" of the attack on Pearl Harbor. The rest of the eight-page memo defends the removal operation and the conditions in the internment camps, praises the character of President Roosevelt and Secretary Stimson against allegations of racism, and condemns the movement for apology by the U.S. government.[29] An op-ed by McCloy, similar in substance but less emotional in tone, was published in the *New York Times* the following Sunday.[30]

McCloy's contemporaneous notes from February 1942 show that he knew that his actions would one day be judged. That day came in the winter of 1982 and 1983, as a new generation that scarcely remembered the war came to reckon with one of its most ignoble legacies. Though he had anticipated that day for four decades, McCloy's memorandum to Schuler shows that he was not fully prepared for it. He remained rooted in the thoughts, impressions, experiences, uncertainties, and—undoubtedly—fears that he and most others in the government carried on their strong shoulders in early 1942. McCloy's legal experience in prosecuting Germany's bombing of American munitions plants in 1916 and 1917 would have underscored in his mind the risk of sabotage on U.S. soil. Several years before the creation of the CIA and with three federal intelligence agencies with different mandates, McCloy could only rely on an intelligence apparatus that today would be considered rudimentary.

No matter how McCloy may have sought to justify his decision in 1942, however, his reaction in 1983 was not inevitable. McCloy's misgivings, inchoate as they were, are evident in the title he gave to the memo he dictated and sent to Schuler. McCloy could have expressed his regrets without rushing to qualify them. He could have done so without disavowing his own and the rest of the Roosevelt administration's earnest—and human and fallible—efforts to protect the country. He could have said I'm sorry that you suffered. He could have said that he did his best, and that we must do better.

9 Reckoning

The astonishingly swift defeat of Norway, France, and the Low Countries led many in Europe and the Americas to assume that Germany must have been aided by vast numbers of undercover agents attacking from within, undetected—a fifth column. The reality was defeat of a far more ordinary and ignominious nature.

Contrary to American newspaper accounts at the time, the fifth column played little role in the invasion of Norway. In his postwar study of the Nazi fifth column threat, Dutch historian Louis De Jong reported that, in Norway, "Hitler and the generals wished to keep their plans completely secret, and this precluded making full use of any military fifth column." Vidkum Quisling, the leader of the Norwegian national socialist movement who offered to organize internal assistance for the Nazis, was distrusted by the Nazis and written off by one official as "of no importance, held to be a dreamer of phantasy." A plan to sabotage Norwegian railways and mines by fifth column agents was discussed, but the explosives designated for the project still sat in the German embassy in Stockholm as of the invasion on April 9. De Jong concluded that "the success of the German invasion, taking into account the too unsuspecting attitude of the

Norwegians, must undoubtedly be mainly ascribed to the purely military aspect of the German operations."[1]

Historians have attributed the rapid fall of France and the Low Countries to conventional military and political failures of the French and supporting British forces: aging leadership, outdated strategic thinking, slow mobilization, fragmented command structures, and lack of modern technology.[2] The notion of German agents sneaking around the French hinterlands giving false orders is without support. De Jong concluded that "[i]n the French military literature on the struggle of 1940 there is not one single truly convincing Fifth Column case of this nature described." The only fifth column activity noted in the diary of one French general was that, on his unit's retreat from the Belgian frontier into France, he and his troops were branded as fifth columnists by a hysterical person who was promptly placed into custody.[3]

In Holland, the Germans did send in some troops near the border disguised as Dutch soldiers, but the uniforms were so poor (with cardboard helmets, no less) that few were fooled. De Jong did not find a single German military document referring to a fifth column in Holland. Moreover, there was not a single documented case of the Germans "dress[ing] their forces in the western part of the country in Dutch, British, Belgian or French uniforms. Nor is there any case on record in which their parachutists, airborne troops or accomplices operated in the disguise of farmers, policemen, postmen, conductors, delivery boys, priests, nuns, maid-servants or nurses." Even the use of parachute troops was limited to a few locations.[4]

In the United States, the fifth column threat was almost entirely illusory. Hitler, nervous about provoking war with the United States, for which he was unprepared, ordered in April 1940 that no sabotage plans be pursued in the United States. In June, the order was given to recall to Germany the "only agent deserving consideration." While a few efforts at fifth column sabotage were considered after the onset of war between the United States and Germany in 1941, the only one ever undertaken was the disastrous (for Germany) Operation Pastorius in the summer of 1942.[5] This plot to blow up railways, disrupt New York's water supply, and cause general confusion was undermined from the start by a longtime New York waiter named George Dasch, who turned the entire group in to the FBI upon arrival and was one of only two of the would-be saboteurs to escape the death penalty.[6]

But Goebbels's clever insinuation of a fifth column threat worked perfectly. Even Roosevelt was not immune to the fear. Within two weeks of the German invasion of France and the Low Countries, he reversed a decision he had rejected for a year, placing the immigration courts under the control of the nation's top law enforcement officer. They have remained there ever since.

10 Un Día de Fuego

On September 5, 2001, President George W. Bush and his wife Laura—
well rested after a month-long working vacation at their Texas ranch—
hosted the first state dinner of Bush's presidency.[1] The guests of honor
were Vicente Fox, the swashbuckling president of Mexico and a friend of
President Bush since his days as governor of Texas, and Fox's wife, Marta
Sahagún de Fox. The evening was spicy and colorful, literally and meta-
phorically. Mrs. Bush wore a "hotly hued gown" by fashion designer Scaasi,
the *Washington Post* style section reported, with a bodice of red lace over
hot pink silk and a red taffeta skirt—a look Mrs. Bush said reminded her
of the colors of Mexico. The menu "combined the spicy flavors of the
Southwest with sophisticated American cuisine," including Maryland crab
and chorizo pozole, bison crusted in pumpkin seeds, and a dessert of
mango and coconut ice cream with fresh peaches and raspberries, red chili
pepper sauce, and a tequila sabayon. President Fox said that he and his
friend "Jorge" shared not only a penchant for wearing western boots (as
both did that evening) and relaxing at their ranches, but also a common
desire "to see things happen." President Bush said that it was "like a family
gathering" and that "the United States has no more important relationship in the world than our relationship with Mexico." After dinner, the two

couples retired to the Truman Balcony to watch a nearly twenty-minute fireworks show of "pyrotechnic virtuosity" (albeit one that annoyed some White House neighbors who were awakened on a school night).[2]

That spectacular evening must have seemed light years away when Bush stepped off the helicopter onto Ground Zero nine days later. Although shocked by the view from the air, he was still unprepared for what he saw on the ground. "We had just started the drive to the disaster site when something on the side of the road caught my eye," the president would later recall in his memoirs. "It appeared to be a lumbering gray mass. I took a second look. It was a group of first responders covered head to toe in ash." Bush asked the driver to stop. He got out and shook hands with the men, thanked them for all they had done. "Several had tears running down their faces, cutting a path through the soot like rivulets through a desert." Approaching the disaster site was like "entering a nightmare," Bush recalled. "There was little light. Smoke hung in the air and mixed with suspended particles of debris, creating an eerie gray curtain."

After a few minutes of handshakes and condolences, Bush began to sense the rage of those undertaking the harrowing task. One first responder cut off the president's attempts to comfort him. "George, find the bastards who did this and kill them." The president took no offense at being called by his first name. "Do not let me down!" one man yelled. Another shouted in the president's face, "Whatever it takes!" Recalling the moment years later, Bush would say that "[t]he bloodlust was palpable and understandable." Bush climbed on top of a mound of rubble that he would later learn was a crumpled fire truck. A staffer handed him a bullhorn. Trying at first to console, to offer prayer, he was cut off. They couldn't hear him. "I can hear you!" he shouted back. They cheered. He changed course.

"I can hear you. The rest of the world hears you. And the people who knocked these buildings down will hear all of us soon!" The crowd exploded. Chants of "USA! USA!" filled the air with something besides dust, debris, and despair. "It was a release of energy I had never felt before," Bush would recall. He had chosen his path.[3]

George W. Bush was raised in Texas and served as governor of that state beginning in 1995—the year after NAFTA destabilized Mexican labor markets and contributed to a tide of Mexican immigration, much of it unauthorized, across the border into the United States. For Bush, as for many Texans, immigration from Mexico was part of the fabric of life. At age thirteen in 1959, he had opened the door of the Bush family home to find a young woman named Paula Rendón, alone in the rain and looking tired and scared. Rendón, a Mexican immigrant, "became like a second mother to my younger brothers and sister and me," Bush recalled. She took care not only of the Bush children but of her own family, whom she eventually moved from Mexico to Houston. Bush said that Rendón came on a permanent work visa, but he knew that many others came through temporary programs or entered unlawfully. "As governor and president, I had Paula in mind when I spoke about immigration reform," he would later say.[4]

Bush's interest in immigration reform was refined during his years as governor of Texas and shaped by his friendship with President Fox. At their first meeting, in the Texas governor's office, Bush gave Fox a baseball. The two had an opportunity to talk one on one at a later meeting at the University of Texas. In 2000, Bush campaigned for president with proposals to "make America more welcoming to new immigrants," including plans to expand a temporary guest worker program and to relax visa policies for spouses and children of permanent residents.

Shortly after Bush's election as president, Bush and Fox met for the third time at Fox's ranch in San Cristóbal in February 2001. The two began to collaborate closely. "Every day, communication; every day, discussing; every day, coming with new ideas; every day, thinking about the families and the people of our countries," Fox said.[5] The Bush administration focused little on the status of the immigration courts; administratively, Bush's goals focused on separating the processing of visa and citizenship applications from the enforcement of the immigration laws, both functions then operated by INS.[6] But the president's proposed reforms would have offered an alternative to illegal entry and removal proceedings in thousands of cases, and his friendship with Fox suggested that Bush might persist until he had persuaded a reluctant Congress to pass reform legislation.

9/11 changed all that. Describing his efforts on immigration reform in his memoirs, Bush first recalled his childhood in Texas, his ideas for reform, and his partnership with President Fox. "Then 9/11 hit, and my most serious concern was that terrorists would slip into our country undetected," Bush said. "I put the idea of a temporary work program on hold and concentrated on border security." When his focus shifted back to immigration reform in 2006, it was too late. "[T]he House, which had been focused on border security alone, couldn't get a comprehensive bill done before the midterm elections in November 2006," Bush wrote. Democrats took control of both bodies in 2007 and the politics of immigration reform were upended.[7]

"FOREIGNERS WHO HAD INFILTRATED THE UNITED STATES"

Throughout the summer of 2001, CIA director George Tenet later told the 9/11 Commission, "the system was blinking red" with the threat of terrorist attacks. But the U.S. intelligence and law enforcement communities were hampered by tunnel vision, imagining threats as either foreign or domestic—not both. As the 9/11 Commission would conclude,

> [t]he September 11 attacks fell into the void between the foreign and domestic threats. The foreign intelligence agencies were watching overseas, alert to foreign threats to U.S. interests there. The domestic agencies were waiting for evidence of a domestic threat from sleeper cells within the United States. No one was looking for a foreign threat to domestic targets. The threat that was coming was not from sleeper cells. It was foreign—but from foreigners who had infiltrated the United States.[8]

Exploiting this void, the 9/11 terrorists took advantage of administrative inefficiencies and compromise immigration policies. For example, regulations at the time allowed individuals who entered on standard six-month tourist visas to file applications for student visas from within the country. Because INS often took several months to process the student visa applications, individuals frequently began their programs of study while their student visa applications were still pending. Aware of the backlogs, officials and schools looked the other way during such gaps. Two of the 9/11 terrorists, Mohammed Atta and Marwan Al-Shehhi, followed this path to begin flight training months before their flight school visa applications were reviewed.[9]

In truth, the void ran deeper than delays in student visa processing. Even if the terrorists had been required to receive approval for student visas before they began training (as they would be today),[10] there was no evidence that the officers reviewing those applications would have had any information about suspected terrorist activities—just as the State Department consular officers lacked any such information about the terrorists when they applied for the visas they used to enter the country. In the investigation following the 9/11 attacks, Assistant Secretary of State Mary Ryan raised the ire of Senator Diane Feinstein and other lawmakers by insisting that State was not at fault because it had been excluded from intelligence information-sharing by the FBI and CIA.[11] Though Secretary of State Colin Powell would ask for Ryan's resignation in 2002, Ryan's successor, Maura Harty, said that Ryan "put her finger right on it as a much broader and complex event than the visa iteration."[12]

In the post-9/11 world, Americans were aware that "foreigners . . . had infiltrated the United States," and with devastating results. The attacks raised the specter of the "fifth column": In a multiethnic United States in an era of global travel, nearly anyone might come and go unremarked. It seemed that the scenario Roosevelt had feared sixty years earlier had come to pass—saboteurs who passed as locals being trained abroad by enemies of the United States and then returning to the country to attack from within. The events of 9/11, and the fears it engendered, would radically change the course of immigration policy in the twenty-first century.

TINKERING WITH REFORM IN THE COLD WAR ERA

Before 9/11, immigration reform had been headed in a different direction. In the Immigration Act of 1990, Congress created the bipartisan U.S. Commission on Legal Immigration Reform.[13] A first report in 1994 focused on illegal migration and how to control it. In September 1997, the Commission issued its second report, which recommended substantive immigration law reform and also addressed what it viewed as serious structural problems with the administration of the immigration laws. "While the Executive Branch has taken significant steps to address many of the weaknesses in current operations," the Commission stated, "the organization of the immigration system undermines reform efforts."[14]

Though the executive branch had, as the Commission stated, implemented some reforms to immigration administration after 1940, those limited reforms did not occur without prodding and were often reversed as quickly as they were made. For example, INS received a reform mandate in 1950 when the Supreme Court decided that deportation proceedings had to be conducted in accordance with the APA, passed in 1946. The majority opinion in *Wong Yang Sung v. McGrath* was written by Justice Jackson, a decade after he had warned Roosevelt not to transfer INS to Justice. As the Court noted, both the legislative history of the APA and a study of immigration law administration ordered by the Secretary of Labor in early 1940 had condemned the commingling of investigative, prosecutorial, and adjudicative functions then characteristic of deportation proceedings. This contravened the APA, Justice Jackson wrote:

> When the Constitution requires a hearing, it requires a fair one, one before a tribunal which meets at least currently prevailing standards of impartiality. A deportation hearing involves issues basic to human liberty and happiness and, in the present upheavals in lands to which aliens may be returned, perhaps to life itself. It might be difficult to justify as measuring up to constitutional standards of impartiality a hearing tribunal for deportation proceedings the like of which has been condemned by Congress as unfair even where less vital matters of property rights are at stake.[15]

INS was entirely unprepared for this new requirement to comply with the APA. After appointing temporary hearing examiners to conform to the Court's ruling in the short term, INS appealed to Congress for an exemption. Congress obliged in an appropriations rider seven months later.[16] The quick fix afforded by the appropriations rider was embedded by Congress two years later in the INA. That law included some modest reforms of immigration court procedures, such as the appointment of special inquiry officers for the first time in deportation as well as exclusion proceedings. In the words of an immigration officer at the time, however, the INA "eschewed the opportunity to initiate fundamental reforms" to the old INS procedures.[17]

The new system faced a Supreme Court challenge as well, but this time fared better. In May 1955, the Supreme Court decided a challenge to the administrative procedures of the INA in a case called *Marcello v. Bonds*.[18] Marcello challenged his deportation on the grounds that the new procedures of the INA still permitted the adjudicator to serve as prosecutor or investigator. The Supreme Court was unsympathetic, noting that Senator McCarran and Congressman Walter had sponsored both the APA and the INA. "[W]hen in this very particularized adaptation there was a departure from the Administrative Procedure Act—based on novel features in the deportation process—surely it was the intention of the Congress to have the deviation apply and not the general model," the Court stated.[19] The case was decided 5–3, with Justices Black, Frankfurter, and Douglas dissenting; Justice Harlan did not take part in the decision. Justice Jackson had died the previous October.

The Court's decision was definitive but unpopular. The lack of separation of functions continued to be criticized by academics and immigration lawyers; it had also been criticized earlier in 1955 by a special commission on government organization chaired by former president Herbert Hoover, as well as by the American Bar Association.[20] In response to the criticism, INS changed course voluntarily, initiating in 1956 what an immigration officer called "truly radical changes . . . in the INS hearing structure." Under the new INS rules, the INS district director was required to appoint a separate "examining officer" in any contested deportation case. Other reforms included replacing the arrest warrant with an order to show cause, and creating a record file for hearing officers that excluded any prejudicial or inadmissible material that may have been in the general file.[21]

The immigration laws underwent dramatic substantive changes in 1965, when Congress eliminated the national origins quota system and with it the last vestiges of overt racial and ethnic discrimination in the immigration acts.[22] The Act of 1965 made no major procedural changes to removal proceedings, however. The next set of major changes—at least in appearances—occurred in 1973 as INS and DOJ sought to increase the credibility of immigration hearings. An INS regulation that year provided that the term "immigration judge" could be used interchangeably with the term "special inquiry officer" in the statute; subsequent amendments to the statute entirely eliminated the unfortunately inquisitional title.[23] Also in 1973, DOJ authorized immigration judges to wear black judicial robes after a "vigorous campaign" by the judges themselves for greater dignity and credibility.[24] An EOIR policy memorandum from 1994 made the wearing of black robes mandatory anytime an immigration judge conducted a hearing with one or more of the parties present. The policy was intended "[t]o enhance the solemnity of the proceedings" through the uniform use of this "traditional symbol of dignity and authority," according to the Chief Immigration Judge's memorandum.[25]

These semantic and cosmetic changes lent an air of greater formality to removal proceedings but did not alter the underlying authority of the attorney general over the immigration courts. In 1983, DOJ made a long-sought (by immigration judges) step toward immigration court independence by issuing a regulation creating the Executive Office for Immigration Review, tasked with administering the work of immigration judges and the BIA.[26] Although the creation of EOIR placed the day-to-day administration of the immigration courts under the new Office of the Chief Immigration Judge instead of the attorney general, the new agency remained within DOJ and subject to attorney general self-referral authority and DOJ regulatory policy—a chain of command that would be used to discipline Judge Morley for failing to fulfill Attorney General Sessions's expectations in the *Matter of Castro Tum* case in 2017.

These changes were most likely among the steps to which the U.S. Commission on Immigration Reform referred in 1997 when it mentioned improvements the executive branch had made to the function of the immigration courts. Nevertheless, the Commission concluded, the system was due for legislative reform. "Experience teaches that the review function works best when it is well insulated from the initial adjudicatory function and when it is conducted by decisionmakers entrusted with the highest degree of independence," the Commission stated. "Not only is independence in decisionmaking the hallmark of meaningful and effective review, it is also critical to the reality and the perception of fair and impartial review."[27]

In canvassing the structure of review of immigration-related decisions, the Commission noted that enforcement decisions were primarily conducted by EOIR within DOJ, while the review of benefits adjudications was scattered among several agencies, including Justice, Labor, and State. The commission recommended consolidating the review function and considered several options: separate reviewing bodies in Justice (for enforcement decisions) and State (for benefits adjudications); consolidation of all decisions within EOIR; or the creation of an Article I immigration court. Ultimately, the Commission recommended a fourth option: the creation of an independent agency, called the Agency for Immigration Review, still within the executive branch but independent of the Department of Justice or any other existing department. The Commission noted that consolidating appeals within the existing EOIR was "an attractive option," and recognized the relative independence that EOIR had achieved since its creation by regulation in 1983. The Commission concluded, however, that the administrative structure was not sufficient to ensure immigration court independence going forward:

> EOIR remains located in the Department of Justice, ultimately and predominantly a law enforcement agency. Further, existing procedures permit the Attorney General to reverse or modify any decision reached by the BIA. The Commission, as well as other commentators, find this practice troubling because, at a minimum, it compromises the appearance of independent decisionmaking, injects into a quasi-judicial appellate process the possibility of intervention by the highest ranking law enforcement official in the land, and, generally, can undermine the BIA's autonomy and stature.[28]

WARNINGS AND HINDSIGHT

The Commission's report was released on September 30, 1997. Around the same time, another commission had its origins—one focused on the shape of potential threats to U.S. security in the coming century. That fall, Speaker of the House Newt Gingrich approached President Bill Clinton and Secretary of Defense William Cohen about the need for a comprehensive study on the changing national security environment and the government policies and organization that would be needed to respond to it, which he hoped Congress would fund and direct. When that had not occurred by July 1998, the Department of Defense instead chartered the study. The U.S. Commission on National Security/21st Century (better known as the Hart-Rudman Commission after its chairmen, Gary Hart and Warren Rudman) was still very much a Gingrich creation: when the Commission gathered for its first meeting at the Pentagon on October 6, 1998, it was Gingrich who addressed the members about his vision for their work.[29]

Phase I of the Hart-Rudman Commission report, *New World Coming: American Security in the 21st Century*, was delivered to the Secretary of

Defense and released to the press on September 15, 1999. The report was disturbing—and prescient. Part of its "View of the Future," the Commission reported, was that "[w]e should expect conflicts in which adversaries, because of cultural affinities different from our own, will resort to forms and levels of violence shocking to our sensibilities." Increasing U.S. cultural, economic, and political power would result in American influence that is "both embraced and resented abroad," the Commission concluded. "States, terrorists, and other disaffected groups will acquire weapons of mass destruction and mass disruption, and some will use them. Americans will likely die on American soil, possibly in large numbers." The changing nature of communications and allegiances would also strain the traditional notion of citizen-state loyalty and border security; the report concluded that "[a]ll borders will be more porous; some will bend and some will break."[30]

These two currents were swirling, contending, and intermingling in U.S. policy at the turn of the century—the desire to ensure impartiality of immigration adjudication in an increasingly globalized world, and the need to defend against a new species of security threat. In August 1999, Senators Spencer Abraham, Edward Kennedy, and Chuck Hagel would introduce the INS Reform and Border Security Act of 1999, which would have created a new immigration affairs agency within the Department of Justice headed by an associate attorney general for Immigration Affairs, with separate bureaus for "immigration services and adjudications" and for "enforcement and border affairs." The bill—which would have expressly left EOIR and the immigration courts unchanged—died in committee, but then-Governor Bush would campaign for office the following year on a nearly identical immigration platform. Calling immigration "not a problem to be solved, but the sign of a successful nation," Bush's platform emphasized INS reform for the purpose of "[w]elcoming legal immigrants" before outlining plans to fulfill the "federal responsibility to secure the border."[31]

Only a month into Bush's first term, the Hart-Rudman Commission would release its final report, with recommendations for government reorganization to increase national security to deal with the new threats. A House bill by Representative Mac Thornberry would heed the call issued by Hart-Rudman, introducing a bill on March 21, 2001, to create a cabinet-level National Homeland Security Agency consisting of the Federal Emergency Management Agency, the Customs Service, the Border

Patrol from INS, the Coast Guard, and four infrastructure security offices from the Department of Commerce and the FBI. Thornberry's National Homeland Security Agency Act began with a finding, taken from the first Hart-Rudman report, that "[a]ttacks against United States citizens on United States soil, possibly causing heavy casualties, are likely during the next quarter century."[32]

Some at the CIA and National Security Council felt the new administration failed to appreciate the gravity of the threat. CIA Director George Tenet wrote in his memoirs that he had asked in March 2001 for the authority to plan and carry out operations to kill Osama Bin Laden without capturing him. According to Tenet, an NSC senior director and CIA staffer called his chief of staff, John Moseman, the next day with the administration's response, something to the effect of "[w]e need you to take . . . the draft covert-action finding back," Tenet recalled. "If you formally transmit these to the NSC, the clock will be ticking, and we don't want the clock to tick just now." The administration wanted time to craft its policy on terrorism—time that Tenet felt they did not have.

The intelligence continued to get worse throughout the summer. On July 10, Tenet was given a briefing by counterterrorism staff that "literally made my hair stand on end." It alarmed him so much that he picked up the phone on his desk that had a secure connection to National Security Adviser Condoleeza Rice and asked to meet with her immediately. "I can recall no other time in my seven years as DCI that I sought such an urgent meeting at the White House," Tenet later wrote. According to Tenet, Rice immediately arranged for the meeting and Tenet went to the White House with CIA Counter-Terrorism Center director Cofer Black and an agent that Tenet identified in his memoirs only as "Rich B." At the White House, they joined Rice, Deputy National Security Advisor Stephen J. Hadley, and NSC counterterrorism expert Richard A. Clarke. Tenet requested they sit around a conference table rather than on the couch so everyone could focus on the briefing charts. Rich gave the briefing: Bin Laden and his network were reporting a "big event" in the coming weeks, a "stunning turn of events" involving "decisive acts." "Multiple and simultaneous attacks are possible, and they will occur with little or no warning," Tenet recalled Rich saying. "Al-Qa-ida is waiting us out and looking for vulnerability."

After the briefing, Tenet recalled Rice turning to Clarke. "'Dick, do you agree? Is this true?' Clarke put his elbows on his knees and his head fell into his hands and he gave an exasperated yes," Tenet wrote. Rice asked for a recommendation, and Tenet or Black recommended that the country immediately shift to a "war footing," authorizing the authority to kill bin Laden that the CIA had requested in March. The 9/11 Commission report did not mention the meeting, though Tenet said he informed them in his classified testimony in early 2004.[33]

The new Department of Defense may have felt that the greatest threat was not bin Laden but Iraq. In his memoirs, Clarke recalled a meeting with Deputy Secretary of Defense Paul Wolfowitz in April 2001 in which Clarke attempted to focus attention on bin Laden. Wolfowitz reacted with skepticism and attempted to steer the discussion to Iraq, Clarke later wrote. "You give bin Laden too much credit," Clarke recalled Wolfowitz saying. "He could not do all these things like the 1993 attack on New York, not without a state sponsor. Just because FBI and CIA have failed to find the linkages [to Iraq] does not mean they don't exist."[34]

Neither Bush nor Rice refuted the substance of Tenet's and Clarke's claims that the new administration hesitated to implement a plan to kill bin Laden before 9/11 and focused instead on crafting a comprehensive strategy to deal with the terrorism threat. The president later told Bob Woodward that bin Laden was not his or his security team's focus prior to the attacks. "I have no hesitancy about going after him," Bush said. "But I didn't feel that sense of urgency and my blood was not nearly as boiling."[35] Rice, questioned about these statements by the 9/11 Commission, would ask, "Whose blood was nearly as boiling prior to September 11?"

Moreover, as Rice would later tell the 9/11 Commission, Tenet had told the president that killing bin Laden would not be a "silver bullet" to eliminate the terrorist threat. "And in fact, I think that some of us felt that the focus—so much focus on what you did with bin Laden, not what you did with the network, . . . not what you did with the regional circumstances, might in fact have been misplaced," Rice testified. In hindsight, Rice concluded that the administration would indeed have "gone off course" had it followed the CIA's original recommendations, which focused on the Afghan Northern Alliance rather than bin Laden's center of operations in the south.[36]

Everyone in the intelligence community and the White House focused on "the wall"—the legal limits on the intelligence service sharing information with domestic law enforcement. To many Americans, spying within the United States smacked of the Gestapo and brought back bad memories of J. Edgar Hoover and the FBI spying on civil rights leaders like Martin Luther King, Jr., and of the Clinton administration's receipt of FBI files on political opponents.[37] As Rice would tell the 9/11 Commission, "[w]hen it came right down to it, this country, for reasons of history, and culture, and therefore, law, had an allergy to the notion of domestic intelligence, and we were organized on that basis. And it just made it very hard to have all the pieces come together."

Hindsight is, notoriously, 20/20. Perhaps the actions of the president, the NSC, the CIA, the FBI, and the FAA were as aggressive as they could legally and reasonably be in countering a growing—but never precisely identified—threat in the months before 9/11. But there's no question that, as the president himself would later write, the attacks "redefined my job." He had spent the month of August 2001 at his Texas ranch; in addition to morning briefings by his staff, his activities included jogging, fishing, clearing brush with a chainsaw, and relaxing with his wife. For months after, he received six intelligence briefings a week detailing about four hundred threats each month, and "would wake up in the middle of the night worried about what I had read." For as long as he held office, the terrorist attacks—and the voices of grief and rage that yelled in his face and called him by his first name that day at Ground Zero—would drive him. "I would pour my heart and soul into protecting the country," he said— "whatever it took."[38]

11 President Bush's Department

There wasn't going to be a Department of Homeland Security, at least if you had asked the president and his advisors as late as May 2002. On October 11, 2001, Senator Joseph Lieberman had introduced a bill to create a Department of National Homeland Security, but President Bush opposed it and instead created the Office of Homeland Security within the White House.[1] In addition to his instinctive reticence to a large new government department, he feared the inefficiencies of a major reorganization in the middle of a crisis. Quoting an advisor, he reflected, "'[w]hen you are in the process of beating swords into plowshares, you can't fight and you can't plow.'"[2] On May 30, 2002, Office of Homeland Security Director Tom Ridge told reporters that if Congress approved a bill creating a Cabinet-level department, "I'd probably recommend he veto it."[3]

Ridge's comment was disingenuous. In fact, sometime that spring, the president had had a change of heart about the new homeland security department. Since late April, five White House staffers had been meeting secretly—in the bunker from which Vice President Dick Cheney had managed the September 11 crisis while the president was on Air Force One—to craft a plan for a new Department of Homeland Security. Ridge was among the few officials invited in for the top-secret meetings. Most Bush aides and affected Cabinet members didn't find out about the plan until June 5, the day before Bush publicly announced it. According to news reports, the only two lawmakers briefed before the speech—House speaker J. Dennis Hastert and Senate minority leader Trent Lott—were told during the congressional picnic on the South Lawn of the White House that evening, while Asleep at the Wheel played its ironic brand of Western swing and hundreds of members of Congress devoured Texas barbecue. Even Senator Lieberman was not given a heads-up.[4]

Why the intense secrecy? Partly to minimize bureaucratic infighting, which happened anyway—for example, Joe Allbaugh, director of the Federal Emergency Management Agency, immediately vowed to resign as soon as the transfer of FEMA to the new DHS took effect, a promise on which he made good.[5] Perhaps the Bush administration learned a lesson from Roosevelt's ill-fated Presidential Committee on Administrative Management, which spent three years navigating around the turf battles of Cabinet officers only to have most of its recommendations deep-sixed by a skeptical Congress. Or perhaps they just knew better than to invite trouble.

Bush's about-face was triggered, at least in part, by a politically devastating gaffe by INS. On March 11, 2002, the Florida flight training school Huffman Aviation International received immigration documents in the mail for Mohammed Atta and Marwan Al-Shehhi—two of the hijackers who had perpetrated the 9/11 attacks. This was not a belated INS approval of known terrorists; the visas in question had been approved in July and August 2001, before INS had any information linking Atta and Al-Shehhi to terrorist activities. The flight school was merely receiving its record copy of the approvals six months later, after data entry by an INS contractor, in accordance with the contract in effect at the time. Although the student visa system was riddled with inefficiencies and information gaps, the mailing of the Atta and Al-Shehhi I-20 forms was in accord with standard practice, "analogous to buying an item with a check and not receiving the receipt for six months," INS commissioner James W. Ziglar explained to the House Subcommittee on Immigration the following week. The error was in failing to recall the paper document from the contractor after the attacks.[6]

It didn't matter; the political fallout was severe. President Bush learned of the incident by reading about it in the newspaper on March 13. "I could barely get my coffee down," he said at a press conference later that day. This "sloppy error," as he termed it, was one of the things that convinced him that a departmental reorganization was necessary. Ridge was also having difficulty managing and coordinating dozens of different agencies, spread across numerous departments, with homeland security responsibilities. In any event, the White House was clearly on the losing end of the debate in the first half of 2002, as Senator Lieberman's homeland security bill gained steam in Congress. By developing his own plan, Bush could control the debate and shape the office that he would have to lead.

The timing of Bush's public announcement of the plan confirms the administration's chagrin over federal law enforcement failures. The president announced the plan in a nationally televised speech from the White House at 8 PM on Thursday, June 6. Earlier that same day, the Senate Judiciary Committee heard testimony from FBI director Robert S. Mueller and Minneapolis-based FBI agent and whistleblower Colleen Rowley. In a private letter to Mueller two weeks earlier that was leaked, Rowley had criticized the FBI culture and bureaucracy, claiming that FBI supervisors in Washington had thwarted Minneapolis agents' investigation of Zacarias Moussaoui, who was linked to the 9/11 plot.[7] In his speech, President Bush referenced the Senate hearings, tacitly approving of Rowley's decision to write to Mueller and to speak publicly about her concerns. "If you're a front-line worker for the FBI, the CIA, some other law enforcement or intelligence agency, and you see something that raises suspicions, I want you to report it immediately. I expect your supervisors to treat it with the seriousness it deserves," Bush said. The duty was not limited to law enforcement, however. With echoes of Roosevelt's radio address warning Americans of fifth column activities, Bush told Americans to "go about your lives, but pay attention to your surroundings. Add your eyes and ears to the protection of our homeland." In the final segment of the thirteen-minute speech, Bush proposed a Cabinet-level Department of Homeland Security tasked with four related missions: controlling the nation's borders, responding to emergencies, developing defensive technologies, and synthesizing all intelligence and law enforcement information. Obscuring several years of congressional leadership on the issue, he noted that only Congress could create a new government department and, therefore, he said, "I ask for your help in encouraging your representatives to support my plan."[8]

A version of the White House proposal was introduced in the House by Representative Richard Armey on June 24 as H.R. 5005. The original bill would have effected a wholesale transfer of INS to the new department under the supervision of the under secretary for border and transportation security.[9] This concerned members of Congress, particularly Democrats, who noted that the written version of Bush's own proposal had planned to reform INS by separating its enforcement functions, such as investigation and prosecution, from its services functions, such as adjudication of visa, green card, and citizenship applications.[10] Similar reforms, which had been recommended by the Commission on Immigration Reform in the 1990s, had passed the House that April in a bill sponsored by Representative James Sensenbrenner, called the Barbara Jordan Immigration Reform and Accountability Act of 2002, or H.R. 3231.[11]

None of those proposals—H.R. 3231, the Bush plan as proposed, or H.R. 5005—would have affected the location or structure of the immigration courts. But two senators—Democrat Edward M. Kennedy of Massachusetts and Republican Sam Brownback of Kansas—had been studying the issue and saw an opportunity to increase immigration court independence as part of the reorganization.

KENNEDY-BROWNBACK

On June 26, Senator Kennedy convened the Senate Judiciary Committee's Subcommittee on Immigration for hearings addressing reform of the immigration services. On May 2, Senator Kennedy had introduced legislation, S. 2444, that would have abolished INS and created a new agency with separate bureaus for services and enforcement. That bill expressly left EOIR and the attorney general's authority untouched. Opening the June hearings, however, Senator Kennedy mentioned growing concerns in Congress about the independence of the immigration courts, particularly if they were moved into the new department then under discussion. "Moving [EOIR] into a new security department would undermine its ability to independently hear and decide important immigration matters," Kennedy said. "Support[] is growing to create an independent agency to oversee this important function."[12]

In the year since Bush's arrival in Washington, the relationship between Senator Kennedy and President Bush had started wary, grown warm, and then turned chilly as tornado-level political winds buffeted them both, the country's most prominent Democrat and its most prominent Republican. Bush had arrived in Washington looking for another Bob Bullock, the Democratic lieutenant governor with whom he had worked successfully in Texas. Among those he set about courting was Kennedy, the ranking Democrat on the Senate committee that drafted education legislation. In his memoirs, Bush emphasized their differences: he grew up in West Texas, not Cape Code; Kennedy had spent forty years in Washington, while Bush was "relatively new to town." These differences were exaggerated. Political views aside, both men were heirs to New England political dynasties that had shaped U.S. politics for most of the twentieth century; both were educated at the Ivies; and both had come to Washington with very big shoes to fill.[13]

Moreover, both were known by friends and colleagues as warm, engaging, and quick to laugh, and it wasn't long before they had formed a bond. In January 2001, Bush and his wife invited Kennedy and others to the White House theater to watch *Thirteen Days*, a movie about President John F. Kennedy's handling of the Cuban Missile Crisis. As Bush came downstairs to greet his guests, Kennedy congratulated him on the confirmation of John Ashcroft as attorney general, which Kennedy had pointedly opposed. Kennedy sensed an initial coolness in the president's response, but political differences soon faded in the light of both men's signature good humor. Bush showed Kennedy that he had chosen to use the *Resolute* desk used by President Kennedy; Senator Kennedy brought Bush a framed photograph of the elder Kennedy brother at the desk. Bush was charmed by Kennedy's trademark accent and "great Irish glow"; Kennedy appreciated Bush's dinner menu (hamburgers, hot dogs, and chili) and the president's enjoyment of the film's feisty portrayal of Kennedy's beloved brother, Bobby.[14]

Perhaps most importantly, both sensed a capable ally in their shared desire to reform federal education policy. It was that legislation, which became known as No Child Left Behind, that President Bush was promoting at Emma E. Booker Elementary School in Sarasota, Florida, on the morning of September 11. In the urge for bipartisanship that filled Washington and the country after September 11, No Child Left Behind managed to overcome earlier partisan disputes about vouchers and bureaucratization, passing by what Bush called "a bipartisan landslide" in December. Kennedy called it a "big victory" for the president on his "signature issue"; Bush praised Kennedy before a Boston crowd, recalling how Kennedy had hosted and comforted Laura on the morning of September 11, as she had been preparing to testify before his committee. "Not only are you a good senator, you're a good man," Bush said.[15]

But the good vibes had begun to wear off before the ink was dry on the new education law. Kennedy would write in 2009 that he was deeply disappointed by the president's failure to include a request for agreed-upon funding for the bill in the budget he sent to Congress a few weeks later. Bush, in his memoirs, discounted the "common claim" that the law was underfunded, pointing to a 39 percent increase in education spending during his eight years in office. Kennedy's later disappointment may have been colored by his eventual disagreement with the president over Iraq, a war Kennedy strongly opposed. In October 2002, Kennedy said on the Senate floor that the proposed invasion "flies in the face of international rules of acceptable behavior." In July 2004, he called it "a fraud, cooked up in Texas" for the president's political gain. In his memoirs, Bush would call Kennedy "a decent man" and regret that he had never sat down with the senator to discuss the war, which "might have persuaded him to tone down his rhetoric."[16]

In the summer of 2002, Senator Kennedy's desire to ensure the independence of the immigration courts had bipartisan support on the committee. In an opening statement at the hearing on June 26, Senator Brownback, a Kansas Republican who co-sponsored the INS reform bill, acknowledged Kennedy's concerns about moving EOIR from DOJ to the new department. "We certainly do not want to compromise unbiased courtroom review of immigration cases," Brownback said, "and we should either keep the immigration court system with the Department of Justice or set up an independent agency." Brownback proposed that, in addition to the four divisions of the new department outlined by President Bush in his speech and included in H.R. 5005, Congress add a fifth division for Immigration Affairs to handle immigration services but not removal cases.[17]

Brownback's interest in immigration grew largely out of his faith (once an Evangelical Christian, Brownback converted to Roman Catholicism in

2002). He once told a reporter that his support for immigration reform was based on biblical edicts to welcome the stranger, such as Matthew 25:35: "I was hungry and you gave me something to eat, I was thirsty and you gave me something to drink, I was a stranger and you invited me in."[18] As ranking member of the Subcommittee on Immigration in 2001, Brownback looked to hire counsel with expertise on immigration issues. He reached out to David L. Neal, then a staff attorney for the BIA who would later spend a decade as its chairman before retiring in 2019.

   But times were about to change—Neal's second interview for the position with Senator Brownback occurred on September 10, 2001. Brownback, and by extension Neal, would soon find themselves in the line of fire as the rhetoric in Washington shifted from bipartisan support for immigration reform to border enforcement and tighter restrictions on admission. "When I interviewed with Senator Brownback's office, being a pro-immigration Republican was not an issue, but after September 11 it very much was an issue," Neal said.[19] Nevertheless, Brownback worked closely with Kennedy in 2001 and 2002 to restructure INS, motivated by his religious principles and his views at the time on the value of immigration reform for Kansas farmers. The two "were joined at the hip on this effort," recalled Esther Olavarria, then counsel to Senator Kennedy.[20]

   The bill introduced by Kennedy, Brownback, and others on May 2, 2002, S. 2444, was titled the "Immigration Reform, Accountability, and Security Enhancement Act of 2002" and built on an earlier bipartisan effort between Kennedy and then-chairman Senator Spencer Abraham of Michigan. The bill focused on two issues that would become lines in the sand for Brownback: creating separate offices with unified supervision and funding for immigration services and immigration enforcement; and separating supervision of unaccompanied minors from immigration enforcement operations. The bill mentioned the immigration courts only in expressing that the bill did not affect the authority of EOIR.[21]

   The omission was casual but not accidental. While Senate staffers would debate the various permutations while drafting immigration reform bills—fully independent immigration courts, a restructured office within DOJ, no change to EOIR—those conversations lacked political momentum in an era when attorneys general rarely got involved in immigration court functions. "Before [the Trump] administration, there were instances of abuse, but there wasn't a program of destroying the independence of the immigration courts," Olavarria said. As a result, some drafts of legislation included immigration court reform, often driven by lobbying from the immigration judges' union, while other versions omitted it.[22]

Early proposals over the shape of the new homeland security department raised the stakes of the issue, however. H.R. 5005, introduced by Armey on June 24, provided a twelve-month "transition period" for the president to transfer agencies to the new department. During the transition period, "[w]hen an agency is transferred, the President may also transfer to the Department [of Homeland Security] any agency established to carry out or support adjudicatory or review functions in relation to the agency." Although EOIR was not explicitly mentioned in the bill, this provision allowed the president to punt for the moment on the question of its location and to decide, within twelve months after passage, to move EOIR into DHS without further congressional scrutiny.[23]

Two days after the introduction of H.R. 5005, at Kennedy and Brownback's hearings on S. 2444, the witnesses addressed the location of the immigration courts in any reorganization. Much of the testimony centered on the need to further separate EOIR's adjudication functions from INS's enforcement and prosecution functions. "[W]ho wants a boss who is dealing with both the prosecutor and the judge?" said Kathleen Campbell Walker, an El Paso immigration lawyer who spoke on behalf of the American Immigration Lawyers Association. Walker and most other witnesses believed that this separation should be accomplished by moving INS to the new DHS while locating the immigration courts in one of three possible locations: a new independent executive branch agency; an Article I court system within the judicial branch; or, if necessary, the status quo within the Department of Justice.[24]

Former Representative Bill McCollum, a Republican who had served on the House Committee on Immigration for eighteen of his twenty years as a member of Congress, also submitted written testimony. McCollum prosaically described the cost of the current system not only to the American justice system, but to the image of the United States to other nations:

> While we call them Immigration Judges, those performing adjudicatory tasks in immigration matters are attorney employees of the Department of

Justice just as the attorneys of the INS are. They are judges in name only. Yet they are called upon to make adjudicatory determinations that will grant or deny individuals the right to remain or not in the United States and to ultimately become a citizen or not. In the way that they affect the lives of people and project to the rest of the world the long established image of America as a land of immigrants open to limited migration through a fundamentally fair process, they are in an entirely different league from Administrative Law Judges or any other adjudicators in the Executive Branch.[25]

These witnesses recommended that Congress create either an Article I court or an independent executive agency; opinions varied depending upon how the witnesses balanced questions of judicial independence, executive policy coordination across branches, and cost savings. They agreed on one thing, however: Not one witness recommended that the immigration courts remain in DOJ. At best, witnesses viewed this as merely a "stop-gap solution" to separate the courts from investigation and prosecution while looking for a better home for the courts.[26]

Only one witness, law professor and former INS general counsel David A. Martin, differed in any material respect with the recommendation of creating an independent executive agency or Article I court. Martin's concern was primarily with executive efficiency. On occasion, he noted, the immigration courts would be deployed to handle an emergency influx of cases at the border or some other coordination with enforcement services might be needed. For that reason, he favored transferring the immigration courts to DHS along with INS, while acknowledging reasonable concerns about the need for separation of investigatory and adjudicative functions. He minimized concerns about the agency head's self-referral authority, describing this power as "carefully structured" and a "specialized and infrequent function" that might be carried out by counsel to the secretary of DHS.[27]

Throughout the hearing, the ghost of President Roosevelt's decision of May 1940 was a silent presence. Walker began the day of testimony by referring to Senator Brownback's proposal to add a fifth division for immigration services to the four DHS functions enumerated in President Bush's plan. She chose her words carefully. "[W]hat we are hoping you would consider is perhaps a fifth prong, as Senator Brownback mentioned," Walker said. "We have been struggling that we should not use the 'fifth column' reference."[28]

THE HOLDOUT

Later that summer, the location of the immigration courts would get pulled into the fight between the White House and the Senate over the shape of the emerging Homeland Security Act. As immigration reform became incorporated into the homeland security bill, Neal recommended that Senator Brownback prioritize three issues: coordination of enforcement and services; moving responsibility for unaccompanied minors out of the enforcement agencies; and keeping EOIR from moving to DHS to ensure the separation of enforcement and prosecution from the adjudication functions of the immigration courts.

In Neal's view, no news was good news when it came to immigration court restructuring. As long as investigation and prosecution functions seemed destined to move to the new DHS, a bill that was silent on immigration courts would leave the courts in DOJ and ensure the separation that Neal believed essential. "If you want judges making non-biased, non-ideological decisions, you have to insulate them," Neal said. The regulation of 1983 that separated EOIR into its own office within DOJ was a move in the right direction, he believed; pulling the courts into DHS would once again have commingled enforcement and adjudication.[29] Senator Kennedy's office agreed. "This was a department that was being created whose principal mission was to focus on national security, fighting terrorism," Olavarria said. "It was almost exclusively an enforcement agency. That would have been the worst place for the immigration courts."[30]

As the Bush administration became involved in shaping the Senate bill that summer, their original plans for the new DHS omitted any mention of EOIR. During a presentation of the White House plan to congressional staffers, however, Neal recalled another staffer raising her hand and asking about the immigration courts. "Their response was, 'If you don't see it up here, it's not part of the President's plan,'" Neal said. The question may have spurred White House staff, however. Soon thereafter, new White House charts showed the immigration courts moving to DHS. From that point on, Neal said, the White House was "adamant" that EOIR's functions move to DHS. "That's when the drama began," Neal recalled.[31]

Although the early negotiations between the White House and the Senate were bipartisan, Democrats were later excluded from the talks. In meetings with Senate Republicans, White House staff leaned heavily on Brownback and Senator Orrin Hatch, at that time the only other Republican holdout on the White House's plans for immigration. Neal recalled Senator Brownback receiving calls from Secretary of State Colin Powell and Homeland Security Director Tom Ridge. Hatch eventually changed his position and the pressure on Brownback mounted. Neal urged the senator to stand his ground on the immigration courts, unaccompanied minors, and coordination of enforcement and services.[32]

Brownback was in a strong position to resist. During the summer of 2002, Democrats controlled the Senate; the White House could not afford to lose a single Republican, much less the ranking member of the Subcommittee on Immigration. Even if Brownback were kept on board, however, the chances at that time of the Republican minority prevailing on their version of the bill in the Senate were low. As the momentum for a homeland security department mounted, Senate Democrats quickly crafted a substitute bill. The Senate Committee on Government Affairs led a fast and furious effort to craft S. 4471, eventually introduced by Senator Lieberman, over the August recess.

Immigration reforms from the Kennedy-Brownback bill were among the pending reform proposals that were pulled into the Lieberman substitute. Noting that the existing draft of the Lieberman bill included immigration provisions drawn largely from their legislation, S. 2444, Kennedy and Brownback wrote to Lieberman and ranking member Fred Thompson on August 28, 2002, describing the intent behind the language. The letter also mentioned one matter that was not in the Kennedy-Brownback bill: the immigration courts. The move to create EOIR by regulation in 1983 had been a response to criticism that the judge and prosecutor should not be part of the same office, Kennedy and Brownback wrote. "Even parsed into separate components, however, concerns remain that the immigration courts are still too closely aligned with the immigration enforcers." Moreover, the letter continued, "[c]oncerns about the impartiality of a court system located in a law enforcement agency are certain to be exacerbated if the court system is relocated to a security agency." To create greater separation of functions, the authors recommended that the statute include provisions ensuring that the immigration courts remain in the Department of Justice if INS were to move to the new Department of Homeland

Security. "The immigration courts make potentially life-or-death decisions every day and are therefore too important to exist only in regulation," Kennedy and Brownback concluded.[33]

When the Lieberman substitute was introduced in the Senate six days
later, it contained a section reforming the immigration court system without moving it to DHS. Lieberman's bill would have abolished EOIR alto-
gether and created a new agency, the Agency for Immigration Hearings
and Appeals, still within DOJ but with additional protections for judicial
independence. For one thing, it provided that the director of the agency
would be confirmed by the Senate after presidential appointment, and
that the director would appoint the other officers and judges within the
new agency. The director, rather than the attorney general, would have
had responsibility for promulgating rules and regulations for the new
agency, for appointing the chair and members of the BIA and the lead
administrative judge for the immigration courts, and for appointing and
fixing the compensation of all personnel. To limit political manipulation
of decisions, immigration judges and BIA members would have been
required to "exercise their independent judgment and discretion" in cases
coming before them. Immigration judges and Board members would have
been removable only by the director, in consultation with the other officers, and only for "good cause, including neglect of duty or malfeasance."
Perhaps most significantly, the bill provided that "[t]he decisions of the
Board shall constitute final agency action, subject to review only as
provided by the Immigration and Nationality Act and other applicable
law." This provision might be read to eliminate the attorney general's self-
referral power, which exists only by DOJ regulation, not by statute.[34]

THE SENATE FLIPS

The Democrats had effectively controlled the Senate since May 2001,
when Senator Jim Jeffords of Vermont changed his affiliation from
Republican to Independent and began to caucus with the Democrats.
With the Democratic majority, the Lieberman substitute would likely have
passed had Senate leadership been able to bring the matter to a vote.
Republicans, however, succeeded in opposing Democrat-sponsored

cloture motions, which would have ended debate and forced a vote, on four occasions between September 19 and October 1, 2002.[35] Republicans opposed cloture based on a debate about the scope of the labor rights of federal security agency workers. News reports said that Republicans sought to eliminate traditional civil service protections, which White House officials claimed made it hard to fire ineffective workers or promote good ones.[36] President Bush, however, would later characterize the dispute as one over "extensive collective bargaining rights that did not apply in any other government agency."[37] Regardless, the issue provided grounds for Senate Republicans to block a vote on the Lieberman substitute, and as of October, the Senate appeared to be at an impasse awaiting the November elections and a possible shift in power when the new Congress assembled in January.

In a tragic turn, the political balance would actually shift even before the elections when Senator Paul Wellstone, a Democrat from Minnesota, and seven other people were killed in an airplane crash near Eveleth, Minnesota, on October 26. Wellstone's public memorial service three days later included several partisan speeches and advocacy on political issues, not to mention some crowd members tossing around a beach ball. Minnesota governor Jesse Ventura, who had previously indicated his intent to name a Democrat to the seat vacated by Wellstone, was offended by the display and instead appointed Dean Barkley, an Independent, to fill the seat on November 4.[38] When Barkley announced his intent to caucus with Republicans, the Senate was split 50–50. With Vice President Cheney as the tie-breaking vote, Republicans now had control of the chamber.

Bush would describe the election results later that week, in which Republicans gained two Senate seats, as a vindication of his version of the Homeland Security Act that spurred him to immediate action, though he failed (perhaps out of decorum) to mention Wellstone's death and the early shift in Senate control.[39] Three days after the election, Bush urged Representative Armey to get the Homeland Security Act passed. A flurry of meetings between members of key House and Senate committees and the president ensued. "In light of some of the concerns that we knew were fairly well known to us on the other side of the building," Armey said on the House floor the following week, "we were able to very quickly move through those issues that still remain, fully vet them with all interested parties, . . . and work out what we believe will be in the form of the bill before us right now a bill that can comfortably pass both bodies and be sent to the President for signature." The compromises were few. The result, as Armey noted on the House floor, was "essentially the same bill that was passed by the House of Representatives last July."[40]

One change, however, was necessary to secure the vote of Senator Brownback. The earlier House bill, H.R. 5005, had not included any statutory recognition of EOIR. Although Republicans now effectively controlled the Senate, they still could not afford any defections. Brownback was willing to compromise on one of his three immigration reform priorities: In the final version of the Homeland Security Act, immigration services under the new USCIS were separated (and separately funded) from the enforcement offices within DHS. Brownback would note his concerns on the subject in the brief Senate debate on the bill.[41] The transfer of responsibility for unaccompanied minors had already carried that summer in the House, but the issue of the immigration courts was still to be worked out.[42]

Despite continued pressure, Brownback held firm. The compromise was reflected in the new House version of the bill, H.R. 5710, which deleted the immigration court provisions that had been offered by the Lieberman substitute but gave statutory recognition to EOIR as an office in the Department of Justice. The new provisions, Section 1101 and 1102, meant the immigration courts and the BIA could not be moved to DHS or eliminated by the executive branch. However, Section 1102 also solidified attorney general control over the immigration courts and clarified that the attorney general would have the power to make rules and regulations and to "review . . . administrative determinations in immigration proceedings."[43]

H.R. 5710 passed the House on November 13, 2002, one day after it was introduced. Six days later, the Senate passed S. 4901, based on the original House version plus a small number of changes, including adoption of the provision recognizing EOIR. The House agreed to the Senate version on November 22, and President Bush signed the Homeland Security Act into law on November 25.[44] On the Senate floor, Brownback gave the subtlest of nods to his hard-won victory on the immigration courts. "I want to quickly commend this legislation for keeping the Executive Office for Immigration Review within the Department of

Justice," he said. "It didn't move over [to] homeland security. I think permitting the Attorney General to retain control of the immigration court system is going to be positive."[45]

"A RECIPE FOR MISTAKES AND ABUSE"

For immigration court independence, the victory was important but, as future events would confirm, incomplete. David A. Martin, the former INS general counsel who testified at the Subcommittee on Immigration hearings in July, would later write critically of the solution chosen by Congress—moving INS into DHS but leaving the immigration courts under the control of the attorney general. It accomplished neither the policymaking efficiency that he had supported, Martin argued, nor the judicial independence that other witnesses had advocated. "[I]f that vision of fairness is the objective," Martin wrote in 2003, "then placing adjudication in another Cabinet department rather than in an independent body—and at that a Cabinet department deeply involved in general law enforcement—is at best a curious step." The decision, Martin speculated, was perhaps best viewed as a temporary fix by "weary legislators who thought they could placate both sides and ran out of time and energy to think through the full implications of either alternative." Martin hoped this was a "mere way-station," and concluded that "it would be better for the adjudication system to move on to its final structural destination sooner rather than later."[46]

The immigration court provisions went unnoticed in the debates by every other member of Congress except Senator Kennedy, who argued that the bill "will seriously undermine the role of immigration judges." The bill, he argued,

> vests the Attorney General with all-encompassing authority, depriving immigration judges of their ability to exercise independent judgment. Even more disturbing, the bill gives the Attorney General the authority to change or even eliminate appellate review. This result is a recipe for mistakes and abuse. An independent judicial system is essential to our system of checks and balances. Immigrants who face the severest of consequences deserve their day in court.[47]

For his part, President Bush would never again be the cavalier cowboy who had welcomed his friend Vicente to the White House to discuss a new relationship for people migrating across their nations' shared border. Bush soon became consumed with the impending attack on Iraq and needed Mexico's vote in the UN Security Council implicitly authorizing a U.S.-led attack. Fox held out, soured by the president's sudden loss of interest in a U.S.-Mexico migration deal. In the fall of 2002, Fox invited Bush to attend a meeting in Mexico the following summer to announce progress on an immigration deal or at least conduct meetings, but Bush declined, sources told the *New York Times*. "President Bush came back and said, 'Well, maybe we'll be at war then, and you may not want me to come because maybe it won't be a popular war,'" a source said. "'The fact is, he wasn't addressing the issue that President Fox was bringing up.'"[48] Fox would later call Bush a "windshield cowboy," and the prospect of immigration reform receded in the rearview mirror.[49]

PART III

The Future of the
Immigration Courts

12 Checks and Imbalances

Just as the immigration courts are not really "courts," immigration judges are not really "judges" in the traditional sense of Article III of the Constitution but rather attorneys who work in the Department of Justice under the supervision of the attorney general. Since DOJ is a law enforcement agency, immigration judges in fact decide cases brought by the client they represent, the United States, against a private individual. Imagine going to court and discovering that your case will be decided by a lawyer who works for the party who sued you. Like your chances? That's the situation noncitizens face when they appear in immigration court.

As assistants to the attorney general, immigration judges can be incentivized, disciplined, reassigned, or removed by that official (at least within the limits of their contracts and, at least for now, assisted by their union). Their job performance is evaluated by the attorney general and his delegates. And, using the self-referral power that was established by DOJ regulation in 1940, the attorney general may redecide any case heard by any immigration judge at any time and for any reason. In short, immigration judges contravene the will of the attorney general at their own professional peril.

NEMO IUDEX IN CAUSA SUA

There's a maxim of law known as *nemo iudex in causa sua*, which means "no man can be a judge in his own cause." This principle was articulated by the year 534 in a codification of Roman law, the *Codex Justinianeus*, which cited older references to the notion. It was recognized as part of the common law of England in 1610, when Sir Edward Coke ruled in *Dr. Bonham's Case* that a judge could not be paid with the fines he imposed. The maxim was included by Coke in his *Institutes of the Lawes of England* in 1628.[1]

The principle was foundational to American law. The idea that no man should judge his own case was recognized by James Madison in *The Federalist* No. 10, and Thomas Jefferson called it a rule "of immemorial observance" in his manual on parliamentary practice for the Senate.[2] For nearly a century, the United States Supreme Court has cited the maxim as part of the guarantee of due process of law under the Fifth and Fourteenth Amendments. In the case of *Tumey v. State of Ohio* from 1927, the Court rejected Ohio's laws that allowed judges, law enforcement officers, or executive officials to sit as judges and be paid out of the fines received upon convictions. To begin with, the decision by Chief Justice Taft stated that "it certainly violates the Fourteenth Amendment and deprives a defendant in a criminal case of due process of law to subject his liberty or property to the judgment of a court, the judge of which has a direct, personal, substantial pecuniary interest in reaching a conclusion against him in his case." Observing that the principle had been called "a maxim which is among the fundamentals of judicial authority," the Court concluded that, unless the amounts in question were *de minimus*, there was no established rule "either at common law or in this country, that [the Ohio practice] can be regarded as due process of law."[3] The principle was later extended by the Court beyond cases of direct pecuniary interest. In 1955, the Court held in *In re Murchison* that the rule precluded a judge who sat as the "judge-grand jury" from also sitting as the judge in contempt proceedings arising out of the attorneys' conduct before the "judge-grand jury."[4]

But the maxim is as limited as it is venerable. As noted, the principle at common law applied only to cases in which the judge had a direct pecuniary interest in the outcome, and most of the recent expansions by the

Supreme Court involved cases in which the judge had personally been the target of abuse or criticism by the litigant.[5] Federal courts of appeals have invoked *nemo iudex* where the adjudicator has made statements indicating a prejudgment of the facts in the very case before him, but the Supreme Court has expressly declined to extend the principle to all cases in which the adjudicator has previously served as an investigator or expressed an opinion about the legal questions presented.[6] In *Withrow v. Larkin,* the Court considered and rejected arguments based on the *nemo iudex* principle in holding that the Wisconsin Board of Medical Examiners could both investigate a complaint against a physician and order the suspension of the physician's license.[7] The Court's extensive survey in *Withrow* of cases involving challenges based on *nemo iudex* does not yield any clear rule as to when an adjudicator may not sit in judgment in a case. According to the Court, that is precisely the point:

> The issue is substantial, it is not new, and legislators and others concerned with the operations of administrative agencies have given much attention to whether and to what extent distinctive administrative functions should be performed by the same persons. No single answer has been reached. Indeed, the growth, variety, and complexity of the administrative processes have made any one solution highly unlikely.[8]

Because of the wide variety of situations in which government agencies conduct adjudication, the courts after *Withrow* would apply a high standard, setting aside cases on the basis of *nemo iudex* only where the conflict was pecuniary or prejudgment of the facts was obvious. "Without a showing to the contrary," the Court held in *Withrow,* "state administrators 'are assumed to be men of conscience and intellectual discipline, capable of judging a particular controversy fairly on the basis of its own circumstances.'"[9] In most cases, the Court stated in *Tumey,* questions of judicial qualification do not implicate due process concerns. "Thus matters of kinship, personal bias, state policy, remoteness of interest would seem generally to be matters merely of legislative discretion."[10]

Since *Withrow,* courts have rarely found due process violations on grounds of judicial bias. In one notable exception, *Caperton v. A. T. Massey Coal Co.,* the Supreme Court required recusal but ultimately did as much to define the limits of the *nemo iudex* principle as to expand it. In that case from 2009, the Court held that a justice of the West Virginia Supreme Court of Appeals should have recused himself in an appeal from a $50 million jury verdict against a company whose chairman had spent over $3 million to help elect the justice after the jury verdict had been entered. On one hand, the Court justified its ruling by pointing out that its precedents requiring judicial recusal were not limited to cases in which the judge had a direct pecuniary interest in the outcome. In *Tumey*, for example, the Court had held that recusal was required not only because of the direct payment to the mayor-judge, but also because of the funds that would flow to the general treasury funds of the mayor's town.[11] In another case, *Ward v. Monroeville*, the Court had required recusal where the fines exacted went only to the town's general treasury, not to the mayor-judge personally; the Court observed that "the mayor's 'executive responsibilities for village finances may make him partisan to maintain the high level of contribution [to those finances] from the mayor's court.'"[12] The Court in *Caperton* held that the West Virginia justice should have recused himself from the case; in the Court's view, there was a serious risk of actual bias where "a person with a personal stake in a particular case had a significant and disproportionate influence in placing the judge on the case by raising funds or directing the judge's election campaign when the case was pending or imminent."[13]

This aspect of the *Caperton* decision casts some doubt on the use of DOJ employees as judges in immigration cases. Immigration judges receive no direct payment based on how often they deny claims for relief, but a system that rates judges "Satisfactory" or "Unsatisfactory" based on deciding claims quickly regardless of the merits appears to place a thumb on the scales against relief. That incentive is enhanced where immigration judges who resist are soon disciplined, and an immigration judges' union that comes to their defense is threatened with decertification. It seems likely that the immigration judges' "executive responsibilities" to the attorney general and the law enforcement mission of DOJ "may make [them] partisan to maintain a high level" of removal orders. And while the chairman of A. T. Massey Coal Co. had a "significant and disproportionate influence" in electing the West Virginia justice, the attorney general has ultimate discretion in hiring and retaining immigration judges (at least subject to the limits of collective bargaining agreements with the now-threatened union).

CHECKS AND IMBALANCES   149

But the Court in *Caperton* emphasized that its holding was not meant to have broad applicability. Calling the facts of the case "exceptional," "an extraordinary situation," and "extreme by any measure," the Court doubted that its holding would cause lower courts much difficulty or lead to a flood of recusal motions. Responding to the dissenters' fears of a slippery slope, the Court stated, "[i]t is true that extreme cases often test the bounds of established legal principles, and sometimes no administrable standard may be available to address the perceived wrong. But it is also true that extreme cases are more likely to cross constitutional limits, requiring this Court's intervention and formulation of objective standards. This is particularly true when due process is violated."[14]

The situation the Court considered in *Caperton* was different than the situation of immigration judges. Immigration judges, as instruments of the attorney general, have a risk of institutional bias, but they generally lack the *"personal* stake in a *particular* case" that troubled the Court in *Caperton.* The Department of Justice might point out, for example, that the performance metrics do not require speedy disposition of *every* case, leaving judges some discretion to determine that some cases require extra time. Nor are immigration judges employed only when the United States has one exceptional and costly case pending; the conflict of interest, to the extent it exists, is institutional—pervasive and ongoing but not particularized. Finally, the Department of Justice is not coextensive with the United States as a litigant. DOJ's law enforcement functions are diverse and some—the investigative and prosecutorial functions—were separated from the adjudication function in the Homeland Security Act, at least in part because of concerns about fairness to litigants. The interest of immigration judges in the outcome of any particular case, then, is likely too attenuated to violate the due process rights of a particular respondent in a particular case.

Indeed, a similar due process claim was raised, and rejected, by the Supreme Court shortly after the passage of the INA. In *Marcello v. Bonds,* the respondent claimed that the INA's procedures violated due process because, before the 2002 reforms of the HSA, adjudicators were under the supervision and control of INS officials who also handled investigation and prosecution. In rejecting the claim, the Court deferred to long-standing practice, judicial vindication, and Congress's "particularly broad discretion in immigration matters."[15] Now that the adjudication function has been separated from investigation and prosecution with the creation of EOIR and DHS, claims of due process violation because of institutional conflicts by immigration judges are unlikely to succeed in the courts.

But not every bad idea is a due process violation. The requirement that Congress respect the Constitution and provide for due process is a floor, not a ceiling, on what makes good policy. Congress might be justified in compromising judicial independence in the immigration courts if it could demonstrate that such a trade-off is unavoidable or necessary to achieve some competing and important goal. The trouble is that, on closer examination, the compromises in immigration court independence through their location in DOJ appear unnecessary, even counterproductive, to other plausible goals in administration of the immigration laws. The institutional design appears explainable only as collateral damage of the national security crises and propaganda-driven fears that dominated the eras in which the design was hastily created.

Adrian Vermeule has argued that *nemo iudex* as a principle is limited (or even useless) because institutional designers sometimes must and do allow for a less neutral decision-maker where other important and countervailing values must be accommodated. Vermeule identifies competing values such as minimizing direct costs, maximizing decision-making expertise, protecting institutional independence, and enhancing motivation and activity of officials. He identifies numerous examples of institutional design in which government officials judge their own cause in order to promote one or more of those values: Legislators draw district boundaries and determine their own qualifications and salaries. The president may pardon his advisors (and, arguably, himself). Judges rule on court jurisdiction, judicial immunity, recusal, and contempt of court. The APA allows the head of an agency (though not anyone else) to participate in investigation, prosecution, and adjudication of the same matter.[16]

Vermeule doesn't argue that the principle of judicial independence is unimportant—just that it doesn't provide a useful policymaking standard when there are so many reasons to compromise it. When you look at the immigration courts, though, none of the arguable reasons for compromise of judicial independence really holds water.

THE LIMITS OF AGENCY EXPERTISE

There's a facially appealing argument that the attorney general's supervision and review powers may be useful to coordinate immigration policy and reduce disparate outcomes. After all, the APA expressly permits other agency heads to participate in investigation, prosecution, and adjudication of a matter in order to capitalize on agency expertise and coordinate agency policy.[17] Although removal proceedings are operated under the INA rather than the APA, one might argue that the attorney general's review of immigration court decisions is no more self-interested than APA agency head review.

This argument overlooks the fact that, apart from removal proceedings, the attorney general has no special expertise in immigration law. The APA allows broad powers to the other agency heads because the agency has unique expertise in the subjects being adjudicated: the Secretary of Education administers the federal education statutes and promulgates regulations under those statutes, the administrator of the Environmental Protection Agency does the same for environmental statutes and regulations, and so on. This was the case for immigration when all of INS, including investigation and prosecution, was located within DOJ, but that changed in 2002.

Concentrating the power over the immigration courts in one person—the attorney general—adds little in terms of agency expertise and contravenes another important administrative principle: collegial review of judicial decisions. As immigration law scholars pointed out in the Senate hearings in 2002, a fundamental principle of judicial administration is that decisions should be reviewed by more people, not fewer, as appeals proceed and stakes get higher. In the federal courts, cases are heard initially by a single trial judge, appealed to a panel of three judges, occasionally reheard by the entire court of appeals, and, if sufficiently important, finally reviewed by the nine justices of the Supreme Court. State judiciaries operate similarly. In contrast, decisions of an immigration judge are appealed to the BIA, where most are now heard only by a single board member (though more difficult cases are assigned to a three-judge panel and, occasionally, reheard en banc by the entire Board). And if a single person—the attorney general—disagrees with the BIA decision, he can change it using the self-referral power. Under this system, the thorniest cases are considered and decided based on only one perspective. "'Although authorized to act independently in its decisionmaking role, the Board hardly can avoid taking into account its perception of the Attorney General's likely view,'" witnesses told the Senate subcommittee.[18]

Moreover, this concentrated power in the attorney general is troubling because of the types of penalties imposed by immigration courts. Only immigration judges have the power to deprive an individual of their liberty—and effectively, in some cases, their life. Sanctions imposed by other agencies involve primarily property interests, not life or liberty interests. Typical sanctions include monetary penalties, cease and desist orders, product recalls, or suspension or revocation of licenses and permits. Even denial of much-needed federal benefits does not directly deprive an individual of life or liberty. In contrast, an order of removal (and detention while the government seeks an order of removal) directly deprives a person of their liberty, and in some cases indirectly leads to loss of life. With stakes of this magnitude, any negligible efficiency gains from plenary review by an agency head with no other immigration expertise are outweighed by the risk of erroneous deprivations of liberty that may result from concentrating the review power in one official.

THE LIMITS OF EXECUTIVE POWER

What about the power of the president? It might be argued that immigration is essentially a law enforcement function, and that Congress should not invade the executive sphere. Perhaps the attorney general is in the best position to transmit executive policy as to difficult issues in removal cases. More broadly still, it may be argued that concentration of removal power in the attorney general provides democratic accountability—citizens displeased with the administration's handling of removal adjudication could say so with their vote in the presidential election.

Neither of these arguments withstands much scrutiny. First, there's no constitutional reason to protect the prerogative of the executive over removal cases because immigration is not exclusively or even primarily an executive branch function under the Constitution. Some conservative constitutional scholars have argued that immigration, which is scarcely mentioned in the Constitution, is not a federal function at all but should be viewed as the prerogative of the states.[19] A more conventional view was expressed by Representative McCollum in his testimony during hearings on the HSA. Denying that reorganization would erode executive power, Representative McCollum said, "[a]ctually, the legislative branch ultimately controls immigration. Except for due process rights, non-citizens have only those rights and privileges granted by Congress." Congress could leave important immigration enforcement powers in the control of the executive branch, McCollum said, even if it transferred the immigration courts to an independent court system.[20] A few Supreme Court decisions have mentioned (without delineating) some inherent power in the executive to control the admission of aliens, but any such inherent power would be, at best, concurrent with congressional power to regulate immigration. This means that Congress would be within its constitutional authority if it were to relocate a particular immigration function to another branch, and the executive could not likely mount a successful challenge based on inherent powers alone where Congress has expressly curtailed executive authority.[21]

Moreover, the immigration judges' union argued in 2002 that the work of applying the immigration laws has evolved from a quasi-regulatory function into a quintessentially judicial function in the years since the passage of the INA:

> In the past decade, for example, Congressional enactments involving immigration matters have provided specific and detailed roadmaps to enforcement, not general goals which require the specialized skill of an agency to provide a methodology to implement or flesh-out. The general trend in the field of administrative law appears to be shifting towards a judicial focus of insuring that Congressional will is implemented, rather than a reliance on agency expertise in interpretation. This is a task which affords far less deference to administrative experience and interpretation, since it focuses instead on a search for Congressional purpose.[22]

Indeed, Congress tacitly acknowledged that removal adjudication did not require regulatory expertise when it separated immigration enforcement from immigration adjudication in the HSA. The fact that EOIR has functioned independently of USCIS and ICE for the past two decades suggests that the immigration judges were correct in characterizing their work as essentially judicial, not regulatory.

Arguably, Congress has already begun to reclaim removal decision-making from the executive branch. As suggested by the statement of the immigration judges' union, in the years since passage of the INA in 1952, Congress has amended the legislation numerous times to add increasingly detailed provisions for both removal and relief from removal. These changes have been driven by two distinct trends. First, in the early years of the INA, individuals would often petition Congress to pass a private bill relieving a family member from what were perceived as unnecessarily harsh impacts of the immigration laws. In the notorious case of Ellen Knauff, for example, the German wife of a U.S. citizen was excluded from the country (and detained at Ellis Island) without a hearing, a decision that was upheld by the Supreme Court on national security grounds in a Cold War climate. Public outcry over the treatment of Ms. Knauff eventually led Congress to introduce several private bills. Though the bills languished, the attorney general under public scrutiny ordered that Ms. Knauff was, in fact, entitled to a hearing, and eventually a favorable decision from the BIA afforded her admission to the country.[23] Seeking to avoid the ad hoc and preferential nature of the private bill system, Congress has increasingly codified the more common bases for exemption, such as humanitarian concerns and hardship to U.S. citizen family members, through amendments to the INA. Immigration courts now routinely interpret and apply those amended provisions of the INA to grant relief in cases where the strict removal provisions would cause unusual hardship.

Second, a trend toward tougher law enforcement in the 1990s and 2000s led to laws increasing the number and types of crimes that could lead to removability, resulting in a finely detailed scheme of "crimmigration" provisions that must be interpreted and applied in removal proceedings.[24] Now that the institutional manipulability of the immigration courts has birthed a political crisis of its own, Congress may be inclined to take the final step in that process of increasing congressional delineation, placing removal proceedings into an independent Article I immigration court system outside the executive branch.

In this context, the argument for democratic accountability through executive control pales. As the constitutional province of another elected branch, the legislature, voters still retain a choice to express their immigration policy preferences at the ballot box. An independent Article I court, while operating independently day to day, is ultimately created by Congress and could be restructured or eliminated by Congress if voters were unsatisfied with it. Moreover, the actual democratic accountability of executive agencies like DOJ has been subject to heated debate since the advent of the regulatory state in the 1930s. Given the common skepticism about the democratic accountability of federal agencies, that value seems no better achieved in DOJ than in an independent Article I court.

Although a change would entail some loss of executive power, not every presidential administration—whether Republican and Democratic—is likely to resist congressional efforts to establish immigration courts independent of the executive branch. A Democratic president would likely respond to public outcry about due process concerns, as evidenced by the self-referral cases of the Obama administration described in chapter 1. In those cases, Attorney General Eric Holder reversed some of the self-referral decisions of the second Bush administration and committed the political questions raised in those cases to the APA rulemaking process. But even some Republican presidents might not strongly resist a congressional move to create Article I immigration courts. Control over most immigration enforcement is committed to DHS, with only one facet—removal proceedings—in DOJ. Some Republican administrations might be unwilling to expend political capital on aggressive intervention in the immigration courts and prefer instead to concede congressional control there and focus resources instead on DHS enforcement efforts.

COSTS AND APPROPRIATIONS

Instinctively, one might think that having the immigration courts located in the Department of Justice would be much cheaper for the government. In reality, though, the cost savings are minimal, because DOJ isn't really in the adjudication business. Apart from the immigration courts, the only other adjudications conducted by DOJ relate to employment violations and fraud provisions of the INA and are conducted by administrative law judges in the Office of the Chief Administrative Hearing Officer against primarily U.S. individuals and businesses. The immigration courts are a separate operation and could be relocated to an independent court system. Aside from one-time costs to make the transition, the biggest change would be to the immigration courts' constitutional authority, not to the physical cost of maintaining them.

The federal process for funding an independent immigration court system is a somewhat trickier issue. Concerns about appropriations have steered some observers toward keeping the immigration courts in DOJ in the past. At heart, the concern is political, not fiscal—the worry is not that the independent courts would cost more to operate but that Congress would fail to adequately fund them if their funding were not tied to DOJ appropriations. As attorney general intervention into immigration courts' decision-making has increased, however, concerns about appropriations may be decreasing in relative importance among many in Congress and in EOIR.

If an Article I court were established, at least two avenues for appropriations would have to be weighed. First, the immigration courts might be funded as part of the appropriations request for the judiciary prepared and submitted annually by the Administrative Office of the U.S. Courts, along with the usual request for funding for other Article I courts such as the Court of Federal Claims and the Court of International Trade.[25] This would have the advantage of insulating the new courts' appropriations from executive control, since the president is required to submit the judiciary budget to Congress without changes.[26] Alternatively, a new Article I immigration court system might be funded like the Tax Courts, which are still included in appropriations for the Department of the Treasury. That model probably evolved as a result of the Tax Court's history as part of Treasury and later an independent executive agency (a history that in some ways foreshadows a move of the immigration courts from the Commissioner of Labor's Board of Review to EOIR to independent Article I status).[27] Funding a new Article I immigration court system as part of DOJ appropriations might decrease worries about appropriations neglect but would not sever the political control of the president and the attorney general, who could manipulate the new Article I court through their appropriations request for the Department of Justice.

EROSION OF CHECKS AND BALANCES

In *The Federalist* No. 51, Madison argued that the cure for self-dealing by one branch of government was to grant powers of resistance to the other branches; in this way would "ambition . . . be made to counteract ambition."[28] Madison could thus justify the mechanisms in which the Constitution tolerated self-dealing by judges, legislators, and executive officials as long as the powers of each were balanced and the balance was carefully preserved. Unfortunately, this principle does not save the immigration courts. Rather than building in powers by the other branches to minimize the potential for institutional bias by immigration judges working for the attorney general, the immigration courts were expressly designed at a time of national security crisis to limit the checks and balances contemplated by Madison.

The primary check on immigration court decisions in DOJ is the right of appeal to the U.S. Court of Appeals. While the federal appellate courts can and sometimes do reverse decisions of the BIA (or the attorney general under the referral power), the immigration laws limit the types of decisions that the courts of appeals may review and the grounds on which cases may be reversed. First, the only appeal that may be taken from orders of removal is directly to the U.S. Court of Appeals; Congress in 2005 eliminated the right to federal habeas corpus from a district court for relief from removal.[29] The district courts also lack jurisdiction to consider claims challenging DHS regulations under the APA to the extent that those claims have the effect of challenging orders of removal.[30] And the scope of federal court review is narrower when challenging the decision of an immigration judge than when challenging a decision made by an agency whose procedures are subject to the APA.[31]

In addition to these limits on judicial checks on the immigration courts, the near elimination of private bills has limited congressional checks. While the move toward more detailed laws in lieu of private bills has the virtue of ending the inefficient and ad hoc private bill system, it also leaves the implementation of the system to the executive branch with little review by Congress of unfair or particularly harsh outcomes. For review of visa and other immigration applications, USCIS has an ombudsman who is required by statute to make an annual report to Congress on the operations of USCIS for the previous year, but no such apparatus exists to oversee the immigration courts within DOJ.[32] While Congress can and occasionally does amend the immigration laws, it generally takes a hands-off approach to their administration.

This agglomeration of the removal power in the executive branch was in fact an intentional part of Roosevelt's plan when he moved immigration services into DOJ. In a memorandum to the president recommending the transfer, Under Secretary of State Sumner Welles reasoned that "[t]here are various aspects of naturalization and of immigration problems, such as deportation, in which the collaboration and cooperation of the courts are essential" and thus "administrative practice would be simplified" by moving immigration to DOJ.[33] Although lawyers for DOJ do frequently appear before the federal courts and are familiar with court procedures, the Constitution prohibits "collaboration and cooperation" between the executive and the judiciary in removal cases (or any other cases or controversies brought by the United States in those courts). Precisely the opposite is contemplated by the separation of powers.

The point was stated even more baldly (and inaccurately) in an unsigned memorandum regarding antisabotage efforts that appeared in the files of Attorney General Robert H. Jackson, dated the same day Roosevelt initiated the transfer. After recommending that the immigration services be moved to DOJ, the author of the memo identified the FBI as "[p]rimary among the agencies of control and investigation" to counter sabotage. "In [DOJ], also," the author continued, "are the federal courts and the machinery for the prosecution of offenders." The author recommended that "these three agencies of the Department of Justice" plus the immigration services should be used to control sabotage attempts. Even more than Welles, the author misapprehended the separation of powers in federal law, actually perceiving the federal courts to be an "agency" of DOJ along with the FBI and the U.S. Attorney's Offices. While the author was clearly mistaken about the facts, the opinion expressed was the same as that urged upon Roosevelt by the more legally sophisticated Welles. When even executive officials assumed an identity of interest between the immigration services and the federal courts in ordering removal of noncitizens, at least the appearance, and perhaps the fact, of immigration court impartiality is fatally compromised.[34]

Representative McCollum, in his statement to the Senate in 2002, emphasized the need for immigration courts that are perceived to be, and truly are, impartial and distinct from federal law enforcement. "The hallmark of our freedoms is the system of checks and balances that our Founding Fathers gave us by creating the three branches of government," McCollum stated. "It is the lack of such an independent judiciary in so much of the rest of the world that impedes the development and growth of democracies, and it is our judiciary that distinguishes our free nation more than any other thing from all other countries of the world." McCollum concluded that "in the area of immigration we have failed to carry forth this basic hallmark of our system."[35]

The principle that "no man shall be made a judge in his own cause" is fundamental to the notion of a fair trial. Although *nemo iudex* may be subject to trade-offs where necessary to achieve other important goals, there is no reason to simply jettison the principle without reason. History and contemporary practice suggest no rational basis for compromising the independence of the immigration courts by placing them under the control of the nation's law enforcement agency. As a matter of institutional design, the structure is irrational.

13 Reforming the Immigration Courts

For the first time in two decades, immigration court reform has become a subject of national political debate. Most Democratic candidates for the 2020 presidential election addressed the issue, some even making it a key plank in their immigration platforms. The first and most vocal was Julián Castro, former Department of Housing and Urban Development secretary and mayor of San Antonio. Castro promised independent immigration courts created under Article I, followed by increased hiring of independent judges to reduce backlog and an end to case completion quotas for immigration judges.[1] At a speech to the American Immigration Lawyers Association in June 2019, Castro's pledge to seek independent Article I immigration courts received a standing ovation.

Castro dropped out of the presidential race at the beginning of 2020, but other candidates also included the issue in their campaign platforms. Elizabeth Warren included a lengthy statement about immigration court independence on her campaign website, and her platform expressly criticized the location of the immigration courts within DOJ and the power of the attorney general to overturn immigration court decisions. In addition to the creation of an Article I immigration court system,

Warren pledged "smart efficiency measures" such as greater docket management authority for immigration judges and recruitment of "highly qualified immigration judges with a diverse set of legal experiences," an apparent indictment of the recent practice of hiring immigration judges with law enforcement backgrounds and promoting those with the highest asylum denial rates without the customary yearlong probationary period.[2]

Bernie Sanders also pledged to reform the immigration courts. His campaign website included pledges to "[r]estore case by case discretion for immigration judges" and to "[e]stablish immigration courts as independent Article I courts, free from influence and interference." He promised to more than double funding for the immigration courts to fully staff the courts and eliminate backlog.[3] Sanders told the American Immigration Lawyers' Association in a survey that he was "open to creating an independent Article I immigration court system but believes that much more must be done to reform our broken immigration court system." He mentioned increasing funding, hiring more judges, ending case quotas, and restoring judges' discretion. Sanders also pledged to "guarantee immigrants a right to counsel"—perhaps a promise to provide representation at government expense (akin to the public defender system), since a right to counsel in immigration proceedings was already recognized by the U.S. Supreme Court but is often unavailable due to lack of resources.[4] Cory Booker and Pete Buttigieg also pledged to support Article I immigration courts.

Of the top Democratic candidates, only Joe Biden took no position on independent immigration courts. Instead, Biden focused on providing more resources to the existing system and doubling the number of immigration judges, court staff, and interpreters.[5]

While support in the White House could move the issue forward politically, the president has no direct power to materially change the immigration court structure. Presidential powers might be sufficient to reform or limit the attorney general's self-referral power, and could certainly curtail the attorney general's use of that authority or of performance metrics for immigration judges. Such changes would be temporary, however, and subject to change by subsequent administrations.

MODELS FOR REFORM

The only way to ensure independence for immigration court judges' decisions is to make the immigration courts independent of the attorney general (or any other law enforcement officer). Because the immigration courts were statutorily recognized and embedded in DOJ by the Homeland Security Act, only an act of Congress could reform the immigration courts into a new, more independent institution. Over the years, a few basic models have been proposed:

1. The narrowest change would be the type proposed in the Lieberman substitute to the HSA: leaving the immigration courts within the Department of Justice, but with a new name and some structural independence from the political process. The Lieberman bill, for example, would have eliminated EOIR and created a new "Agency for Immigration Hearings and Appeals" in DOJ. Checks and balances would have been introduced by providing for a director appointed by the president but subject to the advice and consent of the Senate. Decision-making independence from the attorney general would have been assured in two ways: First, the language provided that all immigration judges and BIA members "shall exercise their independent judgment and discretion" in cases before them. Second, by providing that BIA decisions would "constitute final agency action, subject to review only as provided by the Immigration and Nationality Act and other applicable law," the amendment may have been intended to eliminate the review power of the attorney general, which exists only by regulation, not by statute.

2. A second option would also leave the immigration courts within the executive branch, but as an independent agency outside DOJ or any other Cabinet department. This type of agency—akin to the Environmental Protection Agency—was proposed by the U.S. Commission on Immigration Reform in 1997 and was recommended by the National Association of Immigration Judges in 2002. The 1997 Commission recommended moving review out of DOJ more for efficiency than fairness. The Commission sought to consolidate the review of all types of immigration decisions— including those now made by DHS, State, and Labor as well as EOIR—

and worried about the "inherent difficulty" of having a body within one agency, the Department of Justice, review the decisions of other agencies. These difficulties might include communication inefficiencies or lack of respect for and enforcement of decisions. The Commission preferred an independent executive agency to an Article I court in order to achieve "flexibility and coordination of function, including the review function, by the various agencies in the Executive Branch." The Commission recommended a similar structure to that proposed in the Lieberman substitute (though it did not suggest Senate confirmation of the director). The Commission expressly recommended elimination of any review of BIA decisions by any agency head or other executive branch officer; those decisions would be reviewable only by the federal courts or through congressional action.[6] The immigration judges' union recommended the Commission's approach to the Senate Subcommittee on Immigration in 2002 as a more "feasible" solution than an Article I court (which it also supported).[7]

3. The third approach, a new Article I immigration court, offers the most significant break from the current EOIR model. The immigration judges' union stated in 2002 that "the major distinction between [agency] tribunals and Article I courts is the greater degree of judicial independence which is provided by the latter, due to the insulation of decisionmakers from the agency whose rulings it impacts." The Federal Bar Association, with support from the American Bar Association (ABA), the American Immigration Lawyers Association (AILA), and the National Association of Immigration Judges (NAIJ), has posted model legislation for Article I immigration courts. That model envisions a court structure headed by a twenty-one-member appellate body and a chief judge, each judge serving a five-year term. Appellate judges would earn the same salary as federal district court judges, and trial judges would earn the salary of federal bankruptcy and magistrate judges. All judges could be removed only for cause. Judges of the appellate division would be appointed by the president with the advice and consent of the Senate, and judges of the trial division would be appointed by the appellate division in a merit-selection process. Similar to current practice under EOIR, trial divisions would be located around the country and the appellate body would sit in

Washington, DC. Final decisions of the appellate division would be subject to review in the U.S. Court of Appeals for the region in which the trial division proceedings occurred.[8]

Although proposals for an Article I immigration court have percolated for decades, experts in previous generations often rated an Article I court as roughly equivalent to an independent executive agency, sometimes preferring the latter based on concerns about executive policymaking flexibility or simple political feasibility. Since the dramatic increase in attorney general administrative control over decisions in the immigration courts, however, most experts have insisted that an Article I court independent of the executive branch is the only effective solution. On January 29, 2020, the House Judiciary Committee's Subcommittee on Immigration and Citizenship held hearings on due process and judicial independence in the immigration courts. The Subcommittee heard testimony from representatives of NAIJ, AILA, and the ABA, all of whom supported the creation of independent Article I immigration courts. A witness from the conservative Center for Immigration Studies defended the existing system.[9]

REFORM BILLS IN CONGRESS

Alternatives to a fully independent immigration court system have been pending in the Senate since at least 2018. The bills, all cosponsored by Democrats, offered fairly modest adjustments to the current system, such as measures to increase immigration judge independence under the supervision of the attorney general. Based on campaign statements, these measures appear to represent compromise positions for cosponsors such as Senators Sanders, Warren, and Booker, but may represent the policy preference of other cosponsors who sought the Democratic presidential nomination, including Amy Klobuchar, Kamala Harris, and Michael Bennett.

For example, Harris and Kirsten Gillibrand in 2018 cosponsored a bill called the Immigration Court Improvement Act (S. 2693). That proposal would have provided several protections for the independent decision-making of immigration judges without otherwise restructuring the relationship between DOJ and EOIR. The bill would have mandated hiring immigration judges with legal experience outside of government service; prohibited the discipline of any immigration judge for any good faith legal decision made in deciding cases; allowed the use of completion goals and efficiency metrics only as management tools and for resource allocation requests, not to evaluate individual judicial performance; and made immigration judges subject to the Code of Judicial Conduct, not any code of attorney conduct. The bill was introduced by Mazie Hirono of Hawaii.[10] The bill was reintroduced in 2019, this time cosponsored by Booker, Sanders, and Klobuchar as well as Harris, Gillibrand, and others.[11]

Another Senate bill, the "Stop Cruelty to Migrant Children Act," S. 2113, though not styled as immigration court reform, would arguably have snuck in more important safeguards for immigration court independence than S. 2693. The bill focused primarily on improving the asylum process at the border. Perhaps the most important change to the immigration courts would be to statutorily return the power to immigration judges to administratively close cases where the noncitizen appears to have a meritorious claim for a visa or other immigration benefit and has an application pending before a federal agency. Such a provision would largely abrogate the attorney general's decision in *Matter of Castro Tum*. Moreover, S. 2113 would prohibit the attorney general from using appropriations to implement performance metrics "or other standards that could negatively impact the fair administration of justice by the immigration courts." The bill also would require the hiring of seventy-five new judges and prohibit giving preference to candidates with government experience. The bill was cosponsored by most of the Democratic presidential candidates in the Senate, including Sanders, Warren, Booker, Klobuchar, Harris, Bennet, and Gillibrand.[12]

Another, more modest adjustment was included in the proposed Central America Reform and Enforcement Act (S. 1445), introduced in May 2019. That bill focused primarily on changing U.S. strategy for advancing reforms in Central America that drive migration and for combatting drug trafficking, but also included a few provisions to shore up the existing immigration court system. The bill, introduced by Charles Schumer, was also cosponsored by most of the Democratic presidential candidates. The court reform provisions aimed primarily at reducing delays by adding at least seventy-five immigration judges in fiscal years 2019 through 2022, increasing the number of BIA staff attorneys by twenty-three from 2019 to 2021, and requiring EOIR to implement modernized case management and electronic filing systems. The bill included a small nod toward impartiality in the immigration courts by prohibiting the attorney general, in hiring new immigration judges, to give preference to candidates with prior government service over those with immigration law expertise from nonprofits, private law practice, or academia.[13]

Ultimately, however, none of these Senate bills would redress the fundamental fault line in the immigration court system: the control of the nation's law enforcement agency over cases brought by that nation against individuals. Past generations of lawyers, scholars, and policymakers viewed this structure as incongruous but mostly innocuous. Because past attorneys general had not usually interfered with immigration judges' decision-making, most assumed that future ones wouldn't either. Now that the manipulability of the immigration courts has been illustrated, future administrations are likely to do the same to achieve whatever political or policy goals the president may hold.

A model like the one contemplated by the U.S. Commission on Immigration in 1997—an independent executive agency—would remove the immigration courts from the supervision of the attorney general, but would still leave them in the executive branch, answerable to the president and subject to the shifting winds of politics. Only an Article I immigration court would fully divorce the immigration courts from law enforcement and shifting executive policies. Congress now has an obligation to correct the current, flawed structure.

Epilogue

PORTRAIT OF AN AMERICAN IN
THE TWENTY-FIRST CENTURY

George W. Bush was shocked to find himself with nothing to do. It's a feeling many people experience after retirement, but the dislocation was extreme after the peripatetic office of the modern presidency. By 2010, he had published his memoirs, in tandem with a groundbreaking ceremony for the new George W. Bush Presidential Center and interviews with Oprah Winfrey, Matt Lauer, and Candy Crowley—carefully scheduled for the week *after* midterm elections. His public approval rating was recovering, but still shaky. A Gallup poll that July had found that 45 percent of Americans viewed the former president favorably, up from 34 percent when he left office but still lower than either President Barack Obama or former President Bill Clinton. After two more years of retirement, the former president decided to take up a new hobby. During the long days at his Dallas home and Midland ranch, the self-described "art-agnostic," then sixty-six years old, began to paint.[1]

At first this was a purely private affair and might have stayed that way but for a Romanian hacker named Marcel Lazar Lehel. The hacker, better known as "Guccifer," obtained images of several of Bush's paintings from the email account of Bush's sister, Dorothy Bush Koch. The three Bush paintings disclosed by the hacker in 2013 show the tentative, realistic style of a novice painter, but the subjects and perspectives reveal an inner life that some critics were astonished to acknowledge the former president possessed.[2] Two of the three paintings show Bush alone, bathing. In one, the subject is observed, but at several layers of remove—through the glass of a shower door, to the right of center with his back to us, catching our gaze (or is he avoiding it?) in a small, round shaving mirror in the upper center of the scene. The figure is clearly Bush—the slightly round-shouldered posture of the nude back, even more than the indistinct features in the mirror, delivers a start of recognition to the viewer who lived through a million images of those shoulders clothed in suits, pressed shirts, and trench coats.

The other bathing image brings us much closer, sharing the viewpoint of the subject himself. We see the subject's knees and gently bowed legs as he himself does in the bathtub, toes peeking above the surface of the water, which still pours from the tap of a deep, rectangular tub. Because we know the artist (or thought we did), these two bathing images can't help but evoke Lady Macbeth. "Private baptism; trying to get clean; infantile ecstasies; purification rituals?" wondered art critic Jerry Saltz, admiringly. In both paintings, Saltz noted, the light is soft, "[a]s if the unreal has become a companion to the painter." In both, he is alone, yet still inspected. Bush disclaims any symbolism with his characteristic aw-shucks Texas nonchalanace. He did the bathing paintings, he said, to shock his painting instructor.[3]

But George W. Bush is not just a character defined by our collective national consciousness. He's also a man, an aging and perhaps deepening one with a real facility for painting. Once outed as a painter, Bush increasingly embraced the venture, releasing first a series of portraits of world leaders that generated little new interest, artistic or political—and then, in 2017, a series of portraits of war veterans that decidedly did.[4] If the bathing paintings were "'simple' and 'awkward,' but in wonderful, unself-conscious, intense ways," as Saltz thought, these new portraits of veterans showed a growing artist experimenting with expressionistic color, depth, and texture clearly inspired by his art tutor, Texas portraitist Sedgwick Huckaby.

Response to the book, *Portraits of Courage: A Commander in Chief's Tribute to America's Warriors,* was mixed—not so much in its assessment of the art, which most reviewers found adept and evocative, but for what we should make of it. Peter Schjeldahl of *The New Yorker* found the book "surprisingly likable while starkly disturbing." Though acknowledging that the level of the art was "astonishingly high" for a novice painter, Schjeldahl could not divorce the images from his opinions about the artist. He calls the book not self-congratulatory but self-comforting, an "exercise of Bush's never-doubted sincerity and humility—virtues that were maddeningly futile when he governed, and that now shine brighter, in contrast with Trump, than may be merited." Though the paintings made him uncomfortable enough to reassess in a column, Schjeldahl ultimately remained unforgiving of the former president, both his record and his character. "Having obliviously made murderous errors, Bush now obliviously atones for them. What do you do with someone like that?"[5]

Other reviewers were more sanguine. JJ Charlesworth, senior editor of the London-based publication *Art Review*, acknowledged important questions evoked by Bush's work—as an artist, not just as a president—when an exhibit of the paintings opened at the Kennedy Center in October 2019. "What is the difference between a war memorial and a tribute to warriors? Should we celebrate the lives of courageous people if it risks glorifying futile wars? And what, in the midst of all this, can paintings contribute?" Charlesworth does not gloss over Bush's responsibility for the suffering produced by those wars, noting the seven thousand U.S. troops killed and fifty thousand injured as of 2018, but he rejects Schjeldahl's take on Bush's work as an attempt at "atonement." Charlesworth is more interested in the "everyday-ness" of both the painter's style and his subjects, which lack the traditional emblems of the glorified war veteran—uniforms, arms, insignia. The subjects are "unexceptional, unglamorous" in their depiction, Charlesworth writes; it is "their decency and seriousness" that invites our empathy. They are like us. To Charlesworth, this choice by the artist poses a deeper question than whether a mistaken commander-in-chief deserves to be forgiven. Instead, he sees in the paintings "a yearning for a return to innocence." He notes the growing discomfort in Western democracies to assert the justifications for wars fought in our name and the simultaneous urge to recognize and honor those who fought and suffered in those wars. "Bush's paintings are not memorials to the glorious dead, of course, but celebrations of the living. Yet the question hanging over these portraits is whether a return to normality is ever possible."[6]

If George W. Bush is asking any questions by painting war veterans, he is asking himself, not us. Looking back at the key decisions of his presidency, Bush wrote in his memoirs, "I believe I got some of those decisions right, and I got some wrong. But on every one, I did what I believed was in the best interests of our country."[7] In 2013, he told CNN that he doesn't wait for the verdict of history, because "it's going to take a while for the objective historians to show up. And so I'm pretty comfortable with it. I did what I did. I know the spirit in which I did it."[8]

To a man lying awake in fear of failing to protect those for whom he is responsible, few defensive tactics seem to carry too great a cost. Under those circumstances, the lack of truly independent immigration courts scarcely registered with the Bush administration and most lawmakers in crafting the new Department of Homeland Security. In hindsight, however, some fears may prove illusory—and the cost of protecting against those illusory fears great. The unintended victims of the country's post-9/11 reaction include not only members of the armed forces who have been injured abroad, but also noncitizens in the United States who are injured before immigration courts that fail to offer a tribunal that is separate and distinct from the law enforcement power of the sovereign.

Roosevelt, too, was not immune from such miscalculations. While the fascist threat the country faced in 1940 was extreme, the diabolical Goebbels insinuation that the menace might lurk in every German-American dance hall caused Roosevelt to overcorrect, placing the immigration services hand in hand with J. Edgar Hoover's overweening FBI in the Department of Justice. That decision, unexamined for most of the past eighty years and overtaken by fear of an unseeable foe in 2002, has resulted in an irrationally constructed immigration court system that has been deployed to implement a particular executive policy on immigration enforcement at the expense of the American ideal of justice before an impartial tribunal. Now that it has been unleashed, there is no reason to think that this politicization of the immigration courts will end with the Trump administration. Immigration justice will remain vulnerable to political manipulation as long as the immigration courts remain subject to direct executive control.

But the fundamental premise of a democracy is that we, too, are responsible for the decisions of 1940 and 2002, and we must ask our own questions of ourselves. The increased politicization of immigration adjudication may have created a sufficient domestic crisis to generate the momentum for immigration court reform that has not been mustered since the system was put in place eighty years ago. Congress has the power to change the immigration court structure, but Congress will not act without a consensus by the citizens of the United States that impartial immigration courts are essential to the American ideal of "liberty and justice for all."

Notes

PREFACE

1. *Last Week with John Oliver,* "Immigration Courts," episode 66, HBO, April 1, 2018, www.hbo.com/last-week-tonight-with-john-oliver/2018/66-episode-125.

1. THE ATTORNEY GENERAL'S IMMIGRATION COURTS

1. Matt Stevens, "DACA Participants Can Again Apply for Renewal, Immigration Agency Says," *New York Times,* January 14, 2018 (photo by Al Drago), www.nytimes.com/2018/01/14/us/politics/daca-renewals-requests.html.

2. Sheryl Gay Stolberg, "Ocasio-Cortez Calls Migrant Detention Centers 'Concentration Camps,' Eliciting Backlash," *New York Times,* June 18, 2019, www.nytimes.com/2019/06/18/us/politics/ocasio-cortez-cheney-detention-centers.html.

3. David S. Wyman, *The Abandonment of the Jews: America and the Holocaust, 1941–1945* (New York: Pantheon, 1984); Daniel A. Gross, "The U.S. Government Turned Away Thousands of Jewish Refugees, Fearing That They Were Nazi Spies," *Smithsonian,* November 18, 2015, www.smithsonianmag.com/history/us-government-turned-away-thousands-jewish-refugees-fearing-they-were-nazi-spies-180957324/.

4. "President Donald J. Trump Is Working to Stop the Abuse of Our Asylum System and Address the Root Causes of the Border Crisis," White House, posted April 29, 2019, www.whitehouse.gov/briefings-statements/president-donald-j-trump-working-stop-abuse-asylum-system-address-root-causes-border-crisis/.

5. United States v. Wang, No. 1:12-CR-00941 RPP (S.D.N.Y. Dec. 19, 2013); United States v. Reyes, No. 8:20-CR-111-T-33AAS (M.D. Fla. March 5, 2020); Ailsa Chang, "Thousands Could Be Deported as Government Targets Asylum Mills' Clients," *NPR Planet Money*, September 28, 2018, www.npr.org/sections /money/2018/09/28/652218318/thousands-could-be-deported-as-government-targets-asylum-mills-clients.

6. Ingrid Eagly and Steven Shafer, "Access to Counsel in Immigration Court," American Immigration Council, September 28, 2016, www.americanimmigration council.org/research/access-counsel-immigration-court.

7. Illegal Immigration Reform and Immigrant Responsibility Act of 1996, § 371(c)(2), 101 Stat. 3009 (1996).

8. "About DOJ," United States Department of Justice, www.justice.gov/about.

9. National Commission on Law Observance and Enforcement, *Report on the Enforcement of the Deportation Laws of the United States* (Washington, DC: United States Government Printing Office, 1931), 149–61 (Wickersham Commission Report).

10. *Becoming an American: Immigration & Immigrant Policy* (Washington: U.S. Commission on Immigration Reform, 1997), 147–81, www.hsdl .org/?abstract&did = 437705; Arnold & Porter LLP, *Reforming the Immigration System: Proposals to Promote Independence, Fairness, Efficiency, and Professionalism in the Adjudication of Removal Cases* (Washington: American Bar Association, 2010), www.americanbar.org/content/dam/aba/publications /commission_on_immigration/coi_complete_full_report.authcheckdam.pdf.

11. 8 C.F.R. § 1003.1.

12. In the Matter of B-, 6 I. & N. Dec. 713 (BIA 1955, A.G. 1955) (reversing BIA's grant of termination of deportation for respondent to file application for naturalization and ordering suspension of deportation for Congress to review deportation order in light of mitigating factors); In re: Matter of S- and B-C-, 9 I. & N. Dec. 436 (BIA 1960, A.G. 1961) (resolving conflicting opinions from BIA regarding whether misrepresentation in obtaining immigration documents necessarily renders applicant inadmissible).

13. *See* In re Y-L-, A-G-, and R-S-R-, 23 I. & N. Dec. 270 (A.G. 2002) (withholding of removal unavailable after conviction of "particularly serious crime" of felony drug trafficking despite mitigating factors); In re Jean, 23 I. & N. Dec. 373 (A.G. 2002) (seriousness of crime must be weighed against interests of family unity in considering discretionary relief after conviction of "crime involving moral turpitude" of secondary manslaughter in infant death); In re J-F-F-, 23 I. & N. Dec. 912 (A.G. 2006) (requiring factual showing, not suppositions, that tor-

ture is more likely than not to occur for granting relief under Convention against Torture after conviction for rape). In one other case from this period, the power was used to correct an obvious analytical error by the BIA that would have had the effect of routinely denying humanitarian relief to victims of female genital mutilation. Matter of A-T-, 24 I. & N. Dec. 617 (A.G. 2008).

14. Matter of J-S-, 24 I. & N. Dec. 520 (A.G. 2008) (spouse of person subject to forced abortion or sterilization not per se eligible for refugee status); Matter of Silva-Trevino, 24 I. & N. Dec. 687 (A.G. 2008) (defining test for determining crime involving moral turpitude); Matter of Compean, Bangaly, and J-E-C-, 24 I. & N. Dec. 710 (A.G. 2009) (no right to effective assistance of counsel in removal proceedings).

15. In re R-A-, 23 I. & N. Dec. 694 (A.G. 2005); Matter of S-K-, 24 I. & N. Dec. 289 (A.G. 2007); Matter of R-A-, 24 I. & N. Dec. 629 (A.G. 2008).

16. Matter of Compean, Bangaly, and J-E-C-, 25 I. & N. Dec. 1, 2 (A.G. 2009).

17. Matter of Dorman, 25 I. & N. Dec. 485 (A.G. 2011) (reflecting decision not to defend Defense of Marriage Act before it was declared unconstitutional by Supreme Court); Matter of Chairez-Castrejon and Sama, 26 I. & N. Dec. 796 (A.G. 2016) (proposing to interpret recent Supreme Court decision for determining "crime[s] involving moral turpitude" before Supreme Court itself clarified in subsequent case); Matter of Silva-Trevino, 26 I. & N. Dec. 550 (A.G. 2015) (vacating Attorney General Mukasey's decision regarding test for crimes involving moral turpitude in light of conflicting court cases).

18. Matter of A-B-, 27 I. & N. Dec. 316 (A.G. 2018).

19. Matter of L-E-A-, 27 I. & N. Dec. 581, 588–89 (A.G. 2019).

20. Jeffrey S. Chase, "Matter of L-E-A: How Much Did Barr Change?," Lexis-Nexis Legal NewsRoom, August 11, 2019, www.lexisnexis.com/legalnewsroom /immigration/b/insidenews/posts/matter-of-l-e-a—how-much-did-barr-change ———jeffrey-s-chase.

21. Matter of A-B-, 27 I. & N. Dec. 316 (overruling Matter of A-R-C-G-, 26 I. & N. Dec. 338 [BIA 2014]); Matter of Castro-Tum, 27 I. & N. Dec. 271 (A.G. 2018) (overruling Matter of Avetisyan, 25 I. & N. Dec. 688 [BIA 2012] and Matter of W-Y-U-, 27 I. & N. Dec. 17 [2017]); Matter of L-A-B-R-, 27 I. & N. Dec. 405 (A.G. 2018) (announcing stricter standard for granting continuances than test developed by the BIA since Matter of Hashmi, 24 I. & N. 405 [BIA 2009]).

22. Matter of A-B-, 27 I & N Dec. 247, 247 (A.G. interim decision March 30, 2018) (quoting DHS's Motion on Certification to the Attorney General).

2. WHITTLING AWAY AT ASYLUM LAW

1. Matter of A-B-, 27 I. & N. Dec. 227, 227 (A.G. 2018) (referring decision).

2. Matter of A-B-, 27 I. & N. Dec. 316, 320 (A.G. 2018).

3. United Nations Protocol Relating to the Status of Refugees, Jan. 31, 1967, 19 U.S.T. 6223, 606 U.N.T.S. 267.

4. Section 606 U.N.T.S. 267, art. VII (incorporating United Nations Convention Relating to the Status of Refugees, art. 33, July 28, 1951, 189 U.N.T.S. 137, Art. 33, July 28, 1951).

5. Vijay Padmanabhan, "To Transfer or Not to Transfer: Identifying and Protecting Relevant Human Rights Interests in Non-Refoulement," *Fordham Law Review* 80, no. 1 (October 2011): 81–88.

6. Refugee Act of 1980, Pub. L. 96–212, 94 Stat. 102.

7. 8 U.S.C. § 1101(a)(42)(A).

8. 8 U.S.C. § 1158.

9. 8 U.S.C. §§ 1158(a)(1), 1158(b)(1)(B), & 1158 (a)(2).

10. 8 U.S.C. § 1158 (b)(2).

11. Board of Immigration Appeals, Affirmance without Opinion, Referral for Panel Review, and Publication of Decisions as Precedents, 84 Fed. Reg. 31,463 (Jul. 2, 2019) (codified at 8 C.F.R. Parts 1003 and 1292).

12. Asylum Eligibility and Procedural Modifications, 84 Fed. Reg. 33,829 (interim final rule July 16, 2019) (codified at 8 C.F.R. Parts 1003 and 1208).

13. Marbury v. Madison, 5 U.S. 137, 177 (1803).

14. Chevron v. Natural Resources Defense Council, 467 U.S. 837, 844 (1984).

15. Matter of A-R-C-G-, 26 I. & N. Dec. 338 (BIA 2014); *Matter of A-B-*, 27 I. & N. Dec. at 319.

16. *Matter of A-B-*, 27 I. & N. Dec. at 321.

17. *Matter of A-R-C-G-*, 26 I. & N. Dec. at 389.

18. *Matter of A-B-*, 27 I. & N. Dec. at 346 (quoting Velasquez v. Sessions, 866 F.3d 188, 199 [4th Cir. 2017] [Wilkinson, J., concurring]).

19. 8 U.S.C. § 1101(a)(42)(A).

20. *Matter of A-B-*, 27 I. & N. Dec. at 318.

21. Matter of Acosta, 19 I. & N. Dec. 211, 222 (BIA 1985).

22. Pan v. Holder, 777 F.3d 540, 545 (2nd Cir. 2015); Lopez v. U.S. Attorney General, 504 F.3d 1341, 1345 (11th Cir. 2007); de la Llana-Castellon v. INS, 16 F.3d 1093, 1097 (10th Cir. 1994).

23. *Matter of A-B-*, 27 I. & N. Dec. at 320.

24. *Matter of A-B-*, 27 I. & N. Dec. at 322 (quoting Velasquez, 866 F.3d at 194 [quoting Sanchez v. Attorney General, 392 F.3d 434, 438 (11th Cir. 2004)]).

25. *Velasquez*, 866 F.3d at 191–92.

26. *Matter of A-R-C-G-*, 26 I. & N. Dec. at 389.

27. *Matter of A-R-C-G-*, 26 I. & N. Dec. at 389.

28. *Matter of A-B-*, 27 I. & N. Dec. at 321.

29. 8 U.S.C. § 1158(b)(1)(B)(i).

30. Matter of M-E-V-G-, 26 I. & N. Dec. 227 (BIA 2014).

31. *Matter of A-B-*, 27 I. & N. Dec. at 320.

32. "Guidance for Processing Reasonable Fear, Credible Fear, Asylum, and Refugee Claims in Accordance with *Matter of A-B-*," United States Citizenship and Information Service, July 11, 2018, www.uscis.gov/sites/default/files /USCIS/Laws/Memoranda/2018/2018–06–18-PM-602–0162-USCIS-Memorandum-Matter-of-A-B.pdf. As of June 18, 2020, the language had been redacted from the USCIS memorandum in compliance with an order of the court in Grace v. Whitaker, No. 1:18-cv-01853 (EGS).

33. Memorandum from Tracy Short to All OPLA Attorneys, Litigating Domestic Violence-Based Persecution Claims Following *Matter of A-B-*, July 11, 2018, www.documentcloud.org/documents/4597904-OPLA-Memo-on-Matter-of-A-B.html.

34. Jeffrey S. Chase, "Matter of A-B- Being Misapplied by EOIR, DHS," *Opinions/Analysis on Immigration Law* (blog), July 13, 2018, www.jeffreyschase .com/blog/2018/7/13/matter-of-a-b-being-misapplied-by-eoir-dhs.

35. Redacted decision of Immigration Judge Nadkarni, Arlington Immigration Court, http://immigrationcourtside.com/wp-content/uploads/2019/01 /Nadkarni-Grant-Women-in-Honduras-PSG.pdf; redacted decision of Immigration Judge Hayward, San Francisco Immigration Court, http:// immigrationcourtside.com/wp-content/uploads/2019/01/SF-IJ-Hayward-DV-PSG-grant.pdf.

36. Grace v. Whitaker, 344 F. Supp. 3d 96 (D.D.C. 2018).

37. 344 F. Supp. 3d at 111.

38. 344 F. Supp. 3d at 126.

39. Brief for the Appellants, Grace v. Barr, No. 19–5013, No. 19–5013 (D.C. Cir. June 3, 2019), 55–56.

40. Grace v. Barr, 965 F.3d 883, 897–909 (D.C. Cir. 2020).

41. *Grace*, 965 F.3d at 908; Procedures for Asylum and Withholding of Removal; Credible Fear and Reasonable Fear Review, 85 Fed. Reg. 36,264, 36,292, 36,300, 36,281 (June 15, 2020).

42. Matter of L-E-A, 27 I. & N. Dec. 581 (A.G. 2019).

43. Matter of L-E-A-, 27 I. & N. Dec. 40 (BIA 2017).

44. Matter of L-E-A-, 27 I. & N. Dec. 494, 494 (A.G. 2018) (referring decision).

45. Chase, "Matter of L-E-A."

46. *Practice Pointer:* Matter of L-E-A- (Silver Spring: Catholic Legal Immigration Network, 2019), 6, https://cliniclegal.org/resources/asylum-and-refugee-law/practice-pointer-matter-l-e.

47. Aldana-Ramos v. Holder, 757 F.3d 9, 15 (1st Cir. 2014).

48. Matter of L-E-A-, 27 I. & N. Dec. at 586.

49. 27 I. & N. Dec. at 595.

50. Chase, "Matter of L-E-A-."

51. 27 I. & N. Dec. at 593.

52. *Practice Pointer*, 4–5.

3. POLICING THE IMMIGRATION COURTS

1. Matter of Castro Tum, 27 I. & N. Dec. 271, 278–29 (A.G. 2018).

2. 6 U.S.C. § 279(b); 8 U.S.C. § 1232(c)(2)(A).

3. "About the Program," Office of Refugee Resettlement, www.acf.hhs.gov /orr/programs/ucs/about; Homeland Security Act of 2002, Pub. L. 107–296, § 462 116 Stat. 2203 (2002).

4. Matter of Castro Tum, 27 I. & N. Dec. at 278.

5. "About the Program," Office of Refugee Resettlement.

6. "Guatemala 2019 Crime & Safety Report," Overseas Security Advisory Council, February 28, 2019, www.osac.gov/Content/Report/5f31517e-62bb-4f2c-8956-15f4aeaab930.

7. *Children on the Run: Unaccompanied Children Leaving Central America and Mexico and the Need for International Protection* (Washington, DC: United Nations High Commission for Refugees, 2014), 15–16, www.unhcr.org /56fc266f4.html.

8. "Attorney General Sessions Gives Remarks to Federal Law Enforcement in Boston about Transnational Criminal Organizations," Department of Justice, September 21, 2017, www.justice.gov/opa/speech/attorney-general-sessions-gives-remarks-federal-law-enforcement-boston-about. Similar statements by Attorney General Sessions were quoted in the press. Joseph Tanfani, "Atty. Gen. Sessions Says Lax Immigration Enforcement Is Enabling Gangs like MS-13," *Baltimore Sun*, April 30, 2017, www.baltimoresun.com/la-na-essential-washington-updates-sessions-says-lax-immigration-1492527375-htmlstory.html.

9. 62 Fed. Reg. 10312, 10332, March 6, 1997, codified at 8 C.F.R. § 3.18(b).

10. Pereira v. Sessions, 138 S. Ct. 2105, 2113–14 (2018).

11. Matter of Bermudez-Cota, 27 I. & N. Dec. 441, 442–44 (BIA 2018).

12. *Matter of Castro Tum*, 27 I. & N. Dec. at 279.

13. 27 I. & N. Dec. at 278–79.

14. *Pereira*, 138 S. Ct. at 2112.

15. 27 I. & N. Dec. at 280.

16. Matthew Archambeault, "The Repercussions of How the Administration Has Handled Matter of Castro-Tum," *Think Immigration* (blog), posted August 14, 2018, https://thinkimmigration.org/blog/2018/08/14/the-repercussions-of-how-the-administration-has-handled-matter-of-castro-tum/.

17. *Matter of Castro Tum*, 27 I. & N. Dec. at 280.

18. *Matter of Castro Tum*, 27 I. & N. Dec. at 274–76; Matter of Avetisyan, 25 I. & N. Dec. 688, 690, 694 (BIA 2012).

19. Lorelei Laird, "Whose Court Is This Anyway? Immigration Judges Accuse Executive Branch of Politicizing Their Courts," *ABAJournal*, April 1, 2019, www.abajournal.com/magazine/article/immigration-judges-executive-politicizing-courts.

20. Matter of Castro Tum (BIA 2017), 2–3, AILA Doc. No. 18010530 (on file with author).

21. Matter of Castro Tum, 27 I. & N. Dec. 187, 187 (A.G. 2018) (referring decision).

22. *Matter of Castro Tum*, 27 I. & N. Dec. at 276–78, 283–90 (A.G. 2018).

23. "The End of Administrative Closure: Sessions Moves to Further Strip Immigration Judges of Independence," Catholic Legal Immigration Network, last updated April 4, 2018, https://cliniclegal.org/resources/end-administrative-closure-sessions-moves-further-strip-immigration-judges-independence.

24. "NIJC Condemns Attorney General's Unilateral Decision to Eliminate Access to 'Administrative Closure' for Immigration Judges and Immigrants," National Immigrant Justice Center, May 17, 2018, www.immigrantjustice.org/press-releases/nijc-condemns-attorney-generals-unilateral-decision-eliminate-access-administrative.

25. "Latest USCIS Data Show RFE and Denial Rates Remained High for Key Employer-Sponsored Nonimmigrant Categories in the First Quarter of FY 2020," January 20, 2020, www.fragomen.com/insights/alerts/latest-uscis-data-show-rfe-and-denial-rates-remained-high-key-employer-sponsored-nonimmigrant-categories-first-quarter-fy-2020; Peggy Gleason, "Escalating Cases with USCIS and DHS: Obstacles and Possible Solutions," Immigrant Legal Resource Center, June 2019, 3, www.ilrc.org/sites/default/files/resources/july_3_revised-cases_with_uscis_and_dhs-june_2019-pg-dg-final.pdf.

26. Matter of Avetisyan, 25 I. & N. Dec. 688 (BIA 2012).

27. Grievance Pursuant to Article 8 of the Collective Bargaining Agreement between EOIR and NAIJ at 2 (complaint of the Hon. Steven A. Morley and National Association of Immigration Judges), 2–3, August 8, 2018, https://assets.documentcloud.org/documents/4639659/NAIJ-Grievance-Morley-2018-Unsigned.pdf [Morley Grievance].

28. Archambeault, "The Repercussions of How the Administration Has Handle Matter of Castro Tum."

29. Morley Grievance at 3.

30. Morley Grievance at 1, 4 (quoting 8 C.F.R. § 1003.9[c]).

31. 8 C.F.R. § 1003.9(b).

32. 72 Fed. Reg. 53,673, 53,674 (Sept. 20, 2007).

33. Archambeault, "The Repercussions of How the Administration Has Handled Matter of Castro Tum."

34. Matter of E-F-H-L-, 27 I. & N. Dec. 226 (A.G. 2018).

35. Jeffrey S. Chase, "The AG's Strange Decision in Matter of E-F-H-L-," *Opinions/Analysis on Immigration Law* (blog), March 10, 2018, www.jeffreyschase .com/blog/2018/3/10/the-ags-strange-decision-in-matter-of-e-f-h-l-.

36. Matter of L-A-B-R-, 27 I. & N. Dec. 405 (A.G. 2018).

37. 27 I. & N. Dec. at 405 (quoting 8 C.F.R. § 1003.29).

38. Rebecca Scholtz, "AG Imposes Limitations on Motions for Continuance," Catholic Legal Immigration Network, August 20, 2018, https://cliniclegal.org /resources/removal-proceedings/ag-imposes-limitations-motions-continuance.

39. "Retired Immigration Judges and Former Members of the Board of Immigration Appeals Statement in Response to AG's Decision in *Matter of L-A-B-R-*," American Immigration Lawyers Association, August 17, 2018, www.aila.org /infonet/retired-ijs-former-bia-statement-matter-of-l-a-b-r.

40. *Matter of L-A-B-R-*, 27 I. & N. Dec. at 418–19.

41. 27 I. & N. Dec. 462, 465–66 (citing 8 C.F.R. §§ 239.2[a][6]-[7] & 1239.2).

42. 27 I. & N. Dec. at 466 (quoting 8 C.F.R. § 1239.2[f] [emphasis added by attorney general]).

43. Memorandum of James McHenry, March 30, 2018, www.aila.org/infonet /eoir-memo-immigration-judge-performance-metrics [McHenry Memo].

44. EOIR Performance Plan, Adjudicative Employees, attached to McHenry Memo.

45. Lorelei Laird, "Justice Department Imposes Quotas on Immigration Judges, Provoking Independence Concerns," *ABA Journal*, April 2, 2018, www .abajournal.com/news/article/justice_department_imposes_quotas_on_immigration_judges_provoking_independe (quoting Judge A. Ashley Tabaddor).

46. "Growing Support for an Independent Immigration Court," National Association of Immigration Judges, June 17, 2019, www.naij-usa.org/images/uploads /newsroom/Growing_Support_for_an_Independent_Immigration_Court.pdf.

47. Jeffrey S. Chase, "EOIR Imposes Completion Quotas on IJs," *Opinions /Analysis on Immigration Law* (blog), April 7, 2018, www.jeffreyschase.com /blog/2018/4/7/eoir-imposes-completion-quotas-on-ijs.

48. 531 F.3d 256 (3d. Cir. 2008).

49. *Matter of L-A-B-R-*, 27 I. & N. Dec. at 416–17.

50. *The Attorney General's Judges: How the U.S. Immigration Courts Became a Deportation Tool* (Portland and Montgomery: Innovation Law Lab and Southern Poverty Law Center, 2019), 21, www.splcenter.org/sites/default/files/com_ policyreport_the_attorney_generals_judges_final.pdf.

51. Christina Goldbaum, "Trump Administration Moves to Decertify Outspoken Immigration Judges' Union," *New York Times*, August 10, 2019, www.nytimes .com/2019/08/10/us/immigration-judges-union-justice-department.html?module = inline.

52. Zolan Kanno-Youngs, "Immigration Judges' Union Lodges Labor Complaints against Trump Administration," *New York Times,* September 27, 2019, www.nytimes.com/2019/09/27/us/politics/immigration-judges-union.html.

53. Christine Hauser, "Justice Department Newsletter Included Extremist Blog Post," *New York Times,* August 23, 2019, www.nytimes.com/2019/08/23/us/justice-department-vdare-anti-semitic.html?action = click&module = RelatedCoverage&pgtype = Article&region = Footer.

54. Romero v. Barr, 937 F.3d. 282 (4th Cir. 2019).

55. Auer v. Robbins, 519 U.S. 452 (1997); *Romero,* 937 F.3d at 291 (quoting Kisor v. Wilkie, 588 U.S. ___, 139 S.Ct. 2400, 2414 [2019]).

56. *Romero,* 937 F.3d at 292 (quoting 8 C.F.R. §§ 1003.1[d][1][ii] & 1003.10[b]).

4. A NEW TYPE OF TOUGH IN THE DEPARTMENT OF LABOR

1. Frances Perkins, interview by Dean Albertson, 1951–1955, Part 4, Sess. 1, 62–63, transcript, Oral History of Frances Perkins (OHFP), Columbia University Library Oral History Research Office, www.columbia.edu/cu/lweb/digital/collections/nny/perkinsf/audio_transcript.html.

2. George Martin, *Madam Secretary: Frances Perkins* (Boston: Houghton Mifflin, 1976), 41–51, 205–6, 233–34.

3. Frances Perkins, *The Roosevelt I Knew* (New York: Viking, 1946), 166.

4. Martin, *Madam Secretary,* 231–42.

5. Perkins, *The Roosevelt I Knew,* 4, 9–12.

6. Armond S. Goldman, Elisabeth J. Schmalstieg, Daniel H. Freeman, Jr., Daniel A. Goldman and Frank C. Schmalstig, Jr., "What Was the Cause of Franklin Delano Roosevelt's Paralytic Illness?," *Journal of Medical Biography* 11, no. 4 (November 2003): 232–40; but see John F. Ditunno, Bruce E. Becker, and Gerald J. Herbison, "Franklin Delano Roosevelt: The Diagnosis of Poliomyelitis Revisited," *PM&R* 8, no. 9 (August 31, 2016): 883–93.

7. Perkins, *The Roosevelt I Knew,* 12, 41–43.

8. Frances Perkins to FDR, 11 October 1928, Box 60, Frances Perkins Papers, Columbia University Library.

9. Perkins, *The Roosevelt I Knew,* 4.

10. Frances Perkins to Mary Dreier, 4 May 1945, Box 62, Frances Perkins Papers.

11. OHFP, Part 4, Sess. 1, 96–111.

12. OHFP, Part 4, Sess. 1, 121–29, 205–34.

13. OHFP, Part 4, Sess. 1, 117–19.

14. Immigration Act of 1917, Pub. L. No. 63–301, 39 Stat. 874 (1917); OHFP, Part 4, Sess. 1, 212–14.

15. Handwritten memorandum from JFM to Mr. Mac, Office of the Commissioner-General of Immigration (undated), Official File (OF) 15d, FDR Library. "Mr. Mac" likely refers to Commissioner General of Immigration Daniel MacCormack.

16. OHFP, Part 4, Sess. 1, 214–16.

17. OHFP, Part 4, Sess. 1, 229–32.

18. For a discussion of this period of immigration history, see H. Rep. No. 82–1365, 7–13 (1952) (report accompanying Immigration and Nationality Act).

19. Act of March 3, 1891, ch. 551, 26 Stat. 1084. In the modern immigration code, see 8 U.S.C. § 1182(a).

20. Act of March 3, 1893, ch. 206, 27 Stat. 570; 24 Cong. Rec. 2469–71 (statement of Rep. Stump).

21. Act of Feb. 14, 1903, ch. 552, § 4, 32 Stat. 825; Richard Hume Werking, *The Master Architects* (Lexington: University Press of Kentucky, 1977), 171–72.

22. Act of June 27, 1884, ch. 127, 23 Stat. 60.

23. Act of March 4, 1913, ch. 141, 37 Stat. 736; Lewis B. Swellenbach, "Work and Policies of the Department of Labor, 1913–48: Historical Background of the Department, Principles Guiding Its Work, Fields of Activity, and Specific Programs," *Monthly Labor Review* 66, no. 3 (March 1948): 250.

24. Lochner v. New York, 198 U.S. 45 (1905).

25. E. Pendleton Herring, *Public Administration and the Public Interest* (New York: McGraw-Hill, 1936), 279, *quoting* Lewis Carroll, *Alice's Adventures in Wonderland* (London: Macmillan, 1865), 106.

26. Martin, *Madam Secretary*, 110; OHFP, Part 1, Sess. 1, 314.

27. Act of May 19, 1921, ch. 8, 42 Stat. 5; Act of May 26, 1924, ch. 190, 43 Stat. 153; H. Rep. No. 82–1365, 7–13 (1952).

28. "Overview of INS History," USCIS History Office and Library (2012), 7; https://tinyurl.com/w63vacg; *Wickersham Commission Report*, 42; Sharon D. Masanz, Congressional Research Service, *History of the Immigration and Naturalization Service* (Washington, DC: U.S. Government Printing Office, 1980), 30.

29. Press Release, "Alien Deportation out of Department," Washington State Labor News, 24 March 1933, OF 15d, FDR Library.

30. FDR to Frances Perkins, 28 April 1936, attaching letter from H. L. Mennerick to FDR, 23 April 1936, with handwritten note by Perkins, Box 60, Frances Perkins Papers.

31. Richard Breitman and Alan M. Kraut, *American Refugee Policy and European Jewry, 1933–45* (Bloomington and Indianapolis: Indiana University Press, 1987), 7–21.

32. Herring, *Public Administration and the Public Interest*, 286–87.

33. OHFP, Part 8, Sess. 1, p. 158.

34. Herring, *Public Administration and the Public Interest*, 287–88.

35. Perkins, *The Roosevelt I Knew*, 317.

36. Martin, *Madam Secretary*, 321.

37. OHFP, Part 6, Sess. 1, 302–7.

38. Martin, *Madam Secretary*, 407; OHFP, Part 6, Sess. 1, 324–26, 340–42.

39. Strecker v. Kessler, 95 F.2d 976 (5th Cir. 1938), *modified by* Kessler v. Strecker, 307 U.S. 22 (1939); OHFP, Part 6, Sess. 1, 465–66.

40. Act of Oct. 16, 1918, ch. 186, 40 Stat. 1012, as amended by Act of June 5, 1920, ch. 251, 41 Stat. 1008.

41. OHFP, Sess. 6, Part 1, 465–72.

42. Kessler v. Strecker, 307 U.S. 22, 29–30, 35 (1939).

43. Martin, *Madam Secretary*, 417.

44. "Mr. Bridges and Sec. Perkins," *Detroit Free Press*, February 12, 1938, Box 103, Frances Perkins Papers.

45. A Detroiter to Frances Perkins, 12 February 1938, Box 103, France Perkins Papers.

46. Louis Brownlow, Reorganization Story Manuscript, 1933–39, 14 April 1949, 147, John F. Kennedy Library, www.jfklibrary.org/asset-viewer/archives /LBPP/048/LBPP-048-010.

47. 84 Cong. Rec. 702–11 (1939).

48. Statement of Frances Perkins before the House Judiciary Committee, February 8, 1939; Department of Labor Files, Record Group (RG) 174, National Archives & Records Administration (NARA I).

49. 84 Cong. Rec. 3273 (1939).

50. Martin, *Madam Secretary*, 415–16; H.R. Rep. No. 76–311, at 575 (1939).

51. Transcript of Radio Address by J. Parnell Thomas, 29 March 1939, Box 40, Frances Perkins Papers.

52. Transcript of Radio Address by James M. Mead, 31 March 1939, Box 37, Frances Perkins Papers.

53. Memo from FDR to Edwin M. Watson, 28 July 1939, OF 15d, FDR Library.

54. Unsigned Memo from White House to FDR, 27 July 1939, OF 15d, FDR Library.

55. Martin, *Madam Secretary*, 398, 410.

56. OHFP, Part 6, Sess. 1, 478; Perkins, *The Roosevelt I Knew*, 319.

5. REFUSAL

1. Martin, *Madam Secretary*, 418.

2. Outerlink Bridge Dedication, 5 October 1937, Master Speech File, Box 35, FDR Library, https://fdrlibrary.org/utterancesfdr#afdr093.

3. Marian C. McKenna, *Franklin Roosevelt and the Great Constitutional War: The Court-Packing Crisis of 1937* (New York: Fordham University Press, 2002); Richard Polenberg, *Reorganizing Roosevelt's Government: The Controversy over Executive Reorganization, 1936–1939* (Cambridge, MA: Harvard University Press, 1966).

4. Polenberg, *Reorganizing Roosevelt's Government*, 148–49.

5. Polenberg, 184; Reorganization Act of 1939, Pub. L. No. 76–19, 53 Stat. 561 (1939).

6. Gilbert King, "Sabotage in New York Harbor," *Smithsonian.com*, November 1, 2011, www.smithsonianmag.com/history/sabotage-in-new-york-harbor-123968672/.

7. Kai Bird, *The Chairman* (New York: Simon and Schuster, 1992), 79.

8. Agreement Regarding the Financial Obligations of Germany under the Peace Treaty of 1921, U.S.-Germany, Aug. 10, 1922, 26 L.N.T.S. 358, Art. I., extended by agreement December 31, 1928.

9. Bird, *The Chairman*, 79–84.

10. Lehigh Valley RR Co. v. Germany, 8 Rep. Int'l Arb. Awards 84, 86 (1930).

11. Bird, *The Chairman*, 78–95.

12. Bird, 89–91.

13. Bird, 93.

14. Lehigh Valley R. R. Co. v. Germany, 27 Amer. J. Int'l L. 339–369 (1933).

15. Z&F Assets Realization Corp. v. Hull, 311 U.S. 470 (1941).

16. Letter from FDR to H. H. Martin, 7 May 1940, and memo from FDR to secretary of state and attorney general, 7 May 1940, OF 3603, FDR Library.

17. Louis Brownlow, *A Passion for Anonymity: The Autobiography of Louis Brownlow, the First Half* (Chicago: University of Chicago Press, 1958), 413–19.

18. 84 Cong. Rec. 4741 (1939); 84 Cong. Rec. 5281 (1939).

19. Polenberg, *Reorganizing Roosevelt's Government*, 187–88; Brownlow, *A Passion for Anonymity*, 415; Reorganization Plan No. III of 1940, 5 Fed. Reg. 2107 (1940).

20. Polenberg, *Reorganizing Roosevelt's Government*, 17–19.

21. Memo from Schuyler C. Wallace to President's Committee on Administrative Management, 25 September 1936, Louis Brownlow Personal Papers, Box 45, JFK Library.

22. Letter from Albert Gore to FDR, 25 April 1939, President's Committee on Administrative Management (PCAM) File, Box 24, FDR Library.

23. Letter from Albert Gore to FDR, 9 February 1940, President's Personal File (PPF), Box 15, FDR Library (handwritten note on document dated 20 March 1940).

24. Kyle Longley, *Senator Albert Gore Sr.: Tennessee Maverick* (Baton Rouge: LSU Press, 2004), 33–35.

25. Albert Gore, *The Eye of the Storm: A People's Politics for the Seventies* (New York: Herder and Herder, 1970), 203.

26. Albert Gore, Press Release, 22 April 1939, Albert Gore House of Representatives Papers, Series III: Press Releases, Albert Gore Research Center, Middle Tennessee State University.

27. 84 Cong. Rec. 9532 (1939).

28. 84 Cong. Rec. 10130 (1939).

29. Longley, *Senator Albert Gore Sr.*, 42.

30. Longley, 27–28.

31. Breitman and Kraut, *American Refugee Policy and European Jewry*, 11–27.

32. Diary of Harold D. Smith, 6 May 1939, Box 1, Harold D. Smith Papers, FDR Library.

33. Smith Diary, 6 May 1939.

34. Draft statement, "The Relation of the Immigration and Naturalization Service to the Department of Labor," 24 July 1939, Box 54, Frances Perkins Papers.

35. 84 Cong. Rec. 5281 (1939).

36. 84 Cong. Rec. 5284 (1939).

37. Memo from EK to Frank Murphy, 22 June 1939, Frank Murphy Papers, Box 57, Bentley Historical Library, University of Michigan. "EK" may have been Justice Department lawyer and longtime Murphy associate Edward G. Kemp. Sidney Fine, *Frank Murphy: The Washington Years* (Ann Arbor: University of Michigan Press, 1984), 15.

38. Letter from Frank Murphy to FDR, 22 June 1939, Box 57, Murphy Papers.

39. Memo from FDR to various Department heads, 26 June 1939, Box 57, Murphy Papers.

40. Senate Select Committee to Study Governmental Operations with respect to Intelligence Activities, III Final Reports, 96th Congress, 402–03 (1976).

41. Fine, *Frank Murphy*, 106.

42. *Complete Presidential Press Conferences of Franklin D. Roosevelt*, vol. 14 (New York: Da Capo, 1972), 155.

43. Letter from Lindsey Warren to Edwin M. Watson, 16 November 1939, OF 285c, FDR Library.

44. Memorandum from FDR to Louis Brownlow, 19 December 1939; Memo from FDR to Pa (Edwin M. Watson), 2 January 1940, OF 285c, FDR Library.

45. Memo for attorney general re: Suggested transfer to Department of Justice of functions relating to the administration of the immigration and naturalization laws, 28 November 1939, OF 285c, FDR Library.

46. Memo from attorney general to Judge Townsend, 1 February 1940, Box 90, Jackson Papers, Library of Congress.

47. Letter from Albert Gore to FDR, 6 February 1940, OF 15d, FDR Library.

48. Letter from Robert H. Jackson to FDR, 9 February 1940, OF 285c, FDR Library.

49. Reorganization Plan No. III, 54 Stat. 1231, 5 Fed. Reg. 2107; Reorganization Plan No. IV, 54 Stat. 1234, 5 Fed. Reg. 2421.

6. INVASION

1. James Holland, *The Battle of Britain: Five Months That Changed History, May-October 1940* (New York: St. Martin's, 2010), 27, 70–84, 111; Werner Warmbrunn, *The Dutch under German Occupation, 1940–45* (Stanford: Stanford University Press, 1963), 9–10; Brian Bond, *France and Belgium, 1939–1940* (London: Davis-Poynter, 1975), 158–84; Robert Jackson, *Dunkirk: The British Evacuation, 1940* (New York: St. Martins, 1976), 173–74; Andrew Roberts, *The Storm of War* (New York: Harper Perennial, 2011), 67.

2. Reorganization Plan No. V, 54 Stat. 1238, transmitted May 22, 1940; Samuel I. Rosenman, ed., *The Public Papers and Addresses of Franklin D. Roosevelt, 1940 Volume: War—and Aid to Democracies* (New York: MacMillan, 1941), 194.

3. Reorganization Plan No. IV, 54 Stat. 1234, transmitted April 11, 1940.

4. Diary of Adolf A. Berle, Jr., 7 May 1940, Box 211, Papers of Adolf A. Berle, Jr., FDR Library.

5. Jordan A. Schwarz, *Liberal: Adolf A. Berle and the Vision of an American Era* (New York: Free Press, 1987), 16, 19, 37, 50–55, 110–13, 118–19.

6. Berle Diary, 3 May 1940 and 7 May 1940.

7. Berle Diary, 8 May 1940; Paul F. State, *A Brief History of the Netherlands* (New York: Infobase, 2008), 192–93.

8. Berle Diary, 8 May 1940.

9. Berle Diary, 8 May 1940.

10. White House Ushers Log, 9 May 1940, www.fdrlibrary.marist.edu/daybyday/daylog/may-9th-1940/; Doris Kearns Goodwin, *No Ordinary Time: Franklin and Eleanor Roosevelt: The Home Front in World War II* (New York: Simon and Schuster, 1994), 13–14.

11. White House Ushers Log, 9 May 1940; Memo of Call from FDR to Henry Morgenthau Jr., 10 May 1940, Papers of Henry Morgenthau Jr., Series 1, vol. 261, May 10–11, 1940, FDR Library.

12. Memo of call from FDR to Henry Morgenthau Jr., 10 May 1940, Morgenthau Papers, FDR Library.

13. Berle Diary, 9 May 1940; William Makepeace Thackeray, *Vanity Fair* (Oxford: Oxford University Press, 1983), 359.

14. Thackeray, *Vanity Fair*, 355.

15. "James C. Dunn, 88, U.S. Ambassador to Four Countries After War, Dies," *Washington Post,* April 14, 1979, www.washingtonpost.com/archive/local /1979/04/14/james-c-dunn-88-us-ambassador-to-four-countries-after-war-dies /cbce7e8e-38a2-4bd8-986e-d819a8782bbe/?utm_term = .faf861b56ed2.

16. Berle Diary, 9 May 1940.

17. Summary of Presidential Memorandum for the Under Secretary of State, 14 May 1940, attaching telegram from "Leopold," Bruxelles, Belgium, 13 May 1940 (translation by author), OF 20, FDR Library.

18. Bond, *France and Belgium,* 149–57.

19. Summary of Presidential Memorandum for the State Department, 15 May 1940, forwarding telegram from "Funck," 14 May 1940 (translation by author), OF 20, FDR Library.

20. Transcript of Message to Congress re: Defense Appropriations, May 16, 1940, OF 335, FDR Library, audio available at https://fdrlibrary.org /utterancesfdr#afdr167; Harold L. Ickes, *The Secret Diaries of Harold L. Ickes,* vol. 3 (New York: Simon and Schuster, 1955), 178–79.

21. Telegram C-9x from "Former Naval Person" to President, 15 May 1940, in *Churchill & Roosevelt: The Complete Correspondence,* ed. Warren F. Kimball (Princeton: Princeton University Press, 1984), 37–38.

22. Telegram R-4x from President to Former Naval Person, May 16, 1940, in *Churchill & Roosevelt,* 38–39.

23. Rosenman, *Public Papers,* 197.

24. Joint Resolution of May 3, 1940, ch. 183, 54 Stat. 178 (1940).

25. Rosenman, *Public Papers,* 197.

26. Berle Diary, 16 May 1940.

27. Letter from FDR to Josephus Daniels, 27 July 1918, Box 25, FDR Papers as Assistant Secretary of the Navy, FDR Library.

28. List of Reports Taken by Assistant Secretary, Box 25, FDR Papers as Assistant Secretary of the Navy, FDR Library.

29. Letter from FDR to Eleanor Roosevelt, 2 August 1914, in *The Roosevelt Letters: Being the Personal Correspondence of Franklin Delano Roosevelt,* vol. 2, ed. Elliott Roosevelt (London: Harrap, 1950), 198.

30. Berle Diary, 16 May 1940.

31. Julius Ruiz, "Fighting the Fifth Column: The Terror in Republican Madrid during the Spanish Civil War," in *The Civilianization of War,* ed. Andrew Barros and Martin Thomas (Cambridge: Cambridge University Press, 2018), 49–50.

32. Holland, *The Battle of Britain,* 126; Roberts, *The Storm of War,* 23.

33. Holland, *The Battle of Britain,* 126.

34. Richard Hargreaves, *Blitzkrieg Unleashed: The German Invasion of Poland, 1939* (Barnsley: Pen & Sword Military, 2008), 236. Roberts places the number at seven thousand. Roberts, *The Storm of War,* 23.

35. Holland, *The Battle of Britain.* 126.

36. Peter Gillman and Leni Gillman, *Collar the Lot!: How Britain Interned and Expelled Its Wartime Refugees* (London: Quartet, 1980), 84.

37. Holland, *The Battle of Britain*, 124.

38. Letters from J. Edgar Hoover to Edwin M. Watson, 11 February 1940 and 17 February 1940, OF 10b, FDR Library.

39. Letter from J. Edgar Hoover to Edwin M. Watson, 23 February 1940, OF 10b, FDR Library.

40. Letter from J. Edgar Hoover to Edwin M. Watson, 1 March 1940, OF 10b, FDR Library.

41. Letter from J. Edgar Hoover to Edwin M. Watson, 21 February 1940, OF 10b, FDR Library.

42. Letter from J. Edgar Hoover to Edwin W. Watson, April 23, 1940, OF 10b, FDR Library.

43. Roberts, *The Storm of War*, 41.

44. U.S. Declaration of August 4, 1916, relative to extension of Danish authority over Greenland, U.S. Department of State, 7 T.I.A.S. 62 (1971).

45. Letter from J. Edgar Hoover to Edwin W. Watson, 23 April 1940, OF 10b, FDR Library.

46. State Department memorandum of conversation between Hamilton Fish Armstrong, Mr. Mallory, and Mr. Messersmith, 12 September 1939, Council on Foreign Relations Records: Studies Department Series, Public Policy Papers, Department of Rare Books and Special Collections, Princeton University Library.

47. Isaiah Bowman, "The Strategic Importance of Greenland," in *Studies of the American Interests in the War and the Peace* (New York: Council on Foreign Relations, 1940), 5.

48. Letter from Isaiah Bowman to Joseph H. Willits, 8 August 1940, Box 298, Council on Foreign Relations Records: Studies Department Series.

49. Berle Diary, 26 April 1940.

50. Undated Memorandum, Box 70, Berle Papers.

51. Undated memorandum, Box 70, Berle Papers.

7. THE WELLES MISSION

1. Berle Diary, 8 May 1940.

2. Berle Diary, 9 May 1940.

3. Benjamin Welles, *Sumner Welles: FDR's Global Strategist* (New York: St. Martin's, 1997), 345.

4. Christopher D. O'Sullivan, *Sumner Welles, Postwar Planning, and the Quest for a New World Order, 1937–1943* (New York: Columbia University Press ACLS Gutenberg e-Series, 2008), chap. 3.

5. O'Sullivan, chap. 4.

6. O'Sullivan, chap. 1.

7. Welles, *FDR's Global Strategist*, 26–38, 41–90, 69.

8. Welles, 197, 69.

9. Smith Diary, 22 June 1939.

10. Smith Diary, 25 July 1939.

11. Welles, *FDR's Global Strategist*, 344–53.

12. Welles, 247.

13. Maurizio Vaudagna, "Mussolini and Franklin D. Roosevelt," in *FDR and His Contemporaries: Foreign Perceptions of an American President*, ed. Cornelis A. van Minnen and John F. Sears (New York: St. Martin's, 1992), 157.

14. Stanley E. Hilton, "The Welles Mission to Europe, February-March 1940: Illusion or Realism?," *Journal of American History* 58, no. 2 (June 1971): 93–94.

15. Sumner Welles, *The Time for Decision* (New York: Harper, 1944), 74.

16. Hilton, "The Welles Mission," 95–96.

17. Cordell Hull, *The Memoirs of Cordell Hull*, vol. 1 (New York: McMillan 1948), 737–40.

18. O'Sullivan, *Quest for a New World Order*, chap. 3.

19. Welles, *The Time for Decision*, 73–147.

20. Hull, *Memoirs*, 1:740.

21. Welles, *The Time for Decision*, 90–119.

22. Welles, 119–20.

23. Berle Diary, 12 May 1940.

24. Welles, *The Time for Decision*, 149, 89.

25. Letter from Sumner Welles to FDR, 18 May 1940, OF 15d, FDR Library.

26. Letter from Robert H. Jackson to Sumner Welles, 15 May 1940, OF 15d, FDR Library.

27. Telegram C-10x from "Former Naval Person" to FDR, 18 May 1940, in *Churchill & Roosevelt*, 39.

28. Telegram C-11x from Former Naval Person to the President, 20 May 1940, in *Churchill & Roosevelt*, 40.

29. Warren F. Kimball and Bruce Bartlett, "Roosevelt and Prewar Commitments to Churchill: The Tyler Kent Affair," *Diplomatic History* 5, no. 4 (Oct. 1981): 291–311.

30. Telegram from Louis Brownlow to Edward M. Watson, 13 May 1940, OF 3795, FDR Library.

31. Smith Diary, 22 May 1940.

32. Phone message of 21 May 1940, Box 88, Jackson Papers.

33. Memo to file, 21 May 1940, Box 90, Jackson Papers.

34. Memo from Edwin M. Watson to FDR, 21 May 1940, OF 3795, FDR Library.

35. Smith Diary, 21 May 1940.

36. Smith Diary, 22 May 1940.

37. *Complete Presidential Press Conferences of Franklin D. Roosevelt*, 15–16:352–53.

38. OHFP, Part 8, Sess. 1, 162–63.

39. Francis Biddle, *In Brief Authority* (New York: Doubleday, 1962), 106.

40. Alien Registration Act, ch. 439, 54 Stat. 670 (1940).

41. Draft Message to Congress, 20 May 1940, OF 15d, FDR Library.

42. 86 Cong. Rec. 6637 (1940).

43. FDR, Fireside Chat on National Defense, 26 May 1940, FDR Library, www.fdrlibrary.org/utterancesfdr.

8. ALIEN ENEMIES

1. An Act Respecting Alien Enemies, ch. 66, 1 Stat. 577 (1798).

2. 50 U.S.C. § 21.

3. "COI Came First," Central Intelligence Agency, www.cia.gov/library /publications/intelligence-history/oss/art02.htm.

4. Military Order of 13 June 1942, www.cia.gov/library/center-for-the-study- of-intelligence/kent-csi/vol37no3/html/v37i3a10p_0001.htm.

5. National Security Act of 1947, 61 Stat. 496 (1947), codified as amended, 50 U.S.C. § 3001 et seq.

6. Bird, *The Chairman*, 92, 113.

7. Bird, 113.

8. Letters from John J. McCloy to Henry L. Stimson, 25 September 1940, 7 November 1940, Box 18, John J. McCloy Papers, Amherst College Archives and Special Collections.

9. Letter from L. A. Moyer to Henry L. Stimson, 14 December 1940, Box 18, McCloy Papers.

10. Letter from John J. McCloy to Henry L. Stimson, 25 September 1940, Box 18, McCloy Papers.

11. Bird, *The Chairman*, 118–19, 123–24.

12. Profile, McCloy, John J., Assistant U.S. Secretary of War, July 1944, Box 18, McCloy Papers.

13. Bird, *The Chairman*, 161–65.

14. Paul S. Burtness and Warren U. Ober, "Communication Lapses Leading to the Pearl Harbor Disaster," *The Historian* 74, no. 4 (November 2013): 743–45.

15. Proclamation No. 2525, 3 C.F.R. 1938–1943 Cum. Supp. 273 (1943).

16. Proclamation Nos. 2526, 2527, and 2537, 3 C.F.R. 1938–1943 Cum. Supp. 276, 278, 287 (1943).

17. Proclamation No. 2524, 3 C.F.R. 1938 Cum. Supp. 272–73 (1943).

18. Bird, *The Chairman*, 148–54.

19. McCloy Diaries, 17 February 1942, Box 2, McCloy Papers.
20. E.O. 9066, 7 Fed. Reg. 1407 (1942).
21. Act of March 21, 1942, 56 Stat. 173.
22. Korematsu v. United States, 323 U.S. 214, 233–42 (1944) (Murphy, J., dissenting).
23. Korematsu, 323 U.S. at 242–48 (Jackson, J., dissenting).
24. Trump v. Hawaii, 138 S. Ct. 2392, 2447–48 (2018) (Sotomayor, J., dissenting).
25. Trump v. Hawaii, 138 S. Ct. at 2423 (quoting *Korematsu*, 323 U.S. at 248 [Jackson, J., dissenting]).
26. Commission on Wartime Relocation and Internment of Civilians, *Personal Justice Denied* (Washington, DC: U.S. Government Printing Office, 1982 and 1983), www.archives.gov/research/japanese-americans/justice-denied.
27. Civil Liberties Act of 1988, 102 Stat. 903, § 104(e) (1988); Civil Liberties Act Amendments of 1992, 106 Stat. 1167 §2, (1992).
28. Kenan Heise, "Frank A. Schuler Jr., 88, U.S. Diplomat in Japan," *Chicago Tribune*, May 7, 1996, www.chicagotribune.com/news/ct-xpm-1996-05-07-9605070020-story.html.
29. Letter from John J. McCloy to Frank A. Schuler, Jr., 4 April 1983, Frank Schuler Papers, FDR Library.
30. John J. McCloy, "Repay US Japanese?," *New York Times*, April 10, 1983, www.nytimes.com/1983/04/10/opinion/repay-us-japanese.html.

9. RECKONING

1. Louis De Jong, *The German Fifth Column in the Second World War*, trans. C. M. Geyl (Chicago: University of Chicago Press, 1956), 173–180.
2. Holland, *The Battle of Britain*, 116–21; Roberts, *The Storm of War*, 48–86.
3. De Jong, *The German Fifth Column in the Second World War*, 206.
4. De Jong, 185–87.
5. De Jong, 214–16.
6. David A. Taylor, "The Inside Story of How a Nazi Plot to Sabotage the U.S. War Effort Was Foiled," *Smithsonian.com*, June 28, 2016, www.smithsonianmag.com/history/inside-story-how-nazi-plot-sabotage-us-war-effort-was-foiled-180959594/.

10. UN DÍA DE FUEGO

1. Kelly Wallace, "Bush Vacation Puts Spotlight on Tiny Crawford," *CNN InsidePolitics*, August 7, 2001, www.cnn.com/2001/ALLPOLITICS/08/06/bush.crawford/.

2. Roxanne Roberts and Anne Gerhart, "The State Dinner That Ended with a Bang," *Washington Post*, September 6, 2001, www.washingtonpost.com /archive/lifestyle/2001/09/06/the-state-dinner-that-ended-with-a-bang/2a82b9ff-01f9-4563-90c8-52c83bcca5ca/.

3. George W. Bush, *Decision Points* (New York: Crown, 2010), 147–49.

4. Bush, 301.

5. "Presidents Exchange Toasts at State Dinner," White House, September 6, 2001, https://georgewbush-whitehouse.archives.gov/news/releases/2001/09 /20010906-1.html.

6. George W. Bush 2000, On the Issues: Immigration, www.4president.org /issues/bush2000/bush2000immigration.htm.

7. Bush, *Decision Points*, 301–4.

8. National Commission on Terrorist Attacks on the United States (9/11 Commission), *The 9/11 Commission Report* (Washington, DC: U.S. Government Printing Office, 2004), 259–63, https://govinfo.library.unt.edu/911/report/911Report .pdf.

9. *INS's March 2002 Notification of Approval of Change of Status for Pilot Training for Terrorist Hijackers Mohammed Atta and Marwan Al-Shehhi: Hearing before the Subcommittee on Immigration and Claims of the House Committee on the Judiciary*, 107th Cong. 24 (2002) (statement of James W. Ziglar, Commissioner, Immigration and Naturalization Service); Edward Alden, *The Closing of the American Border* (New York: HarperCollins, 2008), 185–86.

10. 8 C.F.R. 248.1(d)(3).

11. Alden, *The Closing of the American Border*, 150–52.

12. Joe Holley, "Mary Ryan, 65; Embattled Consular Chief," *Washington Post*, April 29, 2006, www.washingtonpost.com/wp-dyn/content/article/2006/04/28 /AR2006042802001.html.

13. Immigration Act of 1990, § 141, 104 Stat. 4978 (1990).

14. U.S. Commission on Immigration Reform, *Becoming an American* (introductory letter of chair Shirley M. Hufstedler).

15. Wong Yang Sung v. McGrath, 339 U.S. 33, 50–51 (1950).

16. Act of September 27, 1950, 64 Stat. 1044, 1048 (1950).

17. Sidney B. Rawitz, "From Wong Yang Sung to Black Robes," *Interpreter Releases* 65, no. 17 (May 1988): 457.

18. Marcello v. Bonds, 349 U.S. 302 (1955).

19. Marcello, 349 U.S. at 308–9.

20. Commission on Organization of the Executive Branch of the Government (Second Hoover Commission), *Legal Services and Procedure* (Washington, DC: U.S. Government Printing Office, 1955), 61–63, 68–72; Justin J. Green, "Influence of Administrative Reform on the Immigration and Naturalization Service," *Administrative Science Quarterly* 15, no. 3 (September 1970): 356.

21. 20 Fed. Reg. 5709, 5730, § 242.9(b) (Aug. 9, 1955) (proposed rule); 21 Fed. Reg. 97, 100 § 242.9(b) (Jan. 6, 1956) (final rule); Rawitz, "From Wong Yang Sung to Black Robes," 458.

22. Immigration and Nationality Act of 1965, 79 Stat. 911 (1965).

23. 38 Fed. Reg. 8590, 8590, § 1.1 (1973).

24. Rawitz, "From Wong Yang Sung to Black Robes," 458; "Evolution of the U.S. Immigration Court System: Pre-1983," Department of Justice, www.justice .gov/eoir/evolution-pre-1983. The authorization to wear judicial robes is often cited to the regulation from 1973 that introduced the term "immigration judge," but robes are not mentioned in the regulation.

25. Memo from Michael J. Creppy, "Operating Policies and Procedures Memorandum Number 94–10: Wearing of the Robe during Immigration Judge Hearings," October 17, 1994, http://web.archive.org/web/20180118205737/https: /www.justice.gov/sites/default/files/eoir/legacy/2001/09/26/94–10.pdf.

26. 48 Fed. Reg. 8038 (Feb. 25, 1983); Rawitz, "From Wong Yang Sung to Black Robes," 458–59.

27. U.S. Commission on Immigration Reform, Becoming an American, 174.

28. U.S. Commission on Immigration Reform, 178.

29. James S. Thomason, The US Commission on National Security/21st Century ("Hart-Rudman") Overview and Observations on Phase I (Alexandria: Institute for Defense Analysis, 2000), 2–6.

30. New World Coming: American Security in the 21st Century: Major Themes and Implications (Washington, DC: United States Commission on National Security/21st Century, 1999), 3–5.

31. S. 1563, 106th Cong. (1999), ¶¶ 103, 105, 109; George W. Bush 2000, On The Issues: Immigration, www.4president.org/issues/bush2000/bush2000 immigration.htm.

32. H.R. 1158 (107th Cong.) (2001); Road Map for National Security: Imperative for Change (Washington, DC: U.S. Commission on National Security/21st Century, 2001).

33. George Tenet, At the Center of the Storm: My Years at the CIA (New York: HarperCollins, 2007), 143–53.

34. Richard A. Clarke, Against All Enemies: Inside America's War on Terror (New York: Free Press, 2004), 231–32.

35. Bob Woodward, Bush at War (New York: Simon and Schuster, 2002), 39.

36. Hearing of the National Commission on Terrorist Attacks upon the United States (9th Hearing, April 8, 2004), 18–19 (statement of Condoleeza Rice, Assistant to the President for National Security Affairs).

37. Immigration Reform and the Reorganization of Homeland Defense: Hearing before the Subcommittee on Immigration, Senate Committee on the

Judiciary, 107th Cong. 34 (2002) (statement of Timothy H. Edgar, Legislative Counsel, American Civil Liberties Union).
38. Bush, *Decision Points*, 151.

11. PRESIDENT BUSH'S DEPARTMENT

1. S. 1534, 107th Cong. (2001); Exec. Order No. 13228, 3 C.F.R. § 13228 (2001).
2. Bush, *Decision Points*, 156.
3. Brody Mullins, "Ridge: Bush Should Veto Cabinet-Level Homeland Security Office," *Government Executive*, May 30, 2002, www.govexec.com /defense/2002/05/ridge-bush-should-veto-cabinet-level-homeland-security-office /11748/.
4. Peter Baker, *Days of Fire: Bush and Cheney in the White House* (New York: Anchor, 2014), 201–02; Dana Milbank, "Plan Was Formed in Utmost Secrecy," *Washington Post*, June 7, 2002, www.washingtonpost.com/archive/politics /2002/06/07/plan-was-formed-in-utmost-secrecy/e09fea5f-ca40-4381-a0fc-f3162197d639/; Remarks at the Congressional Barbecue, *Weekly Compilation of Presidential Documents*, vol. 38 (June 5, 2002), 962–63.
5. Baker, *Days of Fire*, 202.
6. *INS's March 2002 Notification of Approval of Change of Status for Pilot Training for Terrorist Hijackers Mohammed Atta and Marwan Al-Shehhi: Hearing before the Subcommittee on Immigration and Claims of the House Committee on the Judiciary*, 107th Cong. 24 (2002) (statement of James W. Ziglar, Commissioner, Immigration and Naturalization Service).
7. "FBI Whistleblower Describes 'Roadblocks,'" *CNN.com/InsidePolitics*, June 6, 2002, www.cnn.com/2002/ALLPOLITICS/06/06/terror.lapses/index.html.
8. Address to the Nation on the Proposed Department of Homeland Security, *Weekly Compilation of Presidential Documents*, vol. 38 (2002), 963; https://georgewbush-whitehouse.archives.gov/news/releases/2002/06/20020606-8 .html.
9. 148 Cong. Rec. 11,188–189 (2002).
10. George W. Bush, *Department of Homeland Security*, 9–11 (Washington, DC: White House, 2002), www.dhs.gov/sites/default/files/publications/book_0.pdf.
11. 138 Cong. Rec. 5,714 (2002).
12. *Immigration Reform and the Reorganization of Homeland Defense: Hearing before the Subcommittee on Immigration, Senate Committee on the Judiciary*, 107th Cong. 2 (2002) (*Immigration Reform Hearing*).
13. Bush, *Decision Points*, 273–76.
14. Edward M. Kennedy, *True Compass* (New York: Hachette, 2009), 487–88.

15. Bush, *Decision Points*, 274–75; Kennedy, *True Compass*, 488–93; Baker, *Days of Fire*, 182.

16. Kennedy, *True Compass*, 496; Bush, *Decision Points*, 304.

17. *Immigration Reform Hearing*, 107th Cong. 3.

18. Michael Luo, "On the Road: A Week with 'Values' Voters," *New York Times*, October 28, 2007, http://thecaucus.blogs.nytimes.com/2007/10/28/on-the-road-a-week-with-values-voters/.

19. David L. Neal, telephonic interview by author, January 28, 2020.

20. Esther Olavarria, telephonic interview by author, January 28, 2020.

21. S. 2444, 107th Cong. (2002).

22. Olavarria interview.

23. H.R. 5005, 107th Cong., §§ 801–2 (2002).

24. *Immigration Reform Hearing*, 107th Cong. 9 (statement of Kathleen Campbell Walker, American Immigration Lawyers Association).

25. *Immigration Reform Hearing*, 107th Cong. 115 (statement of Bill McCollum, former Member of Congress).

26. *Immigration Reform Hearing*, 107th Cong. 15 (statement Dana Marks Keener, President, National Association of Immigration Judges).

27. *Immigration Reform Hearing*, 107th Cong. 111 (statement of David A. Martin, Doherty Professor of Law and Weber Research Professor of Civil Liberties and Human Rights, University of Virginia).

28. Immigration Reform Hearing, 107th Cong. 8 (Walker statement).

29. Neal interview, January 28, 2020.

30. Olavarria interview, January 28, 2020.

31. Neal interview, January 28, 2020.

32. Neal interview, January 28, 2020.

33. Letter from Edward M. Kennedy and Sam Brownback to Joseph I. Lieberman and Fred Thompson, 28 August 2002 (on file with author).

34. S. 4471, 107th Cong., §§ 1301–7 (2002).

35. Roll Call Votes 107th Senate, Second Session (2002), www.senate.gov/legislative/LIS/roll_call_lists/vote_menu_107_2.htm.

36. Steven Greenhouse, "Labor Issue May Stall Security Bill," *New York Times*, July 28, 2002, www.nytimes.com/2002/07/28/us/labor-issue-may-stall-security-bill.html.

37. Bush, *Decision Points*, 156.

38. Tom Scheck, "Wellstone Staff Apologizes for Memorial Service Rhetoric," *Minnesota Public Radio*, October 30, 2002, http://news.minnesota.publicradio.org/features/200210/30_scheckt_backlash1/.

39. Bush, *Decision Points*, 156–57.

40. 148 Cong. Rec. 22,114 (2002).

41. 148 Cong. Rec. 23,049 (2002).

42. H.R. 5005, 107th Cong., § 462.

43. 148 Cong. Rec. 22,100 (2002).

44. Homeland Security Act of 2002, Pub. L. No. 107–296, 116 Stat. 2135 (2002); www.congress.gov/bill/107th-congress/house-bill/5005.

45. 148 Cong. Rec. 23,049 (2002).

46. David A. Martin, "Immigration Policy and the Homeland Security Act Reorganization: An Early Agenda for Practical Improvements," *Migration Policy Institute Insight* 1 (April 2003): 19.

47. 148 Cong. Rec. 23,009 (2002).

48. Elisabeth Bumiller, "White House Letter; Two Presidential Pals, Until 9/11 Intervened," *New York Times*, March 3, 2003, www.nytimes.com/2003/03/03/us/white-house-letter-two-presidential-pals-until-9-11-intervened.html.

49. Vicente Fox and Rob Allyn, *Revolution of Hope* (New York: Viking, 2007), 199.

12. CHECKS AND IMBALANCES

1. *The Civil Law* 2, Title V, trans. S. P. Scott (Cincinnati: Central Trust Company, 1932), https://droitromain.univ-grenoble-alpes.fr/Anglica/CJ3_Scott.htm#5; *Dr. Bonham's Case*, (1610) 77 Eng. Rep. 638, 652 (C.P.), 8 Co. Rep. 107a, 118a; Sir Edward Coke, *The First Part of the Institutes of the Lawes of England: or, A Commentary upon Littleton* (1628–44; London: J & W. T. Clarke, 1832), 141a.

2. James Madison, *The Federalist No. 10*, Project Gutenberg Etext, 58; Thomas Jefferson, *A Manual of Parliamentary Practice for the Use of the Senate of the United States*, § 17.22 (1801; Washington: Government Printing Office, 1993).

3. Tumey v. Ohio, 273 U.S. 510, 523, 531 (1927).

4. In re Murchison, 349 U.S. 133 (1955).

5. Taylor v. Hayes, 418 U.S. 488 (1974); Mayberry v. Pennsylvania, 400 U.S. 455 (1971).

6. Antoniu v. SEC, 877 F.2d 721 (8th Cir. 1989); Staton v. Mayes, 552 F.2d 908 (10th Cir.) (as amended), *cert. denied*, 434 U.S. 907 (1977); Texaco v. FTC, 336 F.2d 754 (D.C. Cir. 1964), *vacated and remanded on other grounds*, 381 U.S. 739 (1965).

7. Withrow v. Larkin, 421 U.S. 35 (1975).

8. *Withrow*, 421 U.S. at 51.

9. *Withrow*, 421 U.S. at 55 (quoting United States v. Morgan, 313 U.S. 409, 421 [1941]).

10. *Tumey*, 273 U.S. at 523.

11. Capterton v. A.T. Massey Coal Co., 556 U.S. 868, 878 (2009) (citing *Tumey*, 273 U.S. at 535).

12. *Caperton*, 556 U.S. at 878 (quoting *Monroeville*, 409 U.S. at 60).

13. *Caperton,* 556 U.S. at 884.

14. *Caperton,* 556 U.S. at 887.

15. Marcello v. Bonds, 349 U.S. 302, 311 (1955).

16. Adrian Vermuele, "Contra *Nemo Iudex in Sua Causa:* The Limits of Impartiality," *Yale Law Journal* 122, no. 2 (November 2012): 384.

17. Administrative Procedure Act, 5 U.S.C. § 554(d).

18. *Immigration Reform Hearing,* 68 (statement of Susan F. Martin and Andrew Schoenholtz, Institute for the Study of International Migration, Georgetown University) (quoting Peter J. Levinson, "Specialized Court for Immigration Hearings and Appeals," *Notre Dame Law Review* 66 [April 1981]: 652).

19. Ilya Somin, "Does the Constitution Give the Federal Government Power over Immigration?," *Cato Unbound,* September 12, 2018, www.cato-unbound .org/2018/09/12/ilya-somin/does-constitution-give-federal-government-power-over-immigration.

20. *Immigration Reform Hearing,* 118 (statement of former Representative Bill McCollum).

21. Youngstown Sheet & Tube Co. v. Sawyer, 343 U.S. 579, 634–55 (1952) (Jackson, J., concurring). For Supreme Court statements about powers of the political branches over immigration, see INS v. Chadha, 462 U.S. 919, 940 (1983) ("[t]he plenary authority of Congress over aliens . . . is not open to question"); United States ex rel. Knauff v. Shaughnessy, 338 U.S. 537, 542 (1950) (exclusion power "stems not *alone* from legislative power but is inherent in the executive power to control the foreign affairs of the nation" [emphasis added]).

22. *Immigration Reform Hearing,* 91 (statement of Dana Marks Keener, President, National Association of Immigration Judges, attaching position paper of NAIJ, Hon. Dana Marks Keener, and Hon. Denise Noonan Slavin, "An Independent Immigration Court: An Idea Whose Time Has Come").

23. United States ex rel. Knauff v. Shaughnessey, 338 U.S. 537 (1950); Charles Weisselberg, "The Exclusion and Detention of Aliens: Lessons from the Lives of Ellen Knauff and Ignatz Mezei," *University of Pennsylvania Law Review* 143, no. 4 (April 1995): 958–64.

24. Antiterrorism and Effective Death Penalty Act of 1996, Pub. L. No. 104–32, 110 Stat. 1214 (1996); Illegal Immigration Reform and Immigrant Responsibility Act of 1996, Omnibus Appropriations Act of 1996, Div. C, Pub. L. No. 104–208, 110 Stat. 3009 (1996).

25. Barry J. McMillion, *Judiciary Appropriations, FY2020* (Washington, DC: Congressional Research Service, 2020), 19, www.everycrsreport.com /files/20200518_R45965_ad2fe789a59761e5a8ea8ab95c80ac3c59b6f73a.pdf.

26. 31 U.S.C. § 1105(b).

27. Harold Dubroff and Brant J. Hellwig, *The United States Tax Court: An Historical Analysis,* 2nd ed. (Washington, DC: U.S. Tax Court, 2014), 49–238, www.ustaxcourt.gov/book/Dubroff_Hellwig.pdf.

28. James Madison, *The Federalist No. 51*, Project Gutenberg Etext, 333.

29. Real ID Act § 106, 119 Stat. 231 (2005), codified at 8 U.S.C. § 1252(a)(5).

30. 8 U.S.C. § 1252(e)(3).

31. 8 U.S.C. § 1252; 5 U.S.C. § 701.

32. Homeland Security Act, § 452, 116 Stat. 2135, codified at 6 U.S.C. § 272.

33. Memorandum from Sumner Welles to FDR, 18 May 1940, OF 15d, FDR Library.

34. Confidential memorandum, "Observations on, and Recommendations for, the Control of Aliens within the United States as a Measure of Prevention of Sabotage, Espionage, and Other Forms of Subversive Activity," 22 May 1940, Box 90, Jackson Papers.

35. *Immigration Reform Hearing*, 115–16 (statement of former Representative McCollum).

13. REFORMING THE IMMIGRATION COURTS

1. Julián Castro, "AILA 2020 Presidential Candidate Survey," October 10, 2019, www.aila.org/File/Related/19093005h.pdf.

2. "A Fair and Welcoming Immigration System," Warren campaign website, posted July 11, 2019, https://elizabethwarren.com/plans/immigration; Tanvi Misra, "DOJ Changed Hiring to Promote Restrictive Immigration Judges," *Roll Call*,October29,2019,www.rollcall.com/news/congress/doj-changed-hiring-promote-restrictive-immigration-judges.

3. "A Welcoming and Safe America for All," Sanders campaign website, https://berniesanders.com/issues/welcoming-and-safe-america-all/.

4. Bernie Sanders, "AILA 2020 Presidential Candidate Survey," September 30, 2019, www.aila.org/File/Related/19093005d.pdf.

5. "The Biden Plan for Securing Our Values as a Nation of Immigrants," Biden campaign website, https://joebiden.com/immigration/.

6. U.S. Commission on Immigration Reform, *Becoming an American*, 174–82.

7. *Immigration Reform Hearing*, 92–93 (statement of the National Association of Immigration Judges).

8. Federal Bar Association, FBA Model Legislation Establishing an Article I Immigration Court, www.fedbar.org/wp-content/uploads/2019/10/proposed-Article-I-immigration-ct-model-bill-07162019-pdf-1.pdf; Letter from Robert Carlson, Marketa Lindt, Maria Vathis, and A. Ashley Tabbador to Members of Congress,July11,2019,www.fedbar.org/wp-content/uploads/2019/10/19070802-pdf-1.pdf.

9. *Courts in Crisis: The State of Judicial Independence and Due Process in U.S. Immigration Court: Hearing Before the Subcomm. on Immigration and Citizen-*

ship of the H. Comm. on the Judiciary, 116th Cong. https://judiciary.house.gov
/calendar/eventsingle.aspx?EventID = 2757 (testimony of Judge A. Ashley Tabaddor, Jeremy McKinney, Judy Perry Martinez, and Judge Andrew R. Arthur).

10. S. 2693, 115th Cong. (2018).

11. S. 663, 116th Cong. (2019).

12. S. 2113, 116th Cong. § 8 (2019).

13. S. 1445, 116th Cong. §§ 521–23 (2019).

EPILOGUE

1. Peter Baker, "Now Appearing: George W. Bush," *New York Times,* November 6, 2010, www.nytimes.com/2010/11/07/weekinreview/07baker.html?hp; Casey Lesser, "The Artist Who Taught George W. Bush How to Paint," *Artsy,* April 4, 2017, www.artsy.net/article/artsy-editorial-artist-taught-george-bush-paint; Michael Duffy, "George W. Bush Discusses His New Book of Oil Paintings," *TIME,* March 2, 2017, https://time.com/4688206/george-w-bush-painting-book/.

2. Caitlin Dewey, "Guccifer, the Hacker Who Leaked George W. Bush Paintings, Reportedly Arrested in Romania," *Washington Post,* January 22, 2014, www.washingtonpost.com/news/arts-and-entertainment/wp/2014/01/22/guccifer-the-hacker-who-leaked-george-w-bush-paintings-reportedly-arrested-in-romania/; Jerry Saltz, "Jerry Saltz: George W. Bush Is a Good Painter!," *Vulture,* February 8, 2013, www.vulture.com/2013/02/jerry-saltz-george-w-bush-is-a-good-painter.html; Peter Schjeldahl, "George W. Bush's Painted Atonements," *The New Yorker,* March 3, 2017, https://tinyurl.com/sn2h3lg.

3. Kevin Bohn, "The Artist Known as 'W': Paintings Unveil George W. Bush's Softer Side," *CNN.com,* April 4, 2014, www.cnn.com/2014/04/04/politics/bush-paintings/index.html.

4. George W. Bush, *Portraits of Courage: A Commander in Chief's Tribute to America's Warriors* (New York: Crown, 2017).

5. Schjeldahl, "George W. Bush's Painted Atonements."

6. JJ Charlesworth, "George W. Bush's Veteran Portraits Yearn for a Return to Innocence," *CNN Style,* October 7, 2019, www.cnn.com/style/article/george-w-bush-paintings/index.html.

7. Bush, *Decision Points,* 476.

8. "George W. Bush: Snowden Damaged US; Security Programs Protect Civil Liberties," *CNN Press Room,* July 1, 2013, http://cnnpressroom.blogs.cnn.com/2013/07/01/george-w-bush-snowden-damaged-us-security-programs-protect-civil-liberties/.

Bibliography

Alden, Edward. *The Closing of the American Border*. New York: HarperCollins, 2008.

American Immigration Lawyers Association. "Retired Immigration Judges and Former Members of the Board of Immigration Appeals Statement in Response to AG's Decision in *Matter of L-A-B-R-*." August 17, 2018. www.aila.org/infonet/retired-ijs-former-bia-statement-matter-of-l-a-b-r.

Anderson, Charles R. *Day of Lightning, Years of Scorn: Walter C. Short and the Attack on Pearl Harbor*. Annapolis: Naval Institute Press, 2005.

Archambeault, Matthew. "The Repercussions of How the Administration Has Handled Matter of Castro-Tum." *Think Immigration* (blog). August 14, 2018. https://thinkimmigration.org/blog/2018/08/14/the-repercussions-of-how-the-administration-has-handled-matter-of-castro-tum/.

Arnold & Porter. *Reforming the Immigration System: Proposals to Promote Independence, Fairness, Efficiency, and Professionalism in the Adjudication of Removal Cases*. Washington: American Bar Association, 2010. www.americanbar.org/content/dam/aba/publications/commission_on_immigration/coi_complete_full_report.authcheckdam.pdf.

Baker, Peter. *Days of Fire: Bush and Cheney in the White House*. New York: Anchor, 2014.

———. "Now Appearing: George W. Bush." *New York Times*, November 6, 2010. www.nytimes.com/2010/11/07/weekinreview/07baker.html?hp.

Biddle, Francis. *In Brief Authority*. New York: Doubleday, 1962.

Bird, Kai. *The Chairman*. New York: Simon and Schuster, 1992.

Bohn, Kevin. "The Artist Known as 'W': Paintings Unveil George W. Bush's Softer Side." *CNN.com*, April 4, 2014. www.cnn.com/2014/04/04/politics /bush-paintings/index.html.

Bond, Brian. *France and Belgium, 1939–1940*. London: Davis-Poynter, 1975.

Borch, Fred, and Daniel Martinez. *Kimmel, Short, and Pearl Harbor: The Final Report Revealed*. Annapolis: Naval Institute Press, 2005.

Bowman, Isaiah. "The Strategic Importance of Greenland." In *Studies of the American Interests in the War and the Peace*. New York: Council on Foreign Relations, 1940.

Breitman, Richard, and Alan M. Kraut. *American Refugee Policy and European Jewry, 1933–45*. Bloomington: Indiana University Press, 1987.

Brownlow, Louis. *A Passion for Anonymity: The Autobiography of Louis Brownlow, the First Half*. Chicago: University of Chicago Press, 1958.

Bumiller, Elisabeth. "White House Letter; Two Presidential Pals, Until 9/11 Intervened." *New York Times*, March 3, 2003. www.nytimes. com/2003/03/03/us/white-house-letter-two-presidential-pals-until-9-11-intervened.html.

Burtness, Paul S., and Warren U. Ober. "Communication Lapses Leading to the Pearl Harbor Disaster." *The Historian* 74, no. 4 (November 2013): 740–59.

Bush, George W. *Decision Points*. New York: Crown, 2010.

———. *Department of Homeland Security*. Washington, DC: The White House, 2002. www.dhs.gov/sites/default/files/publications/book_0.pdf.

———. *Portraits of Courage: A Commander in Chief's Tribute to America's Warriors*. New York: Crown, 2017.

Carroll, Lewis. *Alice's Adventures in Wonderland*. London: Macmillan, 1865.

Castro, Julián. "AILA 2020 Presidential Candidate Survey." October 10, 2019. www.aila.org/File/Related/19093005h.pdf.

Catholic Legal Immigration Network. "The End of Administrative Closure: Sessions Moves to Further Strip Immigration Judges of Independence." June 6, 2018. https://cliniclegal.org/resources/end-administrative-closure-sessions-moves-further-strip-immigration-judges-independence.

———. *Practice Pointer:* Matter of L-E-A-. Silver Spring: Catholic Legal Immigration Network, 2019. https://cliniclegal.org/resources/asylum-and-refugee-law/practice-pointer-matter-l-e.

Chang, Ailsa. "Thousands Could Be Deported as Government Targets Asylum Mills' Clients." *NPR Planet Money*, September 28, 2018. www.npr.org /sections/money/2018/09/28/652218318/thousands-could-be-deported-as-government-targets-asylum-mills-clients.

Charlesworth, JJ. "George W. Bush's Veteran Portraits Yearn for a Return to Innocence." *CNN Style*, October 7, 2019. www.cnn.com/style/article /george-w-bush-paintings/index.html.

Chase, Jeffrey S. "The AG's Strange Decision in Matter of E-F-H-L-." *Opinions /Analysis on Immigration Law* (blog). March 10, 2018. www.jeffreyschase. com/blog/2018/3/10/the-ags-strange-decision-in-matter-of-e-f-h-l-.

———. "EOIR Imposes Completion Quotas on IJs." *Opinions/Analysis on Immigration Law* (blog). April 7, 2018. www.jeffreyschase.com/blog/2018 /4/7/eoir-imposes-completion-quotas-on-ijs.

———. "Matter of A-B- Being Misapplied by EOIR, DHS." *Opinions/Analysis on Immigration Law* (blog). July 13, 2018. www.jeffreyschase.com/blog /2018/7/13/matter-of-a-b-being-misapplied-by-eoir-dhs.

———. "Matter of L-E-A: How Much Did Barr Change?" LexisNexis Legal NewsRoom, August 11, 2019. www.lexisnexis.com/legalnewsroom /immigration/b/insidenews/posts/matter-of-l-e-a—how-much-did- barr-change——jeffrey-s-chase.

Clarke, Richard A. *Against All Enemies: Inside America's War on Terror.* New York: Free Press, 2004.

CNN.com/insidepolitics. "FBI Whistleblower Describes 'Roadblocks.'" June 6, 2002. www.cnn.com/2002/ALLPOLITICS/06/06/terror.lapses/index .html.

CNN Press Room. "George W. Bush: Snowden Damaged US; Security Programs Protect Civil Liberties." July 1, 2013. http://cnnpressroom.blogs.cnn.com /2013/07/01/george-w-bush-snowden-damaged-us-security-programs- protect-civil-liberties/.

Coke, Sir Edward. *The First Part of the Institutes of the Lawes of England: or, A Commentary upon Littleton.* London: J. & W. T. Clarke, 1832.

Commission on Organization of the Executive Branch of the Government (Second Hoover Commission). *Legal Services and Procedure.* Washington, DC: U.S. Government Printing Office, 1955.

Commission on Wartime Relocation and Internment of Civilians. *Personal Justice Denied.* Washington, DC: U.S. Government Printing Office, 1982 and 1983. www.archives.gov/research/japanese-americans/justice-denied.

Conn, Stetson, and Byron Fairchild. *The Framework of Hemisphere Defense.* Washington, DC: Office of the Chief of Military History, Department of the Army, 1960.

De Jong, Louis. *The German Fifth Column in the Second World War.* Translated by C. M. Geyl. Chicago: University of Chicago Press, 1956.

Dewey, Caitlin. "Guccifer, the Hacker Who Leaked George W. Bush Paintings, Reportedly Arrested in Romania." *Washington Post*, January 22, 2014. www.washingtonpost.com/news/arts-and-entertainment/wp/2014/01/22

/guccifer-the-hacker-who-leaked-george-w-bush-paintings-reportedly-arrested-in-romania/.

Dubroff, Harold, and Brant J. Hellwig. *The United States Tax Court: An Historical Analysis.* 2nd ed. Washington, DC: United States Tax Court, 2014. www.ustaxcourt.gov/book/Dubroff_Hellwig.pdf.

Duffy, Michael. "George W. Bush Discusses His New Book of Oil Paintings." *TIME,* March 2, 2017. https://time.com/4688206/george-w-bush-painting-book/.

Eagly, Ingrid, and Steven Shafer. "Access to Counsel in Immigration Court." American Immigration Council. September 28, 2016. www .americanimmigrationcouncil.org/research/access-counsel-immigration-court.

Fine, Sidney. *Frank Murphy: The Washington Years.* Ann Arbor: University of Michigan Press, 1984.

Fox, Vicente, and Rob Allyn. *Revolution of Hope: The Life, Faith, and Dreams of a Mexican President.* New York: Viking, 2007.

Fragomen. "Latest USCIS Data Show RFE and Denial Rates Remained High for Key Employer-Sponsored Nonimmigrant Categories in the First Quarter of FY 2020." January 30, 2020. www.fragomen.com/insights/alerts /latest-uscis-data-show-rfe-and-denial-rates-remained-high-key-employer-sponsored-nonimmigrant-categories-first-quarter-fy-2020.

Gillman, Peter, and Leni Gillman, *Collar the Lot! How Britain Interned and Expelled Its Wartime Refugees.* London: Quartet, 1982.

Gleason, Peggy. "Escalating Cases with USCIS and DHS: Obstacles and Possible Solutions." Immigrant Legal Resource Center. June 2019. www.ilrc.org /sites/default/files/resources/july_3_revised-cases_with_uscis_and_dhs-june_2019-pg-dg-final.pdf.

Goldbaum, Christina. "Trump Administration Moves to Decertify Outspoken Immigration Judges' Union." *New York Times,* August 10, 2019. www .nytimes.com/2019/08/10/us/immigration-judges-union-justice-department.html?module=inline.

Goldman, Armond S., Elisabeth J. Schmalstieg, Daniel H. Freeman, Jr., Daniel A. Goldman, and Frank C. Schmalstieg, Jr. "What Was the Cause of Franklin Delano Roosevelt's Paralytic Illness?," *Journal of Medical Biography* 11, no. 4 (November 2003): 232–40.

Goodwin, Doris Kearns. *No Ordinary Time: Franklin and Eleanor Roosevelt: The Home Front in World War II.* New York: Simon and Schuster, 1994.

Gore, Albert A. *The Eye of the Storm: A People's Politics for the 70s.* Freiburg im Breisgau: Herder and Herder, 1970.

Green, Justin J. "Influence of Administrative Reform on the Immigration and Naturalization Service." *Administrative Science Quarterly* 15, no. 3 (September 1970): 353–59.

Greenhouse, Steven. "Labor Issue May Stall Security Bill." *New York Times,* July 28, 2002. www.nytimes.com/2002/07/28/us/labor-issue-may-stall-security-bill.html.

Gross, Daniel A. "The U.S. Government Turned Away Thousands of Jewish Refugees, Fearing That They Were Nazi Spies." *Smithsonian,* November 18, 2015. www.smithsonianmag.com/history/us-government-turned-away-thousands-jewish-refugees-fearing-they-were-nazi-spies-180957324/.

Hargreaves, Richard. *Blitzkrieg Unleashed: The German Invasion of Poland.* Barnsley: Pen & Sword Military, 2008.

Hauser, Christine. "Justice Department Newsletter Included Extremist Blog Post." *New York Times,* August 23, 2019. www.nytimes.com/2019/08/23/us/justice-department-vdare-anti-semitic.html?action=click&module=Related Coverage&pgtype=Article&region=Footer.

Heise, Kenan. "Frank A. Schuler Jr., 88, U.S. Diplomat in Japan." *Chicago Tribune,* May 7, 1996. www.chicagotribune.com/news/ct-xpm-1996-05-07-9605070020-story.html.

Herring, E. Pendleton. *Public Administration and the Public Interest.* New York: McGraw-Hill, 1936.

Hilton, Stanley E. "The Welles Mission to Europe, February-March 1940: Illusion or Realism?" *Journal of American History* 58, no. 2 (June 1971): 93-120.

Holland, James. *The Battle of Britain: Five Months That Changed History, May-October 1940.* New York: St. Martin's, 2010.

Holley, Joe. "Mary Ryan, 65; Embattled Consular Chief." *Washington Post,* April 29, 2006. www.washingtonpost.com/wp-dyn/content/article/2006/04/28/AR2006042802001.html.

Hull, Cordell. *The Memoirs of Cordell Hull.* Vol. 1. New York: Macmillan, 1948.

Ickes, Harold L. *The Secret Diaries of Harold L. Ickes.* Vol. 3. New York: Da Capo, 1974.

Innovation Law Lab and Southern Poverty Law Center. *The Attorney General's Judges: How the U.S. Immigration Courts Became a Deportation Tool.* Portland and Montgomery: Innovation Law Lab and Southern Poverty Law Center, 2019. www.splcenter.org/sites/default/files/com_policyreport_the_attorney_generals_judges_final.pdf.

Jackson, Robert. *Dunkirk: The British Evacuation, 1940.* New York: St. Martin's, 1976.

Jefferson, Thomas. *A Manual of Parliamentary Practice for the Use of the Senate of the United States.* Washington, DC: Government Printing Office, 1993.

Kanno-Youngs, Zolan. "Immigration Judges' Union Lodges Labor Complaints against Trump Administration." *New York Times,* September 27, 2019. www.nytimes.com/2019/09/27/us/politics/immigration-judges-union.html.

Kimball, Warren F., ed. *Churchill & Roosevelt: The Complete Correspondence.* Princeton: Princeton University Press, 1984.

Kimball, Warren F., and Bruce Bartlett. "Roosevelt and Prewar Commitments to Churchill: The Tyler Kent Affair." *Diplomatic History* 5, no. 4 (October 1981): 291–311.

King, Gilbert. "Sabotage in New York Harbor," *Smithsonian.com,* November 1, 2011. www.smithsonianmag.com/history/sabotage-in-new-york-harbor-123968672/.

Laird, Lorelei. "Justice Department Imposes Quotas on Immigration Judges, Provoking Independence Concerns." *ABA Journal,* April 2, 2018. www.abajournal.com/news/article/justice_department_imposes_quotas_on_immigration_judges_provoking_independe.

———. "Whose Court Is This Anyway? Immigration Judges Accuse Executive Branch of Politicizing Their Courts." *ABA Journal,* April 1, 2019. www.abajournal.com/magazine/article/immigration-judges-executive-politicizing-courts.

Last Week with John Oliver. "Immigration Courts." Episode 66. HBO, April 1, 2018. www.hbo.com/last-week-tonight-with-john-oliver/2018/66-episode-125.

Lesser, Casey. "The Artist Who Taught George W. Bush How to Paint." *Artsy,* April 4, 2017. www.artsy.net/article/artsy-editorial-artist-taught-george-bush-paint.

Levinson, Peter J. "Specialized Court for Immigration Hearings and Appeals." *Notre Dame Law Review* 66 (April 1981): 644–55.

Longley, Kyle. *Senator Albert Gore Sr.: Tennessee Maverick.* Baton Rouge: LSU Press, 2004.

Luo, Michael. "On the Road: A Week with 'Values' Voters." *New York Times,* October 28, 2007. http://thecaucus.blogs.nytimes.com/2007/10/28/on-the-road-a-week-with-values-voters/.

Madison, James. *The Federalist No. 10 and No. 51.* Project Gutenberg Etext.

Martin, David A. "Immigration Policy and the Homeland Security Act Reorganization: An Early Agenda for Practical Improvements." *Migration Policy Institute Insight* 1 (April 2003): 1–27.

Martin, George. *Madam Secretary: Frances Perkins.* Boston: Houghton Mifflin, 1976.

Masanz, Sharon D., Congressional Research Service. *History of the Immigration and Naturalization Service.* Washington, DC: U.S. Government Printing Office, 1980.

McCloy, John J. "Repay US Japanese?" *New York Times,* April 10, 1983. www.nytimes.com/1983/04/10/opinion/repay-us-japanese.html.

McKenna, Marian C. *Franklin Roosevelt and the Great Constitutional War: The Court-Packing Crisis of 1937.* New York: Fordham University Press, 2002.

McMillion, Barry J., Congressional Research Service. *Judiciary Appropriations, FY2020.* Washington, DC: Congressional Research Service, 2020. www.everycrsreport.com/files/20200518_R45965_ad2fe789a59761e5a8ea 8ab95c80ac3c59b6f73a.pdf.

Milbank, Dana. "Plan Was Formed in Utmost Secrecy." *Washington Post,* June 7, 2002. www.washingtonpost.com/archive/politics/2002/06/07/plan-was-formed-in-utmost-secrecy/e09fea5f-ca40–4381-a0fc-f3162197d639/.

Misra, Tanvi. "DOJ Changed Hiring to Promote Restrictive Immigration Judges." *Roll Call,* October 29, 2019. www.rollcall.com/news/congress /doj-changed-hiring-promote-restrictive-immigration-judges.

Mullins, Brody. "Ridge: Bush Should Veto Cabinet-Level Homeland Security Office." *Government Executive,* May 30, 2002. www.govexec.com/defense/2002 /05/ridge-bush-should-veto-cabinet-level-homeland-security-office/11748/.

National Association of Immigration Judges. "Growing Support for an Independent Immigration Court." June 17, 2019. www.naij-usa.org/images /uploads/newsroom/Growing_Support_for_an_Independent_Immigration_Court.pdf.

National Commission on Law Observance and Enforcement (Wickersham Commission). *Report on the Enforcement of the Deportation Laws of the United States.* Washington, DC: United States Government Printing Office, 1931.

National Commission on Terrorist Attacks on the United States (9/11 Commission). *The 9/11 Commission Report.* Washington, DC: U.S. Government Printing Office, 2004. https://govinfo.library.unt.edu/911/report/911Report .pdf.

National Immigrant Justice Center. "NIJC Condemns Attorney General's Unilateral Decision to Eliminate Access to 'Administrative Closure' for Immigration Judges and Immigrants." May 17, 2018. www.immigrantjustice.org /press-releases/nijc-condemns-attorney-generals-unilateral-decision-eliminate-access-administrative.

O'Sullivan, Christopher D. *Sumner Welles, Postwar Planning, and the Quest for a New World Order, 1937–1943.* New York: Columbia University Press ACLS Gutenberg e-Series, 2008.

Overseas Security Advisory Council. "Guatemala 2019 Crime & Safety Report." February 28, 2019. www.osac.gov/Content/Report/5f31517e-62bb-4f2c-8956-15f4aeaab930.

Padmanabhan, Vijay. "To Transfer or Not to Transfer: Identifying and Protecting Relevant Human Rights Interests in Non-Refoulement." *Fordham Law Review* 80, no. 1 (October 2011): 73–123.

Perkins, Frances. Interview with Dean Albertson. Oral History of Frances Perkins. 1951–1955. Columbia University Library Oral History Research Office. www.columbia.edu/cu/lweb/digital/collections/nny/perkinsf/audio_ transcript.html.

————. *The Roosevelt I Knew.* New York: Viking, 1946.

Polenberg, Richard. *Reorganizing Roosevelt's Government: The Controversy over Executive Reorganization, 1936–1939.* Cambridge, MA: Harvard University Press, 1966.

Rawitz, Sidney B. "From Wong Yang Sung to Black Robes." *Interpreter Releases* 65, no. 17 (May 1988): 453–59.

Roberts, Andrew. *The Storm of War: A New History of the Second World War.* New York: HarperCollins, 2011.

Roberts, Roxanne, and Anne Gerhart. "The State Dinner That Ended with a Bang." *Washington Post,* September 6, 2001. www.washingtonpost.com /archive/lifestyle/2001/09/06/the-state-dinner-that-ended-with-a-bang/2a82b9ff-01f9–4563–90c8–52c83bcca5ca/.

Roosevelt, Elliott, ed. *The Roosevelt Letters: Being the Personal Correspondence of Franklin Delano Roosevelt.* Vol. 2. London: Harrap, 1950.

Roosevelt, Franklin D. *The Complete Presidential Press Conferences of Franklin D. Roosevelt,* Vols. 13–14, 15–16. New York: Da Capo, 1972.

Rosenman, Samuel I., ed. *The Public Papers and Addresses of Franklin D. Roosevelt, 1940 Volume: War—and Aid to Democracies.* New York: MacMillan, 1941.

Ruiz, Julius. "Fighting the Fifth Column: The Terror in Republican Madrid during the Spanish Civil War." In *The Civilianization of War,* edited by Andrew Barros and Martin Thomas, 47–63. Cambridge: Cambridge University Press, 2018.

Saltz, Jerry. "Jerry Saltz: George W. Bush Is a Good Painter!" *Vulture,* February 8, 2013. www.vulture.com/2013/02/jerry-saltz-george-w-bush-is-a-good-painter.html.

Sanders, Bernie. "AILA 2020 Presidential Candidate Survey." September 30, 2019. www.aila.org/File/Related/19093005d.pdf.

Scheck, Tom. "Wellstone Staff Apologizes for Memorial Service Rhetoric." *Minnesota Public Radio,* October 30, 2002. http://news.minnesota.publicradio .org/features/200210/30_scheckt_backlash1/.

Schjeldahl, Peter. "George W. Bush's Painted Atonements." *The New Yorker,* March 3, 2017. https://tinyurl.com/sn2h3lg.

Scholtz, Rebecca. "AG Imposes Limitations on Motions for Continuance." Catholic Legal Immigration Network. August 20, 2018. https://cliniclegal. org/resources/removal-proceedings/ag-imposes-limitations-motions-continuance.

Schwarz, Jordan A. *Liberal: Adolf A. Berle and the Vision of an American Era.* New York: Free Press, 1987.

Scott, S. P., trans. *The Civil Law* 2, Title V. Cincinnati: Central Trust Company, 1932. https://droitromain.univ-grenoble-alpes.fr/Anglica/CJ3_Scott.htm#5.

Somin, Ilya. "Does the Constitution Give the Federal Government Power over Immigration?" *Cato Unbound.* September 12, 2018. www.cato-unbound.

org/2018/09/12/ilya-somin/does-constitution-give-federal-government-power-over-immigration.

State, Paul F. *A Brief History of the Netherlands*. New York: Infobase, 2008.

Stevens, Matt. "DACA Participants Can Again Apply for Renewal, Immigration Agency Says." *New York Times*. January 14, 2018. Photo by Al Drago. www.nytimes.com/2018/01/14/us/politics/daca-renewals-requests.html.

Stolberg, Sheryl Gay. "Ocasio-Cortez Calls Migrant Detention Centers 'Concentration Camps,' Eliciting Backlash," *New York Times*, June 18, 2019. www.nytimes.com/2019/06/18/us/politics/ocasio-cortez-cheney-detention-centers.html.

Tanfani, Joseph. "Atty. Gen. Sessions Says Lax Immigration Enforcement Is Enabling Gangs Like MS-13." *Baltimore Sun*, April 30, 2017. www.baltimoresun.com/la-na-essential-washington-updates-sessions-says-lax-immigration-1492527375-htmlstory.html.

Taylor, David A. "The Inside Story of How a Nazi Plot to Sabotage the U.S. War Effort Was Foiled." *Smithsonian.com*, June 28, 2016. www.smithsonianmag.com/history/inside-story-how-nazi-plot-sabotage-us-war-effort-was-foiled-180959594/.

Tenet, George. *At the Center of the Storm: My Years at the CIA*. New York: HarperCollins, 2007.

Thackeray, William Makepeace. *Vanity Fair*. Oxford: Oxford University Press, 1983.

Thomason, James S. *The US Commission on National Security/21st Century ("Hart-Rudman") Overview and Observations on Phase I*. Alexandria: Institute for Defense Analysis, 2000.

U.N. High Commission on Refugees, *Children on the Run: Unaccompanied Children Leaving Central America and Mexico and the Need for International Protection*. New York: U.N. High Commission on Refugees, 2014. www.unhcr.org/56fc266f4.html.

U.S. Commission on Immigration Reform. *Becoming an American: Immigration & Immigrant Policy*. Washington, DC: U.S. Commission on Immigration Reform, 1997. www.hsdl.org/?abstract&did=437705.

U.S. Commission on National Security/21st Century (Hart-Rudman Commision). *New World Coming: American Security in the 21st Century: Major Themes and Implications*. Washington, DC: United States Commission on National Security/21st Century, 1999. www.hsdl.org/?view&did=2087.

———. *Road Map for National Security: Imperative for Change*. Washington, DC: U.S. Commission on National Security/21st Century, 2001. www.hsdl.org/?view&did=2079.

Van Vleck, William C. *The Administrative Control of Aliens*. New York: Commonwealth Fund, 1932.

Vaudagna, Maurizio. "Mussolini and Franklin D. Roosevelt." In *FDR and His Contemporaries: Foreign Perceptions of an American President*, edited by

Cornelis A. van Minnen and John F. Sears, 157–70. New York: St. Martin's, 1992.

Vermuele, Adrian. "Contra *Nemo Iudex in Sua Causa:* The Limits of Impartiality." *Yale Law Journal* 122, no. 2 (November 2012): 384–420.

Wallace, Kelly. "Bush Vacation Puts Spotlight on Tiny Crawford." *CNN Inside-Politics,* August 7, 2001. www.cnn.com/2001/ALLPOLITICS/08/06/bush.crawford/.

Warmbrunn, Werner. *The Dutch under German Occupation, 1940–45.* Stanford: Stanford University Press, 1963.

Weiner, Tim. *Legacy of Ashes.* New York: Doubleday, 2007.

Weisselberg, Charles. "The Exclusion and Detention of Aliens: Lessons from the Lives of Ellen Knauff and Ignatz Mezei." *University of Pennsylvania Law Review* 143, no. 4 (April 1995): 933–1034.

Welles, Benjamin. *Sumner Welles: FDR's Global Strategist.* New York: St. Martin's, 1997.

Welles, Sumner. *The Time for Decision.* New York: Harper and Brothers, 1944.

Werking, Richard Hume. *The Master Architects.* Lexington: University Press of Kentucky, 1977.

Woodward, Bob. *Bush at War.* New York: Simon and Schuster, 2002.

Wyman, David S. *The Abandonment of the Jews: America and the Holocaust, 1941–1945.* New York: Pantheon, 1984.

Index

In this index, *v.* (in italics) follows the standard use in titles of legal cases. Vs. (in roman lower case) signifies disagreement or disapproval between two parties. For example, the conflict between various immigration judges and Attorney General Jeff Sessions is expressed "immigration judges vs. Sessions." It can mean "against" as in "immigration laws against Japanese immigrants." It is also used in negative comparisons such as Courts of Appeals vs. immigration courts.

Cabinets and governmental agencies with numerous mentions are posted by their acronyms. Those with fewer mentions are posted by the first word of that Cabinet office or agency's designation. In all such postings, a *See also* cross reference is given.

Founded in 1893,
UNIVERSITY OF CALIFORNIA PRESS
publishes bold, progressive books and journals
on topics in the arts, humanities, social sciences,
and natural sciences—with a focus on social
justice issues—that inspire thought and action
among readers worldwide.

The UC PRESS FOUNDATION
raises funds to uphold the press's vital role
as an independent, nonprofit publisher, and
receives philanthropic support from a wide
range of individuals and institutions—and from
committed readers like you. To learn more, visit
ucpress.edu/supportus.